Just Another Day

JASON RANDAZZO

Copyright © 2020 Jason Randazzo
All rights reserved
First Edition

PAGE PUBLISHING, INC.
Conneaut Lake, PA

First originally published by Page Publishing 2020

ISBN 978-1-64584-875-2 (pbk)
ISBN 978-1-64584-876-9 (digital)

Printed in the United States of America

Foreword and Acknowledgments

I was born in Lutheran Medical Center, which is located in Sunset Park, Brooklyn, and briefly lived near Eldert Lane in East New York, also in Brooklyn. After my parents separated, my mother moved us to an apartment just off Jamaica Avenue, in the neighborhood where I was raised, Richmond Hill, which is a town within Queens County, one of the five counties that comprise New York City. The apartment was located in a six-story building, ten apartments per floor, in an area predominantly comprised of ethnic backgrounds of Italian, German, Irish, and a smattering of other European cultures. My bedroom of the apartment overlooked the east end of the 111th Street station of the J train. Although I adapted my sleep to the roar of the engine as it left for the Lefferts Boulevard stop, I would miss parts of my television shows for a minute. My two oldest friends, whose parents were paradoxically born in Italy and Ecuador, couldn't have been more diverse in their respective ethnic backgrounds but similar in all other ways, especially in humor. Unfortunately, their similarities extended to their use of drugs, which claimed the life of one friend at a young age of forty and severely disrupted the life of the other.

My father fought in World War II and then had taken over the family business after his brother moved to California. The business dealt with insurance and travel and was located at 426 East 14th Street in Manhattan on the Lower East Side, right on the border of Alphabet City, which got its name from the alphabetized avenues of A through D. The office was situated between First Avenue and Avenue A, and as a young adult, I would walk over to the De Robertis

Pasticceria on First Avenue for a cappuccino each for Pauline, who handled the travel business in the front of the store, and me and a double espresso for my father.

On occasion, I would also go to Veniero's on East 11th Street between First and Second Avenues for some of their treasured pastries. But rarely would I venture the other direction, for Alphabet City was more known for the drug dens of the time rather than for the hipsters of today. Years later, while working at the FBI, I would find surveillance photographs of Italian organized crime meetings taken inside the pasticceria.

Besides the businesses for which my father was able to earn a living, as a first-generation Italian American who was fluent in Italian and a very well-read individual, he was also an informal "ambassador" to other Italian-speaking people who knew and trusted him. He sat behind a giant mahogany desk in the rear of a railroad-style office and would translate and decipher letters and documents sent to them from entities, both private or public, for these people who spoke little or no English and provide them information and advice, when appropriate, on the contents, often at little to no cost to them. Although he had a fervor for gambling and cigarettes, the latter of which led to his premature death, I had some great memories going to Italian restaurants in either Little Italy in Manhattan or near his old stomping grounds of New Utrecht in Brooklyn. As we talked about many different topics for which he seemed to always have an intimate knowledge, we dined on some of the finest meals I have ever had. Eventually, the restaurant owner would sit with us, having brought a bottle of wine, and talk, mostly to my father, in their native tongue.

My mother stayed home and provided me with the most grounded upbringing a single parent who never remarried could give me. She was at home when I arrived from school, and again at night, after I hung out with my friends in the schoolyard. Those friends, many of whom were pretty evenly divided on falling to the left and right of the line that divided the moral compass, helped me to form many of my ideals and principles. A lot of them, including me, passed the entrance for the New York City Police Department, and we attended the academy together.

I had done this after attending Saint John's University for a short time, when I realized after two attempts that I wasn't going to be the sensational walk-on to the baseball team that had produced a few Major League players back then, and then to Nassau Community College, which I only gave the opportunity to reject me from the team once. After receiving my associate's degree in criminal justice there, I decided to take myself more seriously and finish getting my bachelor's degree at John Jay College of Criminal Justice in Manhattan before entering the NYCPD Academy, which was located at that time on East 20th Street between First and Second Avenues in Manhattan, on July 16, 1984.

After graduating from there five months later, I was assigned to patrol with Neighborhood Stabilization Unit 6, which encompassed the 25th, 28th and 32nd Precincts in the sections of East and Central Harlem, for six months. I then transferred to the Manhattan North Task Force, which conducted patrols in the high-crime areas of Upper Manhattan from the border of 59th Street to the top of the island, mostly working in Harlem and Washington Heights. At that time, the 34th Precinct in Washington Heights, which then included West 155th Street to the top of Manhattan, would lead the city in homicides almost every year.

I remained there in the MNTF for approximately five years.

Upon my entry into the FBI Academy on April 23, 1990, I had the privilege to meet Mr. Bob Rogers, my physical education instructor there, whose "Never say die!" way of teaching gave me the mental fortitude to never let a bad guy win. There was many a day that I cursed him while doing laps around the gym or throughout the landscape of Quantico, Virginia, on a nice day. We ran in the same alphabetical order as we sat in class, and many runs continued until Mr. Rogers would shout out, "Two more laps!" Most of us never knew when or why he decided the run was over, until we later learned that whenever a classmate named Testani puked, that was the marker that the run was long enough.

It wasn't until after our graduation that I realized that his principal purpose wasn't to teach us how to fight and defend ourselves; our time at the academy was limited too much to have us excel at learning to be a skilled fighter. But he was determined to give us an overriding will to survive, an "extra gear" to kick in when you may be fighting for your life against a perp and think you've given it your all and have no more to give, an inner strength to reach for and subdue the perp and effect the arrest.

So I would like to express the undying gratitude I have for my mother, Eleanor, who made many sacrifices in her life to avail me the opportunities to be the person I am today, and for my father, Salvatore, for expanding my horizons in the relatively short time that I knew him and showed me many varieties of life.

I would also like to thank the NYCPD for allowing me the opportunity to gain valuable experience with many situations with both the best and worst of humanity and gave me the ability to have a sense of calmness in the face of unfamiliar, and sometimes adversarial, places and situations. And finally to my mentor, Anthony John Nelson, who drafted me into the venerable Squad C-9, known at that time as the Fugitive Squad of the New York Office. Anthony later became the supervisor of the Truck Hijacking Squad before taking over the NYPD/FBI Joint Bank Robbery Task Force. He was a guiding influence not only on the way of investigating crimes but also on treating victims in such a way that, even though you may not be able to make them feel whole again through the process of the criminal justice system with an arrest and/or a conviction, you can still show them true empathy so they understand that, although they may not find justice in the end, someone does care. That can mean more than anything.

And please be advised that the opinions contained within these pages are expressly those of the author and not at all of the FBI.

"Stop!"

As we drive down East 158th Street east from Broadway toward Amsterdam Avenue, my partner jumps out of the passenger seat of the RMP, police parlance for Radio Motor Patrol, or as the public would call it, a police car, and takes chase after him. I do not realize it at first, but Keith has just seen a Hispanic male walking down the steps from one of the tenements that line both sides of the street in this area called Washington Heights with a bulge in his waistband that looks anything but natural. At the sight of Keith, who this individual with the gun later learns at trial to be Police Officer Keith Jones, coming at him, he takes off down the sidewalk toward Broadway with his right hand holding the object in his waistband in place. Placing the car in park and taking the keys with me as I get out, knowing full well if I leave the keys in the car it will be gone by the time we get back, I run parallel with them in the street. Keeping as good an eye as possible on the two of them through the parked cars between us as they run through the summer night around people hanging in front of their building, I amble along after them with what seems like fifty pounds of police equipment around my waist.

It never stops. Drugs flourish and customers are abundant in this area that encompasses the top of Manhattan that, by some of us, is known as the Heights. The majority of the cops that patrol this area are from the "three-four." Poor bastards, they were highly accountable.

If there's a 10-54, a sick call, you go. If there's a 10-53, car accident, you go. Run from one job to the next, do the paperwork, and don't let the sergeant catch you "holding a job," sitting somewhere while the 911 dispatcher still has you out, 'cause there will be hell to pay. And then there's the Glory Boys, both the plainclothes cops known as Street Crime Unit or Anti-crime Unit that drive in the cars that, although unmarked, everyone in the street knows are the police. And then there are the cops who are dressed "in the bag" (meaning in uniform) and in a marked unit but, like the plainclothes cops, are not slaves to the radio, handling those service-related calls for people in need, but rather running to the calls of "Shots fired" and "Man with a gun." Because we work in different precincts each night, we are not accountable to the dispatcher, which allows us to prowl the night, looking to take the guns off the streets and arrest those who are holding or using them.

The neighborhood has got to be the most densely populated place in New York City. Every block is lined from corner to corner with six-story buildings. Double-parking is the norm; triple parking is sometimes tolerated as well. The area swells from the constant immigration of those who come from the Central and Caribbean nations, particularly the Dominican Republic. With the combination of poor immigrants with the innate ability to smuggle high-quality cocaine coupled with their landing in a place that is easily accessible by bridges from the Bronx, Queens, New Jersey, Westchester, as well as places farther in any direction, this place is not only a drug user's paradise but a potential booby trap at every turn as well.

Because of the logistics, we engage in a different form of racial profiling. White kids from those areas driving through are pounced on by police like lions on their prey. After they and their car are "tossed" for drugs, and if none are found, they will be verbally berated before they hightail it back across the bridge. But if someone is "looking for a collar" that evening, they will go from one car to the next until drugs are found. It doesn't take long, and the only reason any of these cars turn up dry is that we get them before they cop their drugs. Very few people get lost there, and tourists are most rare in this part of the city.

The three-four has led the city in homicides and drug seizures a number of years running, hence the adage "Where there's drugs, there's guns." And since an aggressive cop who had worked there, by the name of Michael Buzcek, was killed chasing a suspect who, unbeknownst to him, had just robbed a drug dealer and was fleeing the apartment building, it is in the back of everyone's mind, including my own, that every situation can be a dangerous one. This was also on the heels of a separate incident, which occurred approximately fifty blocks away when another police officer identified as Christopher Hoban was also killed in a shoot-out while conducting a narcotics transaction. On October 18, 1988, NYPD history was shattered as two police officers were killed in the line of duty in separate incidents on the same night.

Unfortunately, as most people in this line of work do, we throw ourselves into these situations with reckless abandon, because no matter how much you think about what could have happened, when the adrenaline is flowing, you're through that door, over that fence, or around that car faster than Superman. The civilians, who, for the most part and by the nature of our business, are saner than us, run the opposite way. Cops, who are sometimes inspired by a feeling of omnipotence, run to the scene of trouble and, unfortunately, sometimes harm. But no matter what a cop has experienced, instinct usually sets him in drive without much thought process involved.

As Keith quickly seems to be gaining ground, I slowly feel a sense that this chase is coming to an end. Since both of us have been on a dead run to catch this knucklehead, neither of us have called over the radio for assistance. It's a funny thing about calling for help. Some cops will call if they're chasing a kid with a nickel bag of pot, while some cops won't call unless they're fighting for their lives with an armed perpetrator. Some of it falls back on what the Hispanics call *machismo*, where they feel it's a sign of weakness to call for help. That's why cops like to use the slang term "10-84 FORTHWITH" over the radio rather than "10-13." A 10-84 means a cop needs assistance, whereas 10-13 means a cop needs help. Rarely will you hear a cop in the street call a 13, because in a way he's saying for all to hear on the radio, "I'm losing a battle." And from the first day in the Police Academy throughout your entire career, either by instructors at the academy or your peers at your command, you're always told that there is no such thing as losing, because you're a cop and cops *don't* lose.

As Keith now reaches for the shirt collar of the perp, suddenly the man stops and ducks down, sending Keith tumbling over him to the pavement. The man now does a U-turn and begins to run back up the block, people cheering and laughing at the police like we're idiots who fall all over themselves trying to catch this guy. I briefly think to myself, *Yeah, you're hanging out in front of your building on a weeknight at 2:00 a.m. with your infant children, and I'm the idiot,* before continuing the chase back up the street after him while Keith is down.

As we run, my heart pounds out of my chest and my legs grow heavy, but both adrenaline and pride allow me to pursue him alone diagonally across Amsterdam Avenue. I watch as he turns down 157th Street, losing sight of him after he clears the corner. As I come closer to the corner, I instinctively unholster my .38 revolver and hold it at my side until I see a figure hovering in a doorway, breathing as heavily as me and seemingly fumbling by his waistband.

"STOP! DON'T MOVE!" I yell out as I now point my weapon on the middle of his back.

At Rodman's Neck, which is on a small island that is part of the Bronx, they train you over and over to shoot at paper targets on a sunny day with a cool breeze at your back in a sterile environment. But nothing can prepare you for the intensity of a situation in which you confront another man on a city street whose only means of escape is, literally, over your dead body. You can't shoot unless you or someone else is threatened by him, but he plays by no rules. The longer he has time to think about it, the more likely he thinks he can get away from you. *Act fast.*

I quickly come up behind him and kick him in the small of the back, a 9 mm semiautomatic flying to the floor from where he has been holding it by his midsection as he braces himself with his hands from hitting the wall with his face. As responding cars come screeching to the scene, I pull him to the ground face-first by the same collar that Keith had been reaching for minutes earlier. Placing my cuffs on him, I think about how both of us will now see another day.

*****

JUST ANOTHER DAY

The institution that structured my formative years was Public School 51, which was located in the town of Richmond Hill, the borough of Queens, the city of New York. It was a three-story brick building where I attended kindergarten to fifth grade. Adjacent to the building was a cement yard. Although most schools nationwide were layered with lush green grass, or at least dirt, ours was coated with a three-inch blanket of concrete. The only visible signs of chlorophyll were at both extreme ends of the yard. One end was used as a dump by the school custodian for expended coal from the school's furnace. The other end had some tall hedges that we called the baja. We would ride our bikes through the hedges on a trail of whatever vestiges of grass there had been that was made worn by our tires.

New York City became the stage, but Queens was my stomping grounds in my formative years. This school near my house not only provided the environment inside its walls for my formal education during my learning years, but the schoolyard also provided me with some understanding about human frailty. Through my early years, this primitive venue was the site of many games, from softball, football, and basketball to Johnny-on-a-Pony, hide-the-belt, and ring-a-levio. Since most of the yard was topped with cement and there was very little grass within the fenced-in area, we had to play a lot of condensed versions of games. After I had been elevated to the position of the captain of the School Safety Patrol, my friends and I, who were my "subordinates," were summarily dismissed because instead of attending to our posts, safely guiding the younger kids through intersections, we were constantly playing Johnny-on-a-Pony on the side of the school.

My friends and I would hang around the schoolyard for much of our adolescence. Older brothers and their friends would occasionally pass by from their houses to their usual haunts with their friends. As they stopped, they would impart their version of wisdom upon us, sometimes with an open hand, sometimes closed. But it was all a part of the process; they bullied us as we would bully the kids younger than us. A vicious cycle, or maybe just a rite of passage. For some of us, it toughened us up for the adversity that we would face later in life. For others, it could have been a part of other nasty troubles that accounted for either a life in prison or death.

The introduction of drug use came through these sporadic interludes. Of course, it started so harmlessly with marijuana.

It began as an occasional event at night inside one of the outdoor vestibules on either side of the school. I do admit, I smoked it on a number of times that I could count on one hand and would have a finger or two to spare. But whether it was psychosomatic or not, I would experience a sharp pain in my side while playing ball that I attributed to it. Whatever it was, this justified in my own mind—which, despite the peer pressure, was the only excuse I needed—that it wasn't for me. However, my friends did not have the same deterrence.

As time went on, my friends discovered that there was a variety of drugs that could be experimented with. It didn't seem like drug abuse awareness was a hot topic in those days, and the Dome, which was once described in a *New York Daily News* column by Jimmy Breslin as the "biggest drug marketplace on the East Coast," was a three-minute car ride away. The Dome was a landmark aptly named because it referred to the Seuffert Bandshell, a crescent-shaped structure located inside Forest Park. While by the day it was legitimately used for its intended purpose by theatre goers, nocturnal mayhem permeated the parking lot adjacent to it as it transformed into an open-air drug bazaar. The Dome itself would then be relegated as a shield from those in the parking lot while on the other side others would use it as a place to either relieve themselves or engage in sexual acts.

Although there were always neighborhood people hanging out there, the weekends brought out people from everywhere. It looked like one huge tailgate party—only there were no barbecues going on here. Cocaine, mescaline, mushrooms, quaaludes, LSD—all the recreational drugs of choice—were easily available. Although heroin was not a real drug of choice at that time, angel dust, also known as PCP, was a winner for those who really sought adventure.

Dust, as it was more commonly referred to, was smoked like marijuana, but it was treated with some kind of chemical that gave it an odor that reminded me of turpentine. This drug was so potent that, if placed in a nickel or dime bag made of paper, it would seep through the bag and into your skin. When ingested, it gave the person a sense of euphoria in which they not only felt as strong as Hercules but also had a feeling of omnipotence. This led to a lot of people, especially police officers, getting hurt when confronting or subduing these users. The drugs also made people try out their Superman-like powers they suddenly thought they had, like being able to fly from tall buildings.

Unfortunately, long-term use of this drug later showed to erode speech and motor skills. A phenomenal baseball player I knew, named Joey, had played in a Catholic Youth Organization league, which featured many of the premier players of the region. Joey pitched and batted clean-up on one of the elite teams in the league. He was nicknamed Bam-Bam because of his good looks and stout build. But Joey had the misfortune to be friends of some of those older brothers.

As Joey's skills deteriorated, he found employment as a laborer but still harbored the same enthusiasm that he always had for the game of baseball. Although he no longer had the talent he once had, Joey and I would later play ball together on some teams that were lacking in players and would take anyone. Since he lived two blocks from me, he would meet me every Sunday morning by my car, always waiting there for me, until one particular Sunday when he wasn't. He was found a couple of days later inside a rolled-up carpet. Joey, who did not believe in banks and always carried his pay from work until he spent it, had no money on him. He was just a jovial guy who was killed by a pack of bloodthirsty savages. Although the killers were never found, I had heard through the neighborhood that he had been stabbed to death and robbed by people that he knew. People that I knew.

After his untimely death, I would see one of these people on a semiregular basis through mutual friends. Because I never saw evidence or heard from a firsthand witness, for years I had mixed feelings whenever I shook Sammy's hand. It also didn't help that he was one of the local drug dealers, and most of the time, when I did see him, it was because one of my friends was buying drugs from him.

But as the years wore on and I would see him at weddings and funerals, I learned that he sincerely turned his life around, which was confirmed by a police source that I met while I worked at the FBI, I had wanted to ask him for years if the rumors were true. Was he involved in Joey's death? But by the time I became comfortable enough to ask, my feelings of anger had dissipated and I saw that it was something that was better left unsaid and in the past at this point in life.

Joey was only one of the many tragedies that ended potentially viable lives. A guy nicknamed Weedhopper fell under a train during one drug-induced haze and lost parts of both feet and an ear. Under another haze, he later fell from a tree, trying to climb through the window of his house, and died. There was the night I walked with Danny after hanging out from the schoolyard to his house. As he went inside and I continued home, I stopped, thinking that I had heard him call out my name, but, after not hearing him again, continued on my way home. It was not until the following day that I learned that his brother had fatally shot his mother. He was in a drug frenzy, looking for money from her, and when she refused, he shot her with a rifle in the front vestibule. I still could not imagine the frightening scene he came upon and the shock that must have overcome him.

Although I did not bear witness to these events, the facts always seemed to filter their way through the neighborhood. I knew many of these people, because we were all the fabric that comprised the younger community of this neighborhood. I'd been in bars and other gathering places with them, characters so affable that it was hard to conceive the crazy things that you heard about them. When I would shake hands with them, it left me with a feeling of ambivalence.

Sometimes I would wonder what went through the minds of individuals who could joke with you one minute then eviscerate you with a Swiss army knife the next.

Those who were involved in the drug trade, like Joey, fell into a lifestyle that often led to one of two paths. There was John Burke, a local drug dealer who was very much feared by those that didn't know him well but only knew him by reputation, as well as they should. John controlled a lot of the local drug dealing, and as time and bad deeds went on, his well-known reputation grew, which led to a loose association with Italian organized crime. But while I was still in high school, John, who was a few years older than I was but, like many of my friends, long removed from any formal schooling, came into conflict with another local drug dealer named Danny Z. Danny, who claimed an area called Smokey Park as his turf, thought he had a big enough reputation and group of friends that he could deal his own wares. A small war broke out between these two dealers in which Danny drew first blood. His mistake, which led to his demise, was that he didn't finish the job.

Danny caught John in a position where he was able to shoot him, but the bullet went through his neck and he survived, causing him after his recuperation to sport a long scar along the side of his throat. But I remember seeing John afterward with the tracheae tube protruding from the gap below his jaw, his gravelly voice then temporarily brought to a whisper. Danny must have thought that John would not have enough balls to take this any further, that this would end the war between them and keep John at a distance. For most people, it probably would have and they would take this as a sign that they got lucky this time and maybe they ought to look for a new line of work to accumulate their gains, ill-gotten or otherwise. But unfortunately for Danny, John was not like most people.

Time passed. I don't know if they ever had arranged some kind of truce or just kept their distance. Danny might have been scarce for a while, but eventually he came back and resumed old habits. And John never said a word to police; he apparently had his own ideas regarding retribution. But unlike Danny, he saw his job through. One night, Danny had been sitting in his car by Smokey Park, probably dealing again, just like he always did. The evening was quiet as it was on most nights, but somehow John was able to creep up beside Danny's car without him knowing. As he rose up beside the driver's window, raising the muzzle of a shotgun toward him, he sarcastically yelled out, "Happy Birthday, Danny!" before releasing a barrage of gunfire at the driver. John made sure that Danny would not survive as he once did. As soon as this killing occurred, everyone, including the police, knew who was responsible. But not surprisingly, it could not be proven in a court of law.

The list went on. Billy Estrema was another pretty wild guy.

He had a presence as big as a linebacker and was one of those good-looking Italian guys with the olive skin and short black hair. He was quick with a punch and powerful enough to knock the daylights out of those whom he had a beef with. He first hung out at Smokey Park and did not do drugs, but he pounded on a lot of people as a kid and later went on to work as muscle and a collector for a crew with the Luchese crime family. A story goes that once, while riding in a car, going under a stone underpass, he let a round go off just to hear the acoustics.

Once he had a beef with a guy whose nickname was Freebird, who sported a tattoo from the legendary song by the iconic group Lynyrd Skynyrd. Freebird hung out with my friends Odie and Lardi at a bar called Flight 116, a bar whose owner, in our teens, sponsored our softball team. It was a bar that a few patrons would go outside to smoke a little weed, but later on, we stopped going there after softball games, when the dynamics radically changed and it became a full-fledged drug den, coincidentally courtesy of a mutual friend of both Billy and mine who soon became a well-established figure in a very notable organized crime family.

But back to the beef. Generally speaking, Freebird was not someone to fuck with. Although hard-core bikers were not the most stable people to begin with, around Christmastime each year, they rallied to bring big stuffed animals and other toys to a central point and ride in a Toys for Tots run to deliver the gifts to a children's hospital, then partied afterwards. They first would rally at a bar named Glenn's, which was located on Hillside Avenue just off from where it intersected at Myrtle Avenue. It was the first bar I frequented with my friends regularly as they didn't check for proof of age if they knew you, especially since the drinking age was eighteen. It was the meeting place for most of the guys and girls in Richmond Hill at that time.

Among the bikers at the event were members of outlaw motorcycle gangs such as the Hells Angels and Pagans, who had local chapters on Long Island, who were known to frequent these events, and they made their presence known to all. As I had a fascination with bikers, having ridden a bike myself since 1988, I sometimes attended these events myself, anonymously of course, just to check out the girls and view the gang members in their natural habitat. It was there that I saw Freebird bartending at a makeshift bar under a huge heated tent. You not only had to be tough and respected to deal with these people in that environment—with liquor involved no less—but you also had to have confidence about your toughness.

And one day, Billy left a bar called Lenihan's, which was located not too far from Smokey Park, and drove over to Flight 116, which was less than a mile away. When Billy walked up to Freebird and challenged him over the beef to a street fight, not only he but also his reputation was so fierce that Freebird told him, "Go ahead, Billy. I'm not going to fight you. Do what ya gotta do."

Some bad guys that associated with Billy back then got out in time and turned their lives around to be productive members of society, had families, and created legitimate businesses. But unfortunately for Billy, he did not follow suit. As the headstrong individual that he was, his hogtied body was later found in a dumpster after he was shot in the head. He was another victim of Mob justice for either dating the wrong girl or beating up the wrong guy. Only a few knew for sure.

A side story about the Flight, as it was commonly called, occurred when I was still on my probationary period with the New York City Police Department, which at that time was a year, which included the first six months you were in the academy and then the next six months that you were working on patrol. I was driving with Marty Petersen, God rest his soul, and Benny from one bar to the next when Marty asked to stop and see someone at the Flight. Not thinking much of it at that time or knowing the reputation it had come to achieve, I pulled up on the corner and Marty jumped out and disappeared into the bar as Benny and I waited on the corner in the car. Shortly after he entered the bar, the door to the bar burst open, and his back toward us while flailing punches at a group of guys that were trying to get at him, Marty backpedaled out of there while fending off the drug dealers who were in there, including one guy who was wildly swinging a pool cue at anyone close to him.

Without thinking of the consequences either physically or professionally, as this situation could be career suicide with the trouble I could be getting into, I left the car as the scene seemed to hit a lull. A few guys were facing off with Marty on the sidewalk as the guy with the stick watched the rest of the crowd, looking like he was waiting to hit anyone that came near them. I had my off-duty gun with me, a Colt .38 Detective Special, but I was wearing Frye boots and had it clipped inside my jeans to the top of the boot, not thinking I would need to get to it quickly. Maybe it was fortuitous that I had it in a place where I couldn't draw it easily, which, had I drawn it, might have escalated the situation and created dire results, especially if one of these guys was also carrying a gun. As I had kept my eye on the guy with the stick that was standing not too far from me, I glanced to the guys facing Marty, who were taking slow steps toward him as he backed away slowly while he said to them, "You can talk to me without getting any closer." The next second, I heard a *thwack* and looked back at the guy who was holding the pool cue, which was now broken in his hand.

As I looked down at my boots, I saw droplets of blood starting to rain down on the toes of the boots. Someone who must have been a patron of the Flight in the old days when I went there after softball and was still hanging out there yelled out, "You just hit a cop!" Within seconds, the crowd dispersed, especially the drug dealers, including the guy with the broken pool cue. I walked into the Flight, grabbed napkins off the bar, and as I wiped the blood away, asked the barmaid, "Is this gonna need stitches?" Without waiting for an answer, I walked out of the now-empty bar and got into the back seat of the car. Marty drove away as I asked Benny, who was still sitting in the passenger seat, the same question. Benny looked and said, "Naw, you'll be all right."

Marty pulled the car over to take a look and said, "Benny, are you kidding me?"

Marty drove us to Jamaica Hospital, where I received a number of stitches that crossed my hairline. Fortunately, my hard head received no additional damage. While at work, I wore my hat *everywhere*, even at roll call and around the stationhouse, as odd as it looked, hiding the stitches until they were removed from my head. I never did ask about the dispute Marty had with those guys, because I never cared; I was just glad I still had both a job and my head and another episode that I wanted to put behind me.

*****

Brucie Gotterup bounced at another bar called Jagermeister, which was located at the corner of 102nd Street and Jamaica Avenue. It was a trouble spot for those who were unknown there, but familiar faces were welcome, unless you somehow fucked up. The drug dealing was a known element of the bar. But unfortunately, greedy people sometimes are looking to skim from the top, even from "friends." They justify that they should get more, as we all do in our individual lines of work, but somehow they don't understand that the people they're playing with, "friends," just don't care whether you're considered a friend or not.

And that was what happened to Brucie. He thought that if they ever found out, he would get a beating and be out, if he even got found out to begin with, and that would be the end of it. But he didn't understand that friendship is taken lightly when it rests on a foundation of the nasty business of dealing drugs. Two guys may have been tight when they were kids growing up, but times, perspectives, and values change. Once, they were climbing the sides of buildings for kicks and playing ball on the cement environment of the schoolyard, but now, if they thought their "friend" was screwing them out of drugs or money, things would turn to a very unpleasant happening. Someone told me that during the time that led up to his death, a few informed people that hung in the bar knew what was going to happen to Brucie except, unfortunately, for him. It must be a surreal feeling talking to someone you've known for a good portion of your life, knowing that they're going to die shortly because they couldn't conceive someone they deemed a friend would end their lives over drugs or money. An unfortunate way to find out about human frailty.

Me, the worst act of violence I was ever involved in—not something I'm really proud of—occurred one night when we were having one of our "pit parties." The pit was deep inside Forest Park; you had to park your car on Park Lane South and follow the dirt path that meandered its way through the trees and boulders about a half-mile toward the middle of the park. The pit was a cleared area in the midst of the park that had a huge hole dug out in the center. It was an event with little preparation. A couple of guys who considered themselves outdoorsmen would go to the pit during the day and gather a mountain of firewood. For hours they would stack wood in the pit, while others would siphon gasoline from cars. The word would be put out through neighborhoods, "Pit party, Saturday night!"

People from all around Richmond Hill and the surrounding areas would meander their way through the trees and brush to eventually see a tremendous fire in the distance, loud voices talking over one another, and the blaring music, concealed among the towering trees of the park. As you hung out and partied, more people would arrive, carrying beer and liquor in their hands. They would come drink, smoke, and get crazy around the monstrous inferno. The parties raged until the late hours, unless the Fire and Police Departments came because too many cars were parked on the edge of the park and someone made a call to 911. The fire would be doused, and so would the party. We would have these parties a couple of times a year, but on one particular October night, things almost got a little out of hand.

On this one night, a group of guys from 112 Park were at the party but left to go somewhere nearby in Forest Hills. One of them, a friend whom I played street football with, named Alex, who went by the name Cherokee, came back to say that a large group of guys jumped them on the edge of the park. So a number of us, including Eddie L and my oldest friend in the world, Tony, who were all fueled up on beer, liquor, and whatever else, decided to walk back over there and kick some ass. A small group of us ran over through the park, while the larger group went back to Park Lane South to jump in the cars and drive over.

After we left Forest Park and hopped over the Interboro Parkway (now known as the Jackie Robinson Parkway) at the only point where it came even with the side streets, we walked down Austin Street toward a small park. As we got halfway down the block, a much larger group was coming toward us, carrying some sticks and bats, and a guy right in the front was carrying a fish tank. *A fish tank?* Why would someone bring a fish tank to a fight? I could only imagine that as they walked, he saw it in garbage that was piled out on the sidewalk and thought to himself that this would be a good thing to throw at them as they got close.

We stood there frozen for what seemed like an eternity, watching this group much larger than ours coming at us and not moving. I didn't know whether to run or just shit in my pants.

At that moment, I turned and saw Cherokee come flying over the wall that lined the Interboro, the guys who came over in cars having parked them on one side of the parkway and coming over to join us on the other. Although we were still outnumbered, the sight of these guys coming over like the cavalry and Cherokee banging a stick on the sidewalk and yelling, with a deranged, wide-eyed look, got my alcohol-soused brain caught up in the hysteria. We then ran right at them with a vengeance, like a rabid wolf pack attacking its prey. As we bore down on them, they took off like bats to the hills. Most of them, except for the idiot with the fish tank, who stood there with the look of fear.

A couple of guys took a fighting stance when they reached him, not wanting to wear the aquarium as a glass turban. I ran between them and sent him into the bushes with a flying tackle, fortunately coming out unscathed from the tank. The next thing I felt were the hands of the guys I came with, who were pulling me away from this poor sap to administer the beating of his life. Blows came down around me as they started to pummel the hell out of this guy. He curled up and took the beating as I grabbed the guys who stood over him, telling them that it was enough. As the adrenaline started to come down and everyone started to cool out, I turned to see a police car with lights coming down the street.

We scattered like roaches, and I ran with Tony back into the park. But we ducked into the woods right away and stayed still and waited. But the two minutes we hunched in the brush and stayed motionless seemed like two hours. We thought it was safe enough to walk on Forest Park Drive, which winds through the park, until we got closer to the trail to the pit. As we walked on the drive, another police car approached us from the opposite direction. It stopped in front of us, and the two cops inside got out.

One of the cops asked us where we were coming from and why we were sweating so much. We said that we saw two mobs of guys fighting on Austin Street and didn't want to be involved in the mayhem so we hightailed it outa there. One of the cops then brought us over to the car and asked us if we knew the guy in the back seat. It was Mickey, who lived down the block from me and was with the guys who came over in the cars. He now had his glasses on and his crucifix prominently displayed on the outside of his jacket. We turned back toward the cops and said, "No." They said, "Get in the back seat," and off we went back toward the crime scene. My only time as a civilian in a police car.

On the ride over, all I could think about was how scared I was to be in the back seat of a police car and how even more scared I was thinking how my mom was going to take this. This was my first and only brush with the law, and it was a wide stroke as far as I, and she, would be concerned. Man, my heart was in my stomach! All I could think about was the shame if my mother had to come to the 102 Precinct to take me home or, worse, to bail me out.

When we pulled up to the scene, police cars were all over. One cop got out of the car and talked to another cop at the scene. I didn't see the guy with the aquarium, but another guy, I assumed one of the friends that ran and left him there, was talking to the cops, and as he saw us sitting there in the back of the car, he pointed to us and said, "If you let them out, there's gonna be trouble." The same cop came back to the car, opened the door, and told us to get out. The three of us hopped out and stood there as he said to us, "What's the bad blood between you guys?" We stuck to our stories, feigning innocence as best as we could. I was surprised how calm and consistent I was for someone who had never been stopped by the police before, however thinking that I was going to have a long night ahead of me and a lot of trouble in the near future. He looked at us for a moment then said, "Get outta here."

Tony and I walked in one direction, and Mickey walked in another.

We met back up at the pit and couldn't believe how lucky we were.

After that night, I never heard anything or talked about that incident again.

*****

The stories of those who, though might have not tragically ended their lives, limited their opportunities through life because of their drug activity are numerous. As time had gone, continued on through the drug use era, ball playing consumed gradually less of our time. Although some of my friends had some rare, natural talent athletically, they all succumbed to the enticement of drug use. We had a superior softball team that won a few league championships.

Our semiorganized football team, who played against the other neighborhood gangs, was known as the Convicts, because we had some rough-looking guys who were a ragtag bunch that improvised protective pads with items from the kitchen or the junkyard. But we held our own against teams who had players with names such as Nutty, Nut Job, Nutz (those are three separate, well-named guys), and Big Nick. I found myself becoming more isolated from these people I knew throughout my formative years. Many people move on from their high school years to college and then to the working world. In order to do that, I had to move on early from the monotonous and irrational waste of life to a place of meaning.

However, not all the characters I knew growing up were as tragic as these. There were a bunch of friends that were euphemistically called shirt people. As it turned out, my first form of employment came by way of this group, when a few of my friends who had older brothers among the shirt people got hooked up with jobs selling pretzels at Aqueduct Racetrack in Queens, New York. The guy who ran the operation, Mike, would set you up with a shopping cart filled with pretzels, the cart obviously stolen from the local supermarket, and a small barbecue tray filled with charcoal. After the fire was started and the pretzels were heated up, voilà! "Thirty-five each, three for a dollar!"

Now the downside of this at the racetrack was that, being the newest guy and *not* having an older brother, I got the least-attractive spot, which was in the farthest parking lot, away from everyone else, including most of the customers. As a matter of fact, I was so far away that a shuttle bus would drop people off to get in their cars at the end of the day or whenever their money ran out. Either way, I wasn't getting the big winners, but I was getting the bettors who, if they were leaving early, probably couldn't afford much more than a thirty-five-cent pretzel anyway.

Having worked at the racetrack a while, and getting valued experience at not burning the pretzels but toasting them just right, when the season came around, we wound up going to the big house in Queens, Shea Stadium, which was home at that time to none other than the New York Jets. And as in the racetrack, we worked outside the stadium, since a big corporation had the rights to selling their products inside. A lot of the older guys would work "the boards," which were display boards on wheels that had hats, pennants, and other stuff hooked on to them for all to see. And the younger guys, like myself, would be stuck with the drudgery of the pretzels, for which, of course, you didn't make the same money as the boards. But it was work.

Because I was the newest of the new and the stadium would be busier than the track, Mike put me with his father on Gate A. His father was an old guy who reluctantly took me on. Gate A, being the busiest gate there, would be great making commissions from the sales, but now that I was working with Mike's father, I'd be lucky to walk away with enough to eat and have train money home (although there was always a way to sneak on the train platform if I ran short).

Mike's father was a surly guy, didn't say much except to move out of the way if the sales got busy. Tolerance and patience were definitely not his virtues.

We'd work the crowd at the beginning and the end of the game, so we were out there about two hours before kickoff until the end of the first quarter and again at the beginning of the fourth quarter, until the crowd was gone. The crowd coming in wouldn't be bad, because everyone was coming at staggered times and there was no rush. But when the final gun sounded, it was like sharks attacking meat. They'd be coming out of the stadium like crazy, ordering pretzels two, three, a half-dozen at a time. This was when Mike's father was at his best, at his best of making me feel useless. I understood he liked working alone; there was not a lot of room around the cart, but I would have been better off walking away and coming back when it was over. Not that I wanted Mike to know that, hence being out of a job. I guess Mike's father liked me enough, or maybe he did have some tolerance, to keep me around so I could earn a few dollars to buy Spaldeens to play stickball during the week. Either way, I made it through the season.

The best part of the job was going inside the stadium and watching the game for two quarters. Using change from the smock that we wore, we'd grab empty seats somewhere, get some hot chocolate, and sit and watch half the game. Then when it was all over, after counting leftover pretzels and money, we would have to wait until we got paid, in cash, of course. Since this might take another hour or two, we'd make use of the time by scouring the stadium, climbing into the press booths, walking to the absolute top, and even jumping onto the field.

Most of the stadium workers were gone by then, so we would have the run of the place. We would go into the dugouts of our beloved Mets and run on the field where both they and Broadway Joe Namath were made famous. We'd bring a football and have a game out there on the field. A lot of the time, some faceless maintenance worker would keep the lights on while he worked. Often, as we exited the field after running ourselves ragged, tackling one another in the dirt (or mud if it rained), the lights would shut off as if to say, "Hope you guys enjoyed your fun." To this day, I hope to still think that the person who let us play on that field got as much enjoyment watching us as we did playing.

These places, the racetrack and stadium, were the training grounds for what became known for many of these highly energetic workers as the shirt people. As the years wore on, some ingenious individual saw the amount of profit out there that could be made by these hustlers in the bootleg business. And what better marketable, easily movable and most importantly, concealable product than the T-shirt. So after buying up cases of T-shirts and having a graphic artist festoon the shirt with all the trimmings, the shirt people would take their wares and, with many venues around the metropolitan area, would sell them whenever music groups would travel through town outside the stadiums.

At ten dollars a shirt, there would be plenty of customers from the people who were considering buying similar shirts that were going for twice the price inside. And with virtually no overhead, there was a lot of money to be made. And having the shirts cost them less than a few dollars to make, there was a large profit margin. Only problem was that it was illegal due to the copyright infringement laws. And the people who cared most were, ironically, the same people who were performing onstage and drawing the customers to the arena in the first place. Every shirt sold outside the arena by the bootleggers, or shirt people, was profit not seeing their way into the performers', and their associates', pockets.

Dodging the security people hired by the bands, and the US Marshals who enforced the copyright laws, was part of doing business. Of course, they had their losses, in which they were arrested and later fined and their "merchandise" was confiscated. On one occasion, when I was hanging out in some loud bar in New York, I glanced up to an overhanging TV screen to see a familiar face. But this was no TV personality; this was someone I knew. His nickname was Fitz, shortened from his surname, and he was being arrested outside some stadium. I came to realize that the station was doing a documentary on bootlegging and was actually showing one of the shirt people being arrested. After he received a summons, they interviewed

Fitz upon his release, but I couldn't hear what he was saying over the roar of the bar.

But the business was apparently so good that they made enough money to travel behind the biggest bands at the time and sell shirts wherever they played. When the bands were on the road, so were they. These guys would be gone weeks at time just like the bands—the only difference being instead of playing music, they were selling shirts. They would even go to the NFL Pro Bowl each year, which was held in Hawaii in February, sell shirts on game day, and with the money they made, stay an extra week, with their wives or girlfriends on this trip, and still come home ahead of the game. It was not for everybody; not only was it a long time away, but you *did* have to be a hustler to make money. But it was definitely a different lifestyle to be sure.

*****

Thinking I had left that senseless world behind, I began to hang out with a new group of friends that I had met through those same softball and football teams. Since my immediate friends didn't have a sufficient amount of players to field those teams, we combined with another gang that hung out not too far away from us. And at least these guys had gained more of an appreciation for a legal vice—liquor.

And the place we liked to indulge in that vice was the Shamrock Pub.

The Shamrock was a neighborhood place that had recently opened in Woodhaven, Queens. It had the typical neon lights in the front window with a long bar at the front of the place and tables and chairs in the back. John, one of the owners, was a tall good-looking guy of Italian heritage who was also the president of the South Queens Boys Club. He was slightly older than my friends and me but was viewed as a contemporary, especially on a few occasions when he displayed his speed on the football field when he played a few games with the Convicts. Since some of my friends had been a member of the South Queens Boys Club at one time or another, they had known him, not as someone who was simply a social program bureaucrat who dealt solely in administrative details, but as someone who related to the kids who were sometimes simply looking for a sanctuary away from home. As they say, he was as nice as they come.

Richie, his partner, was a Vietnam veteran, who was, obviously, the senior of the two. He was a tall Irishman with prematurely gray hair, and it was easy to see how he worked well with John behind the bar. They both served the crowd whenever the bar was open. We were there every Friday and Saturday night, usually arriving near midnight and staying almost until close.

We spent New Year's Eve that year as well as watched the Oakland Raiders beat the Philadelphia Eagles in the Super Bowl. Eddie, Pete, Glenn, and I would work Friday nights at the local supermarket, unloading items from the trailer into the store. We would finish late at night, shower, change, and met Pat and Tommy at the Shamrock. There we would spend the rest of the evening with other friends that we would not see during the week. It was our own little safe haven, where everyone pretty much knew one another, and there was rarely any trouble there. We were the unofficial bouncers, which usually meant that we would pull the knuckleheads to separate ends of the bar and get them a drink. More often than not, everyone would laugh at the end. But one night, the laughter stopped.

On April 11, 1981, a rainy Saturday night, the group of us piled into a car, and instead of taking our natural and almost-automatic course to the Shamrock, we decided to head out east to Long Island to hit a club called Speaks in Island Park, a place that always had a rock-and-roll band playing nightly on the weekends. It wasn't an occasion; it was just a change to see different faces inside different walls doing the same thing we did ourselves every weekend. We had delusions of meeting girls who weren't the same girls that we had known intimately well, and listening to live music instead of the same songs repeated over the jukebox.

After a night of heavy drinking, laughing, and running the gauntlet of county police seeking to jail all drunk drivers on the road, of which we were evasive repeat offenders, we escaped back to the city limits. We hit the local diner for our customary burgers, in which one of our stewbum crew would take the dare of drinking the pickle juice from the complimentary jar on the table before heading our separate ways home.

The following morning, I was nursing a head that wanted to be anything else but awake. As I lay in bed, the phone jolted me up at a sound that seemed ten times louder than normal. I answered it to hear the anguished voice of one of the friends that I was out with the night before. For some reason, he was a lot more alert than I expected any of us to be at this hour.

He then told me about a gruesome sequence of events that happened on the one night we decided to do something different. While we partied at points east, it was another night as usual at the Shamrock. Only on this night, the establishment was visited by a patron who was not a regular but was there with his girlfriend. He was from an area of Queens called Howard Beach, which was a predominantly Italian community that was known for a few of its locals being associated with organized crime.

Most of those associated with organized crime, or who wish they were, feel that any show of what they deem is disrespect toward them, either imagined or otherwise, is a sign of weakness if they do not deal with that person swiftly and harshly. While those within organized crime must conduct themselves in a certain fashion in order to maintain their stature with the individuals they do business with, others who emulate these men think that this is the way to deal with the public as a norm. Gangsters are involved in a life in which the strong survive. They must instill in people they see day-to-day a fear in which generates the respect they need. Without that fear, they are no one, and some of them carry that over to how they treat people in general.

While this especially particular patron was sitting at the bar with his girlfriend, someone else at the bar accidentally spilled a drink on her. An argument ensued before John quickly reacted with a calm demeanor and a free drink to all involved. The girlfriend continued to rant about how the spilled drink ruined her dress, and the patron, spurred on by her and obviously not one to back down because, in his mind, he had been disrespected, continued to lace profanities at the person who spilled the drink until John asked him to leave. He now turned his anger on John, the ultimate humiliation in front of his girlfriend of being thrown out of the bar. He continued his arrogant tirade until he was gone, stating that he would be back.

About an hour later, long after the bar had gone back to normal, at approximately 2:30 a.m., the patron returned with two other figures. He had gone to a club and told the wiseguys there, the Goodfellas, that he had been disrespected by a bartender in front of his girlfriend. A few of the guys left with him to go back to the bar and teach the bartender about showing a little respect to one of their own. As much as characters like these are romanticized by the movies, films, and television series, which portray them as fun-loving, affable goons with often funny nicknames, they will smile at you one minute and shake your hand and walk away with your money, your business, your dignity, and if they feel it calls for it, your life the next. And on this night, they went to a bar located at 86-09 Jamaica Avenue and left not only after shooting John to death but also after fatally shooting his partner and friend, Richie.

An arrest was later made for these murders. Unfortunately, the guy that was arrested for these crimes had ties to organized crime that, in turn, had their own tentacles wrapped around certain parts of both the Police Department and the Queens District Attorney's Office. Numerous witnesses interviewed stated that they did not see anything, for obvious reason. The men's and ladies' rooms, which were each the size of a large closet, were all of a sudden able to accommodate most everyone, about twenty to twenty-five people, in the crowded bar at the moment the three animals shot John and Richie dead, and of course, they saw absolutely nothing that happened. And one witness who did give an account of the events at the scene stated that she had just begun dating John. But when the time came for her to testify before the grand jury, she suddenly forgot the facts as she had told the police on that night. But this was not a complete surprise to prosecutors. Not when the girl was the daughter of a crime boss and the niece of another individual named John Gotti, a man who himself was just a few years away from orchestrating a murder of his own that would enable him to become the boss of the Gambino family, which at that time was the most powerful organized crime family in New York.

Another bartender who had also provided an identification of the mutts later lied to the cops and jurors because he knew who these mutts were. The fact that Linda Gotti also recanted her earlier statements, including the photo identification from a high school yearbook of Frank Riccardi, must also have helped with his bout of amnesia.

So after having indicted Ron B during April 1982 for his participation in the murders based on the eyewitness identification, due to the recantation of that eyewitness identification by Linda Gotti and the disappearance of a main witness against Ron B, during May 1983, the indictment was later "dismissed with prejudice" by a quizzical judge when presented with this information by an ADA of the Queens County DA's Office. And although both he and Frank Riccardi were indicted by that same grand jury, Bobby Vernace was mysteriously not identified during those proceedings but continued not to be indicted for his participation in the murders until another ADA was assigned the case years later.

However, unbeknownst to most everyone, during March 8, 1983, a fourteen-hour luncheon at an Italian restaurant in Howard Beach called Altadonna that a known organized crime figure with ties to the Gambino family hosted was attended by a Queens District Attorney supervisor and a deputy police chief. Also in attendance was an attorney who was a former partner with Ron B's attorney, Ron R, who would also represent another of the mutts when his state trial came up in 1998, Bobby Vernace.

During this luncheon, the case involving the double homicide was discussed. When the case was closed at that point, it was closed in a way that this individual could never be prosecuted for it again. There was no legal justification to close the case this way, and it was later determined that the same supervisor who was later appointed as a civil court judge in 1989 approved the dismissal sometime after the luncheon. He stepped down from the bench in 1989, coincidentally a year after the state trial. The deputy police chief, who gave conflicting statements regarding the luncheon, was relieved of his command and resigned in 1987.

Although Ron B could not be brought back to court and literally got away with murder, there were two other participants who could be tried, one of whom was in custody and the other, Frank Riccardi, the patron who started it all, who had been on the run and considered a fugitive since the fateful night. The detective had been working with an agent who was assigned to the organized crime squad involved with investigations concerning the Gambino family to locate Riccardi to no avail. But the son of one of the victims became a newly appointed member of the United States Marshal Service on the West Coast. One of the jobs of the service is the apprehension of fugitives from justice. And as part of the tools they need to apprehend these fugitives, they have access to a dizzying amount of computer databases.

One of the other mutts was put on trial with whatever evidence and testimony the State could muster in 1998. It was here that I saw an attorney I had met during a trial after I became an FBI agent, Ron Rubinstein, who, with another attorney who was the son of a known high-echelon member of an organized crime family, represented Bobby Vernace. I had been reading the *Daily News* when I saw an article about an arrest by a detective of the New York City Police Department who worked with the Cold Case Squad assigned to Queens County. It was then that I reached out to the detective and the assistant district attorney that was prosecuting the case to find out that the case had been mired in what might have been a political scandal. This scandal included a conspiracy by a member of the District Attorney's Office, an NYCPD deputy chief, and a member of organized crime, who, by appearances, had the case summarily dismissed "with prejudice," which means that no matter what new evidence was obtained, the individual could never be prosecuted for that crime, and shuttled away so that no one would ever investigate the other individuals involved.

Having the opportunity to get involved in the hunt for one of those responsible for the death of his father, the son randomly checked the databases with computers that could conduct better searches of records as technology had progressed over the years, and after mixing and matching names with a number of variations of the patron that had fled that night and his family, he came upon someone who was a match after using the first name of the patron and the maiden name of his mother, who had a social security number that was issued the same year that Frank went "in the wind." When he came upon the identity of this individual who had lived in Florida for approximately the same amount of time that the patron had been missing, he turned this information over to the Cold Case detective.

The detective, having stayed in contact with the family since having been assigned the case, followed up on this information and found other similarities that substantiated the need for a trip to the Sunshine State. It was then that it was determined that the individual was indeed identified as Frank Riccardi, which he later admitted in court. He had become a reputable member of the community during his time on the run, but that didn't negate his actions years earlier.

During the time that legal obstacles were being hurdled to bring these two defendants together for trial, an article appeared in some of the local newspapers about Rubinstein. He had been implicated during court testimony by a Mob informer. The informer stated that Rubinstein told him that a member of a small but notorious band of Mafia wannabes who were known as the Giannini crew, named for the café in Ridgewood, Queens, on the border of Bushwick, Brooklyn, where the group often met, had gone "bad," meaning he was cooperating with law enforcement authorities. When Rubinstein took the stand, he repeatedly invoked the Fifth Amendment in response to questions about the witness-tampering charge against his former client, who was a Gambino crime family member and attempted to prevent an informer from testifying.

While on the stand, he was asked by a prosecutor whether he had ever been told by the crime family member that a certain member of the Giannini crew was a "rat," Mob parlance for cooperating with authorities. Rubinstein, now using the amendment that he had counseled numerous clients to invoke and that protects a person from answering questions that would incriminate themselves before a constitutionally recognized court, stated, "I refuse to answer on the grounds that I may incriminate myself." He repeated this answer several times over to other questions, which led the prosecutor to ask, "Would you invoke that privilege no matter what question I asked you?" "Yes, sir" was the response. It was said that Rubinstein was considered "house counsel" to the Gambino family—meaning, he was involved in providing advice in regards to their criminal activities.

When I attended the trial for Bobby Vernace, I met Richie's wife and daughter for the first time, family members who had waited a long time to see justice served for the loss of their loved one. However, it wasn't to be, as the mutt, Vernace, beat the rap after whatever witnesses that eventually did come forward in 1981 either recanted their original statements or disappeared altogether for fear of testifying against mobsters. Linda Gotti, who had given a witness identification to police, recanted her statement, and the bartender who had been working that night and who also provided a statement implicating the mutts was not remembering it at all now. The Police Department mysteriously lost the gun, a .38-caliber revolver that was found by a fisherman on the Cross Bay Bridge that connects Broad Channel with Howard Beach and was linked through ballistics tests to the crime. The Queens DA's office temporarily "losing" the case file and permanently losing some of the reports that were contained therein did not help their cause. Again, the criminal justice system let them down. The two remaining defendants in the Shamrock Bar murders were tried separately, Vernace being judged by a jury of his peers and Frank Riccardi going on a separate trial. Unfortunately for Lady Justice, both of them were acquitted for their crimes.

Ron Rubinstein had represented a number of organized crime figures, including the infamous Ronnie "One-Arm." He was given the moniker due to a childhood automobile accident which left him with a paralyzed arm. But what made people fear him, peers and strangers alike, was that he has absolutely no apprehension of killing. Where most everyone would either be repulsed by the thought of taking a human life or fearful of prosecution for the same, he had neither. Whether it was sitting in *his* regular seat at the local bar or just saying hello to an old friend from high school within his earshot whom he just happened to be dating, he had absolutely no qualms about killing.

Senseless is but one of the many descriptive words that could be used to describe the events that occurred that night. For these cowards to snuff out two lives and affect so many others, friends and loved ones, because of this thoughtless act is incomprehensible to all except themselves. To understand how someone justifies a brazen act like this and has the conscience to live with it for the rest of their lives is beyond normal perception.

The thing that sets these people apart is their lack of an inhibition to kill and the remorse before or after doing it. They'll meet another associate at a club or someone's home, somewhere familiar, where the target will feel safe. They'll smile at him while shaking hands, kiss on the cheeks and a hug, have a drink, and "rock him to sleep" into a sense of false security. They can do all this, all of them knowing (except for the poor soul who's getting whacked!) that, for whatever reason, whether he made money in some scheme and didn't kick up enough or any to them (theoretically stealing from them), he was screwing with the wife or girlfriend of a made member (unless he was a good earner—made a lot of money—for them, then he could get a pass for this indiscretion) or, worst of all, he was a rat or a snitch, cooperating with law enforcement authorities. And it doesn't even have to be true; if they have a suspicion, why take the chance?

And if we had not gone out elsewhere that night, our presence there would certainly have changed this story in some way. Maybe one of us would have known Riccardi or at least have recognized his face from the neighborhood. If that were the case, maybe it wouldn't have happened at all. Anything might have quelled the storm.

Or more likely than not, since we probably didn't know him, and having the loyalty of my friends and me to John and Richie, maybe it would have been a massacre.

*****

The neighborhood where I grew up was bordered by Ozone Park, which was an extension of Howard Beach. Howard Beach has the notoriety of having a group of its citizens chase a black man onto a busy parkway, where he was struck and killed by a car. Unfortunately for him, his car broke down, and when he and his friend stopped at a local pizzeria, they were chased by a bat-wielding mob. Chased him right to where he had no place to go onto the Belt Parkway.

These sons also grew up in a neighborhood where John Gotti lived with his family. They grew up, as many wannabes did, aspiring to be someone like him, a tough "made man" of the Mafia who lived beyond his means, especially for someone who described himself as a plumbing salesman. The only thing modest about him was the house his family lived in. Everything else—his suits, cars, spending habits, attitude—was larger than life to these kids. He also had a son, John Jr., who was about my age.

I had only seen Junior, as his friends, and later the media, referred to him, in person on one occasion. It was at a bar named Port-of-Call. I was there with a couple of friends when I saw him come in to the bar. Jimmy, the brother of one of my friends, walked over and greeted him. Since there was a distance from where I stood to them, I didn't know what the context of their conversation was about. The thing I do remember is that Junior slapped Jimmy—for what, I didn't know and never asked the reason—right in the head. Now, Jimmy is someone I've known through the years as an especially tough guy who has never backed down from anyone, to include a Marine officer that he knocked out, earning himself an early release from the service. But after he recovered from the slap, he stood there calmly and did not retaliate. That was when I knew that this guy was someone not to fuck with.

Baseball was a passion of mine from the days I could throw the ball or swing the bat. Although I did not reach the heights that most every kid dreams about as they progress from Little League to high school and college, I did meet a lot of friends and acquaintances through this venue. One of these friends, whom I played many games with at a field that was a stone's throw from the Dome, was an individual who would later in life take a completely divergent path from my own. His name was John Alite.

John and I met on baseball diamonds that were home to the Rich-Haven Little League, located in Woodhaven. The two fields, which served as the venue for all intraleague games, were adjacent to each other, with the home plate to each field facing northeast, known as Twin Fields. It was there where I started to play "organized ball" as a nine-year-old and learned the fundamentals of the game from fathers and uncles whose sons and nephews were in the league and who gave their time after work to coach us. Since my father had left while I was very young, my mother would take me on the bus to the games until she felt I was old enough to get there on my own.

While playing Little League, I began friendships with many guys who lived in the neighboring section called Woodhaven. I was able to convince some of these friends that, combined with my schoolyard buddies, we could put together a very good street football team, in which we would play against other "gangs" in Brooklyn and Queens. The games would be played in full gear, or as much as each individual person could afford to buy, on park or high school fields. There were no referees, and therefore, no penalties were called.

Infractions were meted out on the field, although no weapons were allowed. We played either running time or until the sun went down. And we coached ourselves.

The gangs that we knew were a loose interpretation of what they are today. There was no hierarchy, no moneymaking enterprises or standardized carrying of either weapons or colors. It was a pretty informal gathering of kids to the street corner or schoolyard closest in proximity to their house, which, as in my case, might be the same place that you attended school. For me, it was Public School (PS) 51. To others, it was PS 90, PS 62, Richmond Hill High School, and outside the educational rim, the Jackson Pond in Forest Park, the Seuffert Bandshell in Forest Park, 79th Street, Smokey Park, and a small park located at 88th Street and Atlantic Avenue. The groups, or gangs, called themselves by the number or name of the school, as in 51 Park or Hill, or other monikers such as the Pond, the Dome, 7-N-9, Smokey Park, and 88 Park, respectively. The 7-N-9 crew had the coolest insignia; they wore denim jackets with two two-sided dice, one of which had a 3 and a 4 (7) on each side and the other a 4 and a 5 on each side (9), with the *N* in between the dice. These gangs weren't doing real criminal activity—at least that I knew at that time.

Fights would happen on occasion, usually through interactions at school, and never over anything that made sense. They would rarely involve weapons, though, either just hands and maybe something that might be close by. Most fights would result in cuts and bruises; sometimes someone would go to a hospital for stitches. These altercations would occur because of egos for the most part, so death was not a necessary end. Only when drugs became the crux of the matter did that occur.

And 62 Park (they hung out at PS 62 not far from us) was led by a kid named John Cennamo. He was a tough kid growing up. He and his group had a rivalry with my friends that would end in fistfights here and there. My oldest living friend, Tony, was the leader of our group, and he and John would tangle in one-on-ones as our "reps" every now and then. Tony's background was that his parents were from Ecuador, which made him one of the few minorities in our crew of white faces, and in all the years that I knew him, sometimes to his detriment, I never saw him back down to anyone. His brother hung out with the older guys that made up the Hill crew, which included one guy who would go forward to use his apprenticeship well, John Burke.

When the fights did occur, whether it was the groups as a whole or just Tony and John, no weapons were used, just fists, the results being bumps and bruises mixed in with a little blood, and the biggest bruise inflicted was on the ego. Again, nothing serious, until in 1984, when John Cennamo was found hanging from a low tree limb behind a self-service laundry in Saint Albans, Queens, a neighborhood not known to be frequented by him. As suspicious as both the circumstances and location were, his death was officially classified as an apparent suicide.

As I continued to play baseball and rise through the age brackets, I was picked to play on a team that was coached by Fred Alite, who was Johnny's uncle. Johnny was also picked to play on that team. We played together for three years, Johnny batting third in the order, with me hitting cleanup. We became fast friends, and I also became a fan of something other than baseball, Johnny's sister Maria. My heart would beat faster whenever she would come down to watch our game with her friends. Although I never grew the courage to ask her out during this time, as I had never grown the courage to ask anyone out at this time, I had harbored an infatuation to last through the seasons.

After finishing playing both Little League and high school ball, where we played at rival high schools, we slowly went our separate ways and I lost touch with Johnny. But then I saw him once during my freshman year of college at a club called Hammerheads on Long Island. I was inside the club with a group of friends when I saw Johnny, clad in a polo shirt embroidered with the Hammerheads logo, which was reserved for staff and security. We exchanged stories and caught up on each other's lives. Since I was overjoyed to see him, it did not faze me when this nineteen-year-old kid escorted me to the bar and introduced me to a bartender, promptly telling him, "Take care of him for the night!" He was too small to be a bouncer, and I didn't see him do much except oversee the crowd.

But some years later, stories started slowly filtering my way about Johnny robbing local drug dealers with relative impunity. These stories included people having been shot in the knees and sometimes in other places. And he was doing it openly, no mask, and it didn't matter if you hung out with the guys at the Pond, 7-N-9, Smokey Park, the Dome, 66 Park, 90 Park, or like me and my friends, 51 Park; if someone in the group was selling and Johnny came walking up to you, pony up your money.

I had not seen him in a while (and being before the time of cell phones and Facebook), but having known the diminutive, good-natured kid myself, these were stories that, as far as I was concerned, had to have been conjured up. But it all became more plausible when I read a newspaper article about a fight that took place at a waterside club in Island Park, Long Island, known as Channel 80.

The article read that John Gotti Jr., whose father was the well-known gangster associated with the Gambino crime family, was involved in a fight with a guy whose girlfriend John had made a pass on. Somehow, Junior, as he was often called, was offended to the point where he and his friends slapped the girl and beat the guy. Although the bouncers of the club were powerless to come to the aid of the couple, the responding cops from the Nassau County Police Department were not under the same circumstances. The entire entourage was arrested and the names printed, to my astonishment, to include John Alite.

Sometime later, I went down to one of the more popular bars on Jamaica Avenue in Woodhaven called the White Horse Tavern, where I thought I might find John. I wanted to dispel the "rumors" of who he was today and find an old friend I hadn't seen in a long time. If I didn't see him there, I hoped I might find a familiar face from our Little League days who might still be in touch with him. But after seeing no familiar faces, I asked someone in there if he knew of him, and with the look that I was given, I knew that I wasn't walking out the same way I walked in.

I soon found myself in the middle of Jamaica Avenue on the ground, wrestling with the one guy I asked about John, surrounded by a bunch of the knuckleheads from the bar. While he held me in a bad choke hold, I just held my ground and kept him from wailing on me. I knew if I got the better of him, it would be lights-out for me by the knuckleheads. As I kept my cool, wondering how I was going to get out of this bad situation without multiple serious physical injuries, a voice said, "Jay, you want out of this?" I recognized the voice of one of the older guys who umpired in the Little League I once played. With a weak "Yeah" from me, he grabbed the other guy and coaxed him to let go of me, taking him and the other knuckleheads back into the bar. Not able to give a thank-you, I sheepishly looked around for a clear coast before taking flight.

It was now apparent that John and my fate were much different.

*****

Obstacles can come at you from anywhere as you maneuver through life, and another one rested squarely in my path while I was involved with a local football team in my late teens. I only played there for one season, but it was a fun year, although a bit aggravating, as we didn't win many games. But the team was comprised of a good group of guys, two of whom were interesting characters who took to me right away. When I came to the team, I was looking to play quarterback and, in the preseason, became friendly with a guy who would've been one of my main receivers. But after having minimal success while lying on my back most of the first few games due to a stout but leaky offensive line, I switched over to the other side of the ball and then played next to the other character.

Neither one of them was tall, but there was an element about them where they weren't to be screwed with. While Carl was a quiet guy who did a good job at linebacker, Mike played tight end and was one of the most intense individuals I ever met. Both of them were tough guys in every sense of the word, but the thing that set Mike apart was an intensity that rose to a level that I hadn't seen in many people then. On occasion, when it was needed, he would give the pregame or the half-time speech, in which he would be literally "foaming" at the mouth. We weren't a good team and knew going in most games that they weren't winnable, but he was so inspiring and passionate about playing with heart that not only did we play for one another but also played for Mike foremost, because we didn't want to disappoint him with poor play. But also, you didn't want to get your ass kicked by him if you did.

During the season, when it became too dark to practice, we would sometimes stop for beers at a local bar on Rockaway Boulevard a few blocks from John Adams High School's football field, which was one of the original artificial turf fields in New York City and was centrally located to most of the guys on the team. Both the field and the bar were a stone's throw from the famous Aqueduct Racetrack. On one of those nights, Mike and Carl got into it with a girl who happened to be hanging at the bar as well. What started as an attempt to make conversation with her turned into a nasty exchange between them and her, where a lot of very unflattering names went her way. So she left, either to have a cigarette outside or to have gone altogether, we thought, and we figured, with the surly attitude that she had, the atmosphere at the bar and the mood of those two guys could only get better. Unfortunately, she went outside to use the pay phone and called her boyfriend, who happened to be a New York City cop.

A little while later, Mike and Carl, who were close friends and happened to be the two guys on the team that associated, and participated, in La Cosa Nostra, or the Mafia, as most people referred to it, walked just outside the bar to smoke and talk. I didn't know what they did in their other vocation, and never would I ask, but like the characters that were portrayed either in the movie *Goodfellas* or the TV series *The Sopranos*, they were both very personable and good-humored. So of course, while they were out there, up walked the boyfriend and approached them in a very heated manner. As soon as punches started flying, the guys inside the bar poured to the area outside, and seeing that Mike and Carl got a quick upper hand on him, we pulled them all apart. We yelled at Mike and Carl to walk away as we saw that the boyfriend was disoriented from the few quick blows that he received at the hands of Mike and Carl. As he stood there wobbling and trying to gather his senses, he muttered something barely audible about "guns" as Mike and Carl walked down the side street and away from the bar. Later on, it was said that a gun was pulled out on Mike and Carl, and instead of backing away like most normal people, they were able to pounce on him and get the gun away before delivering a quick beatdown.

Since the girlfriend was outside, watching the altercation in close proximity to the pay phone, she called 911 for a 10-13 and was able to provide a direction of flight and a very identifiable description, since there would likely be only two guys walking down the block wearing football pants and jerseys. Cops came flying by us while we stood still outside the bar, and zoomed down the same side street in hot pursuit of Mike and Carl.

By the time we arrived at the corner of Centreville Street and Rosita Road, where the cops caught up to them, they were side by side, handcuffed in the rear, backs arched over a small waist-high silver chain-link fence that looked as though it was about to buckle under the weight of both them and the plainclothes and uniformed cops who were shouting at them while reaching over one another with fists, billy clubs, nightsticks, or blackjacks, trying to get a piece of them. Other cops formed a perimeter and kept us back as the yelling of "Where's the guns?" was shouted at them as the blows rained down as well. Neither I nor the rest of the guys there knew it at that time, but they relieved the cop of the two guns he was carrying after he pulled one on them as the argument about what was said to his girlfriend in the bar escalated. They later told me that their intentions were not to steal the guns (as I could believe it, since they were very capable of getting guns on their own) but so they weren't shot by him in the back as they got away from what they knew was a very bad situation.

While they were in the back of the car together on their way to the precinct, knowing that another, possibly more severe beating was coming their way, Carl was able to make it look like he was going into convulsions, and Mike shouted at the cops in the front seat that he was having a seizure, causing the cops to immediately divert their trip to Jamaica Hospital, where there were many more watchful eyes, until the attorney was able to get to them.

I went to the hospital still in my football gear, and as I arrived at the emergency room, looking for them, I saw a guy I hadn't seen since high school graduation. George was a low-key person whom I shared a lot of classes with, until we went our separate ways to college. It was an odd, and soon became awkward, reunion after a handshake and a "How have ya been?" The next obvious question was, "Why are you here?" Much to my chagrin, George told me that his brother, who was a cop, got beaten up by two guys outside a bar on Rockaway Boulevard. Wow, at this point, what do I say to that?

The whole experience, from the fence to the hospital, left me disappointed in the direction of my career choice and almost changed my mind about one day joining law enforcement. But after becoming one of New York's Finest myself, I understood from the other perspective that humans have to react instinctively to situations, often with limited information. And the guy with the cell phone video almost never records the events that lead up to the final incident.

When I did become a cop, there was one incident in which a perp who stole a car led cops on a chase that ended on Park Avenue on the Upper East Side of Manhattan. After ditching the car, he ran until he was caught on the median that divided the northbound and southbound traffic, which was decorated by flowers and potted plants. As we arrived on the scene following a number of other units who were in pursuit, I saw a number of cops swinging wildly downward with sticks and clubs upon the knucklehead who had them chase him by car and then by foot.

Unfortunately for him, adrenaline churns the emotions that usually don't have the time or opportunity to subside, which leads angry humans, who have put both themselves and others at great risk chasing you, to sometimes want to impose a little street justice. It's an immediate penalty if you're caught that may have you think twice about running the next time. Or conversely, a fear of being caught by a number of cops may bear the opposite effect. Either way, nothing good has ever come from resisting arrest.

Later on, after we resumed patrol and got away from that scene as quickly as we got there, I thought back to that night outside of Forest Park and the guy with the fish tank that was getting the shit beaten out of him and how I tried to draw people away from him so he had a chance to survive a bad beating by grabbing them and taking off down the block after the rest of their mob, which at that point I really didn't care to catch. People get caught up in the hysteria, and common sense doesn't come about sometimes until it's too late.

I saw Mike many years later walking along Queens Boulevard after I joined the FBI, older, bespectacled, and a little gray, but still looking like he could handle himself as well now as he did then. I pulled over and we had a nice but short reunion right there on the street through the passenger-side window. He was doing well, and so was Carl. Even though it was a nice chat, I could still sense the intensity that Mike had in him so many years ago. At the end, before we parted ways, I asked him whether he'd be inclined to meet for lunch someday. He said that he would but that it wasn't the right time now; he would reach out to me when the time was right.

I never did hear from him again. I wasn't sure if his reluctance to meet again was because he might have been on either parole or supervised release from prison and didn't want to explain to his parole officer that he was in the company of an FBI agent, or that he was presently being investigated by a law enforcement agency and might have been looking out for me so that I wasn't asked questions by my superiors why I was making undocumented encounters with a known member of LCN (otherwise known as La Cosa Nostra), or lastly, maybe he had self-preservation on his own mind and he didn't want it to get back to his bosses that he was meeting an FBI agent for fear of what they might think our seemingly harmless catching-up-on-old-times discussions were about. Anyway, the reasoning was, I could respect it when I didn't hear from him. Like the jovial character Tony on the HBO series *The Sopranos*, or Tommy from the movie *Goodfellas*, when you were hanging out with them socially, they could be the most engaging and funniest guys in the room. But on the flip side, for those who did any kind of business with them, if they got their claws into you, they didn't let go. Fortunately, not that there was ever an opportunity for that to happen, I never saw that side of them.

Later on, I heard that both Mike and Carl were still involved in the life, had both done some bits of time in prison, and although Mike had been stricken with some type of cancer and seemed to be fading from the business, Carl was still in it, running a trucking business that was affiliated with a known associate of the Gambino family, who also operated a large catering hall in Queens. Despite our divergent paths, if Mike did succumb to the deadly disease, I would have gone to the wake to pay my respects, obviously looking past his transgressions and just remembering even the slightest bit of innocence I experienced with him a lifetime ago on the gridiron, members of a bad football team that played their hearts out.

And about that large catering hall in Queens, actually specifically located in Howard Beach, the owners of that hall originally had a restaurant, a family-owned establishment, in Richmond Hill called Villa Russo. It is still there today, near the corner of 101st Avenue and Lefferts Boulevard. As business went well there for them in the community of what once was a large Italian, Irish, German neighborhood, they were able to expand next door and opened up a catering hall aptly called Il Palazzo, the Palace, a stone-structured building that appeared as though it were a castle. There just happened to be a doctor's office next door to the hall that belonged to the brother of the then-Queens district attorney. Ironic coincidence, huh?

I had friends who worked as busboys and waiters at Villa Russo, and I attended some parties growing up in the neighborhood, having many friends who lived nearby there. Some years later in 1987, the family was able to open the biggest catering hall in New York City, Russo's On the Bay. The place was as opulent as a casino in Las Vegas, three rooms that, in total, could accommodate a capacity of one thousand guests. Many weddings, sweet sixteen parties, and organizational events were held there, as they were "in the business of executing fine events," but one party that wasn't held there dispelled any doubt of mine that it was affiliated with Italian organized crime, when a supervisory agent in the Queens office of the FBI had wanted his retirement party held there in 2013. Although some agents, including members of his own squad, grudgingly agreed to put on the soiree there because of the expense of holding the event, it wasn't until a mutiny by members of Squad C-16, better known as the Gambino Squad for their investigations of the noted crime family, acknowledged that they would not be attending that finally that agent capitulated into holding the affair in the more venerable venue, Terrace on the Park.

Appearances aside of holding an official event there, FBI agents paying the owner of a company for which a cooperating witness in an open federal courtroom testified that one dollar for every patron was kicked back to La Cosa Nostra would go against the principles of fidelity, bravery, and integrity. I think Terrace on the Park is a much nicer place, anyway. It has the location (Flushing Meadow Park), the view, where the catering hall sits high on top of a structure, and is accessed by a direct floor elevator, and the history, the edifice having once been part of the 1964 World's Fair. It was a more than fair tradeoff, and grudgingly so thought that heralded agent.

And as for Mike DeVito, I later heard that he died in May 2015. Unfortunately, I didn't find out until two months later. He toiled in a world where sudden death, although not in his particular case, would not be totally unexpected. However, in the winter of 2014, the life of another friend was tragically cut short through no fault of his own but by a mutt who thought a sucker punch was a noble way to defend the honor of his wife, if you believe someone who steals has any honor. Michael Francis Cavallari was a manager of a Foodtown supermarket on Crosby Avenue near Edison Avenue in the Bronx. He was thirty-two, loved his Ford Mustang and vacationing in San Diego, and played fast-pitch softball Sunday mornings, which was where I saw him regularly during the spring to summer seasons each and every year since he was in his early twenties. Although he lived in Howard Beach, Queens, he was a popular coach in the Throgs Neck Little League, which encompassed the neighborhood where the store was located. He obviously had an affinity for the people, and the kids, who lived there.

As Salvatore Zambuto walked into the store on the night of December 17, 2013, he put on a pair of weighted gloves before asking for the store manager. Zambuto's wife had recently been caught shoplifting at the store and was embarrassingly escorted from the premises by the store manager. Mike, who wasn't the manager on that night but happened to be on duty on this particular night, was approached by Zambuto, who punched him in the face without a warning, breaking his right eye socket and cheekbone. Zambuto, five foot ten and 225 pounds, fled from the store as Mike, five foot six and 140 pounds, went to the hospital to have two metal plates inserted into his head. As Mike was recovering from his injuries, the police put out Zambuto's photo for information leading to his arrest. On Sunday, January 5, 2014, after he had not arrived at his parents' house for dinner, family members went to Mike's house to check on him. He was found lying dead on the floor of his apartment.

Zambuto, who had a number of prior arrests, including assault and aggravated harassment, surrendered to detectives at the 45th Precinct with noted attorney Murray Richman the day before Mike's funeral. *The New York Post* reported that the "Mob-linked thug" had family ties to La Cosa Nostra. As those that loved Mike patiently waited for justice to be done, the medical examiner released the results of the autopsy and found that Mike's death had been due to natural causes. The reason, according to them, was that Mike had a condition called myocarditis of probable vital etiology, a disease marked by inflammation of the heart muscle, which often develops in people who are otherwise healthy, with a viral infection the most common cause of myocarditis, and death.

So Zambuto wasn't charged with homicide, and whether his actions were the catalyst to Mike's death, we'll never know. But New York, and the Bronx in particular, lost a very special person for nothing but his stupidity and cowardly act. As for Mike Cavallari, as Winston Wolf aptly said in the movie *Pulp Fiction*, "It is better to have character than to be a character." You did a lot of good things in your life, Mike, and you will be missed, but you will also be remembered as well.

*****

I was sworn into the New York City Police Department at Brooklyn College on July 16, 1984. For the most part of the first week, we sat in the amphitheater, filling out forms about medical insurance and beneficiaries. When we weren't doing that, they had us stand in the hot summer sun at attention in our business suits. I guess this was the part that was either supposed to build character or break us down, I don't know which, and they never stopped to explain it to us. All I do remember is that one of the members of my company, 84-87, passed out on two occasions from the heat. I don't know how much character you can build while unconscious.

When we finally reached the Police Academy, which was located in an obscure building on East 19th Street in Manhattan, we received training in a paramilitary fashion in one of the preeminent organizations in the world. Only problem was, because of the fiscal setbacks that the City of New York experienced during the mid-70s, they were doing an unprecedented amount of hiring to replenish the police officers that were lost through attrition and layoffs. My class itself was comprised of 2,100 recruits.

They split us into two separate groups that would do their schooling on two separate tours but that still had over a thousand recruits using a facility that was capable of accommodating not much more than half that number.

But they made it work. We would spend much of the day in the classroom, where we would be taught the three main subjects of the curriculum. Police science encompassed the rules and procedures of the Police Department as well as the enormous amounts of paperwork that you will be required to fill out while performing your duties as a *service-oriented* civil servant. Social science allowed the predominantly white male recruits an opportunity to learn what a *cuchifrito* was (that's Spanish for *snack stand*) and understand and become accustomed to the diverse multicultural society of the city that they had sworn to protect. And finally, there was law, which was a matter of learning and understanding the New York State Penal Code, in other words, what constituted a robbery as opposed to a larceny (*larceny* is a theft without the use of force).

Incorporated into the classroom studies was what I called gym, but it wasn't the same kind as in high school. It wasn't too tough; we ran two miles a day in company formation and did calisthenics (which sucked for me, because my company was situated right up front on the gym floor and, therefore, was unable to cheat like those bastards in the back of the gym), simple self-defense techniques, CPR, and the all-important film entitled *Delivering a Baby*.

But the unequivocal worst part of gym was the locker room, in which way too many people were expected to change and shower in a place that was capable of accommodating half the capacity. So you were limited to literally four square tiles of space to place your bag and clothes on the floor while maintaining your balance not to bump into the guy standing naked next to you. And then, after gym was over and you came back to the locker room, all these sweaty bodies running in there, running through the shower and then hopping around in your foot of square space putting on pants, socks, and shoes, now you're just as sweaty as when you were finishing your two-mile run running to your next class. I guess another character builder.

Never understood that either.

Then there was the week we spent at Floyd Bennett Field in Brooklyn, New York. What used to be an airstrip during World War II was now a training field from which to become acquainted with the capabilities of the RMP, which stood for Radio Motor Patrol, or in layman's terms, a police car. With tracks wide enough to hopefully avoid careening out of control and hitting anything animate, these cars were driven at high rates of speed and turning on the dime within cones, teaching principles so cones that were run over didn't become people run over later. It was a forum where you could see how accomplished you could be behind the wheel of an RMP or, if not, how bad you were so that the rest of us could stay very far away.

And of course, we also spent a week out in the Rodman's Neck Firing Range, which was located in the Bronx, where many of us actually held and fired a gun, in this case a Smith and Wesson Model 10 .38-caliber revolver, for the first time. If you have decent eyesight and can hold the gun steady, you can hit the target. It's that simple. Except, to somewhat simulate a situation in which your heart is beating faster, your breath is a bit labored, and the sweat is beading on your forehead, they'll have you run a couple of laps around the range before stopping and immediately firing your weapon. Not so simple anymore. And at Rodman's Neck, nobody was shooting back.

Also, while out at Rodman's Neck, a day was spent at an old house in the middle of a field that was aptly named the Fun House. The caretaker of the Fun House was a police officer / firearms instructor named Woody. Woody was an older gentleman with a witty sense of humor. I guess it came in handy, because Woody's job was to make us aware of the pitfalls of entering a residence while answering a call. And more importantly, how to avoid getting killed.

The Fun House was laid out to represent rooms and hallways of your basic house or tenement. Woody would play the part of the perp, or perpetrator, who had somehow caused your presence to be made as a police officer responding to a call. We would then take turns in teams of two answering the call and, when coming upon an armed and dangerous subject, arresting him. At least theoretically.

Needless to say, without exception, we were all "laid to rest" by Woody. But more importantly, he showed us how to act and what to do to enhance our chances of surviving deadly encounters, possibly without the loss of life, but if there was, hopefully not our own. This lesson was basically the most important one in terms of survival on the street.

Finally, six months later was graduation. Our graduation occurred at "the world's most famous arena," as the announcer proudly proclaims before each and every New York Rangers and Knicks home games, Madison Square Garden. We had been given our guns and shields on, appropriately enough, Gun and Shield Day at the academy, days prior to graduation, but this was the first time that we actually wore them in public. Both of my parents, who had long been divorced, attended the ceremony, which was like none other than I had attended. We practiced standing and saluting in unison the days leading up to this one, and no matter how many times we tried to get it down, with over two thousand newly graduated officers, it did not always come out smoothly.

But just like when a football team practices their goal line play all week but fails to execute it correctly until, with God looking down upon them, they successfully execute it on game day, we also scored a touchdown. The speeches were inspirational, telling the audience how their sons, daughters, husbands, wives, sisters, and brothers, after successfully completing training at the Police Academy, would now venture out to their separate commands away from the sterile environment of the academy and affect many people's lives, not only through depriving their liberties through arrest, but also through interactions in which they will provide aid and comfort to those in need.

But it wasn't until the end of the ceremony, when we rose from our seats, a sea of blue, and crisply snapped a salute of acknowledgment, that the cheers rained down upon us from our loved ones. As the emotions came over me, I tried to betray the feelings of joy and pride by remaining stoic among my new brothers and sisters in arms. Not wanting to defy my *machismo*, as we learned in social science as Spanish for a strong male ego, I bit my lip and tried not to let anyone see that I had emotions that some might perceive to be weak.

But when I peered out of the corner of my eye and saw the glistening of tears on the dark-blue dress uniform of Jerry N, whom I had become friendly with during our trials and tribulations during the last six months, I then realized that it *was* okay to feel human, to express both happiness and relief to have finally made it and officially become one of New York's Finest.

Upon graduation, I was assigned to Neighborhood Stabilization Unit (NSU) 6, which covered Harlem and East Harlem, otherwise known as Spanish Harlem. NSU was the concept at that time in which all the cops newly graduated from the academy would flood areas to show omnipresence, which is a fancy way of saying "We'll stand around on the street together and try to understand the radio transmissions." Most of my class was sent to commands in Brooklyn, which, with its close proximity to my home in Queens, was also desirable to me. However, I and a few of the members of my company were sent to Manhattan North, which included the area from 59th Street to the top of the island. And I specifically was assigned to the area that was now under siege by dealers and junkies, who were the most ubiquitous people out on the streets after dark.

I was to report to the 25th Precinct, which was located on East 119th Street between Lexington and Park Avenues. Early that first morning, I excitedly drove west on the Grand Central Parkway, paid the toll after going over the Triborough Bridge, and noticed a McDonald's sign high up in air in the distance to my right as I crossed a short bridge that led me to Manhattan. The sign, which was anchored down in the South Bronx, stood out in the darkness of the sleepy neighborhood across the river. It was pretty much blackened out all around this sign, which was elevated to about one hundred feet in the air. I realized that it was elevated so that anyone on the Harlem River Drive, Major Deegan Expressway, or flying into LaGuardia Airport would know that a McDonald's existed there, but it was eerie the way it shone in that black hole.

I drove south down 2nd Avenue and turned onto East 119th Street. As I rounded the corner, through the early morning haze I could see from a distance the silhouette of what appeared to be a small adult or child hanging by a noose from the overhanging streetlamp. As I slowed down and peered at the figure closer through the darkness of the early morning, the lamp shone on the figure more clearly for me to realize that this poor unfortunate was inanimate after all, actually being a life-size doll. Whether this was a sign of a different culture for me not to ignore, I was surely going to find out.

At the precinct, or what we would call the command, we gathered together in the Muster Room, where the cops would fall in at the beginning of their tours for roll call. Both new and unfamiliar faces from the academy were there, as well as our field training officers, or FTOs. They introduced themselves as Detectives Charlie P and Mick M. Charlie was a portly guy who was good-natured and had a didactic way about him when it came time to explaining something to you. Mick was a typical Irish cop, dark curly hair, reddened nose, and he would talk out of the side of his mouth like one of the Bowery Boys. He had a rough, no-nonsense exterior but would definitely treat you like "one of the boys" when he knew you were okay in his book.

One of the first things I learned on the street was to never look at a public restroom the same. That first week that we went through an orientation period, in which we sat and listened to Charlie and Mick in the Muster Room, we drove to the command in uniform and, therefore, had no reason to go in the locker room. Since we were not really a part of the 25th Precinct and were fresh out of the academy, no one talked or even looked at us except for Charlie and Mick, and they were actually talking at us and not really looking for any of us to talk back either. Therefore, nobody told me that the restroom that was adjacent to the Muster Room was used *not* by the command personnel but by the perpetrator that were arrested and brought there for processing. This, like many other things, was one of the lessons that I had to learn for myself.

And after that, the first six months on the job were more or less spent on a foot post. If you were walking a post on West 116th Street between 7th and 8th Avenues, otherwise renamed up there as Adam Clayton Powell Boulevard and Fredrick Douglas Boulevard, there were times when you might need a restroom, and unless you commandeered a livery cab, you were not going to make it to the locker room of the 28th Precinct, which was where we primarily worked as a part of Operation Pressure Point II. I had been in the restrooms of some of the most disgusting places you could imagine. Between my own personal experiences and the stories I've heard, to include an unverified report of someone getting crabs from a toilet seat, my cheeks have not touched a public toilet seat since 1985.

So after our orientation period, we were given foot posts to patrol and told not to say anything on the radio unless we needed immediate help. Look and learn! The FTOs would drive us out to the confines of the 28th Precinct, which was Harlem, each in a big van. We would be dropped off on our posts at the beginning of the tour and would be picked up again at the end of our tour. The eight hours in between those times were spent "acclimating" yourself to your uniform, which you were wearing on the street for the first time, your equipment, which was hanging around your waist and couldn't be more cumbersome, and your environment, which, for many of us, was mind-boggling in itself.

Operation Pressure Point was a brainchild by someone in Police Headquarters who decided that one way to drive drugs off the streets was to flood the area with uniformed foot patrolmen. This tactic was first employed in the Lower East Side of Manhattan and was now expanded to Harlem, which were the two neighborhoods in Manhattan that were under siege from the drug trade. Having grown up in Queens, my neighborhood friends and I had met and known people of a few different races, mostly blacks and Hispanics. We had lived near, but seldom traveled through, some minority neighborhoods. The closest one to me was Jamaica, and my mother would travel there on occasion, with or without me, because there was a major shopping area there. It was a thriving commercial area, and quite frankly, we just never thought any more about it.

When they brought us out to our foot posts for the first time, every jaw in the van dropped to the floor. During your sterile stay at the academy, they would try to describe some of the things and places you would see when you left. Having grown up in one of the five boroughs of New York City, I thought I would have been mentally prepared to encounter and deal with other parts of the city. But when I saw this, I could only imagine what was going through the minds of the guys who were from East Cupcake, as they would refer to the suburban counties of Nassau, Suffolk, Putnam, Orange, Rockland, and Westchester.

When I tried to describe this area to friends back home, I told them that this was how I imagined England looked after it was bombed by Nazi Germany during World War II. As we drove past block after block where there used to stand magnificent brownstones and six-story apartment buildings, some of the most unbelievable architecture, there would now stand empty shells of buildings and vacant lots. Some blocks would be leveled completely, with nothing but bricks caked with dry grout lying in their wake. Others would have burnt-out buildings with wooden boards covering the openings that were once protected by glass panes.

Some of the boards would have spray-painted boxes on them. I had remembered back to the instructions my social science instructor at the academy, Officer DeP, had said about those boxes. Officer DeP was a man of very few words; in fact, he tried to interest us in learning sign language. During class, he would often acknowledge a student who answered a question correctly by making a fist, knuckles up toward the ceiling, with the thumb extended between the middle and forefingers, and "nodding" it at you. He would also teach us practical lessons each day, taking from his vast amount of experience as a transit cop. One day he might tell us what the blue lights in a subway tunnel symbolize (electrical current power switch), or another he might advise us to wash our hands at every opportunity while on patrol (germs and bacteria are frequently transferred through touch; therefore, whenever you're near a sink, use it).

On this occasion, he told us that the Fire Department would provide this sign on abandoned buildings to represent how structurally sound the building was sometime after the fire was extinguished. A box alone meant that the building was structurally sound, whereas a box with one line through it meant that if you should go in there, tread lightly and carefully. A box with an X inside meant you shouldn't go in there unless you absolutely have to, and you still shouldn't go in.

Well, at that time in Harlem, there were a lot of boxes on the buildings. There would be buildings on a block with no other buildings remaining around it, standing there like Ice Station Zebra. Some buildings, and few whole blocks, would still be vibrant, with the good people of the community coming out during the day and going to and from work. But at night, those people would more or less stay inside, and the junkies, prostitutes, and thieves would prowl the night. Hence, the formation of the NSU and the attempt to make some people feel a little bit safer, particularly at night.

For the most part, our function was to provide an "omnipresence" to the community and, of course, the perpetrators, or perps, as they were commonly referred to. We were told to stay out on your foot posts and be visible to everyone, including and especially the high-ranking officers that would take the drive uptown from Police Plaza to make sure the troops were out there. An old saying was that "a good cop is never cold, wet, or hungry." Well, whoever made that saying never worked NSU, because with everyone clustered in a confined area, we all had short foot posts with not a lot, if any, places to eat, and during our eight-hour tour, we had to be seen a lot. We trudged around with belts that held our gun, nightstick, radio, mace, flashlight, and handcuffs. The bulletproof vest was great in the winter because it provided you with an extra layer of warmth. But in the summertime, you had better kept hydrating.

So during your tour, your squad sergeant would visit you twice a tour to make sure you were out there, signing your memo book to document that both he and you were there at a specific time. Since there was so much activity there, there was plenty of supervision, meaning there were plenty of ranking officers from throughout the "borough" that would come by, see you, and call you over to give you their "scratch" as well. By the end of the night, you have more autographs than if you were in the tunnel outside the Yankee dugout.

Not that I ever let a little thing like that ever keep me in one spot. On one particular evening, I was walking a foot post on West 124th Street between 7th and Lenox Avenues. The south side of the street was lined with residential buildings, both habitable and abandoned, while the north side of the street was mostly the rears of commercial buildings that faced West 125th Street. As I walked along the south side of the street, I saw some activity in front of one of the buildings that I deemed suspicious for narcotic activity from my several weeks of street experience. I entered a building about four doors down from them, went up to the roof, and walked over to the building that they were standing in front of to come down upon them surreptitiously like a cat. Only problem was, the door on the roof was locked on the inside. So much for that.

    I walked over to the next roof, since most all the buildings along the street, like most of them that were left standing in the area, were attached. You could cross rooftops practically from one avenue to the next. Thinking that maybe I could get down close to them from the opposite side, I went down the steps from the roof landing to the next floor, making my way around the feces, urine, baggies, vials, and other remnants of what had been plenty of partying and, I'm sure, other things that had been happening on that landing. But as I got down to the bottom of those stairs, I found that doors and windows were missing, more garbage was strewn about, and there were holes in the walls and floors. Soon I realize that I had just entered one of those abandoned buildings from the roof.

    After reaching the bottom step and looking around in awe at how something that had once probably been so beautiful, as many of those buildings and brownstones had been when they were built so long ago. With my flashlight, I noticed something at the end of the hallway in one of the open doorless rooms that seemed out of place with the other garbage that was there. Remembering the lesson that Officer DeP had given us but not about to make my way across the floor to an open window to try to look at the "box" by sticking my head outside, I gingerly stepped off the step and walked to the back of the building toward the object. As I got closer, it appeared to be a full-size mannequin dressed in a three-quarter-length down jacket, the bottoms of the feet facing me and the head farthest away. Not making much sense for why this would be here in the first place, I tapped the object on the leg with my nightstick, which was made of solid cherrywood that I dug out of a friend's basement and kept with me rather than the balsa wood nightsticks that they supplied you with in the academy. The figure was solid like a rock. But as I noticed the human lines on the bottoms of those feet that you wouldn't see on a mannequin, I realized I had stumbled across something else.

When the sergeant from the Operation Pressure Point Unit responded to the scene, it wasn't to congratulate me on finding this poor victim of a rape-murder who had languished in that abandoned building for a long period and might have never been found, especially after a wrecking ball had come along and brought down the building. Rather, the first of his inquiry was why I was in that building to begin with and not making my "omnipresence" felt on the street below. After my explanation that I was investigating street activity that appeared to be drug-related, I was promptly reprimanded and told never to do that again before being sent off to the command to begin the ton of paperwork that was awaiting me. While I was still there hours later, when he arrived back to the command, he then informed me about how much work ESU (Emergency Services Unit) had to do to cut the frozen body out of the floor and lower it from the window to get it down to the street below. And then there was the chief that was up from Police Plaza that was looking for me on the street below while I was in the building above, looking to give me my "scratch."

The following day, after such stellar work, I was assigned to another block-long foot post on West 117th Street between 8th and Saint Nicholas Avenues. Whereas the other block had many more habitable buildings and, therefore, more criminal activity, this block had mostly empty lots and little activity, or so they thought. A fresh coat of snow had fallen overnight, and on a vacant lot between two abandoned buildings, I could see footprints that led to the back of one of the buildings. I followed the path around the back to find a bed frame propped up against the wall. A few of the cinder blocks that were used to cover the opening of the abandoned building where the window had once been were knocked out. What perps could I find lurking inside there? I thought to myself. I just couldn't help myself.

Maybe I'll find that drug lab that will make up for my "mistake" yesterday.

After crawling inside the building, I found the place to be much more orderly than the building I was in the day before. Although it was apparent that no one lived there in a traditional fashion, it seemed like someone was taking care of the place. It had not been busted out like most of the other abandoned buildings, but it had been bricked up well enough that it was a little harder for the junkies to get in and trash the place. But someone did get in.

I walked around to the stairs and went up a flight, not seeing anyone around, but although there was no running water or electricity, someone had been here often. All the doors were off the hinges. No one in the rooms. At the next floor, I saw a door propped up against a threshold. With my .38 still out, I slowly and quietly made my way toward the door. As I slowly pulled the door away, I quickly popped my head in and out of the doorway, just as they had taught us at the Fun House, not giving anyone who might be sitting in there with a gun much time to blow my head off. After my quick peek, it started to dawn on me that I just saw a fully dressed man lying on a bed. I quickly peeked in the doorway a second time, at a different spot, so if he did shoot, hopefully he'd shoot where he saw my head the first time. Sure enough, there was a guy lying there, a homeless man who was looking to get out of the cold, and on these posts, I knew that feeling.

As I studied his face, I noticed he was an older gentleman with a lot of gray in his hair, beard, and mustache. I also began to notice that he wasn't breathing. A closer inspection revealed that, sure enough, he was dead. From the "works" that I found close to his body, he apparently overdosed during his heroin fix. Well, slowly I back away from the body as though I had never been there. Put the door back the way I found it. Crawled back through that hole in the cinder block window. Retraced those steps through the vacant lot, back toward the street. Ah, home at last, standing on a sidewalk in the freezing cold in the middle of an uninhabited block, just like I was supposed to be.

Wait a minute. I just left this poor guy in an abandoned house, and unless one of his dope-smoking crackhead friends found him and realized he was not sleeping, this guy could lie there forever. And even if they did find him, they wouldn't want the cops coming in and throwing them out of their crib. Who knew what they would do with the body? Maybe leave it down in the basement and let him rot away.

Now my conscience was going to give me a case of insomnia thinking about this. What to do? Hey, a lot of people make 911 calls anonymously, so why couldn't I then? As long as nobody figured out that I made the call, what was the harm? I was making it from a nearby phone so if the call was traced, that would make sense. Only problem was, how would a guy with my voice, sounding very much Brooklyn and none too black, make this call believable? So I went to a nearby pay phone and, after repeating the droll voice of an indigent black male junkie, picked up the phone and dialed 911.

911 Operator: "Ah, 911 Operator. What's the emergency?"

Me (trying my best to sound like I was strung-out): "Hey! Ya gotta help my friend. He's not breathing!"

911 Operator: "Where's the person located?"

Me: "HELP HIM, MAN! He's on the third floor of this boarded-up building on West 117th Street between Saint Nick and 7th Avenue. C'mon, get someone here, man. He needs help!"

Click.

Didn't want to stay on the phone long, just to get the call in and get off. Besides, I didn't need anyone walking up on me while I was talking like this in uniform on a street corner. As I strolled away from the phone, not more than thirty seconds later, the call came over the radio.

911 Operator: "Ah, 10-54. Aided case in the 2–8. Male not breathing, third floor of an abandoned building on West 117th Street, between Saint Nick and 7th Avenue. Unit to respond?"

Me: "NSU Patrol Post 17 is on the block, Central. I'll respond to that aided case."

I walked back over to the building and started to give that look at it like I was looking for something or some way in, in case someone was watching. Just as I was about to walk around to the back, as I knew it was the only way to get in since the front of the building was still bricked up, Detective Mick turned the corner in one of the police vans and drove up to where I was standing.

JUST ANOTHER DAY

Detective Mick: "Hey, Randazzo. Ahhhh, looks like we got an unfounded call here."

Me: "Well, yeah, Mick, I guess. Nobody could get up into that building."

Detective Mick: "All right, I'll call it in as a 10-90."

Just before he got on the radio, I blurted out, "Mick, can I talk to ya for a minute?"

Hey, at this point in my storied career, I wouldn't trust anyone. But on a recent night prior to this one, a prisoner had to be transported down to Central Booking, which in Manhattan was in the bottom floor of 1 Police Plaza. I was assigned to accompany Mick and transport the mutt, one of the names that we affectionately called perpetrators, there. After delivering him to the arresting officer who was going to take him "through the system" and before returning back to our command, Mick asked me if I wanted some soup.

Being that it was a cold night outside, soup sounded like a pretty good idea. He pulled the van in front of Jeremy's Ale House, located at that time under the Brooklyn Bridge. Jeremy's was a popular watering hole that also served food. Mick emerged with two giant Styrofoam cups that were covered. As he got back into the van, he handed a cup over to me, which I grabbed ahold of, but I noticed that the Styrofoam was cold. Thinking maybe it was some kind of Irish potato soup he was giving me, I pulled off the cover. White foam! Hey, this was the best "soup" money could buy. And the first of a few "soups" while working "on the job."

So after he stepped out of the van, both of us knowing about our "soup" run the previous day and having sized each other up a bit more, I told Mick the story of what happened today, including the 911 call. Mick looked at me, turned to the other two cops in the van, and yelled out, "Let's go!" We walked around to the back, hiked up through the hole, headed up the stairs, and came upon the door. As they stood behind me, I grabbed ahold of the door and said a silent wish, hoping this man was just in a deep sleep and suddenly awoke and walked away.

As I pulled the door away and peered in, I saw that it was not to be. There he was, not moving an inch since I saw him last. Two members of the Emergency Medical Service arrived and checked him out and pronounced him dead. After they left, one of the procedures concerning deceased individuals found in public places was to inventory their personal property. "Well," Mick said to me, "you found him, you search him." Nothing like going through the pockets of a dead person. At least I found his identification, and thank God it was not up to me to notify his next of kin.

During the remainder of my time working in the 28th Precinct while in NSU as part of Operation Pressure Point, I got to see and hear a lot of things about this place, both past and present. The 28th Precinct, being that it was located in Central Harlem, was a stomping ground for the Black Panthers, a criminal organization whose members were not averse to shooting cops who were attempting to arrest them or ambushing cops to promote their "political cause." Officers were "encouraged" to bring shotguns on patrol for protection and to make right turns at red lights, which was against the traffic laws inside New York City, so that they would constantly be on the move and wouldn't be a sitting target while waiting for the light to change.

Although there were incidents of attacks on police officers through New York, the most notable attack within the confines of the 2-8 was a police officer who was killed responding to a call at a mosque located at 116th Street and Lenox Avenue. I ride my bike on a memorial run every April for that officer, Phillip Cardillo.

Some of the saddest sights I saw were the hookers who worked the street on Park Avenue, just south of East 125th Street. People would joke that these girls were the "last stop" on the time line for a career in prostitution. I'm sure there are girls who do this line of work to make money and better themselves in some escort services, but these girls were longtime drug users who had nothing better now or in the future and were far removed from any possibility for bettering themselves. This was something they did for a fix, and it was going to continue that way until the end, however that would come.

A couple of sights while I was working on foot posts in the 2-8 still stay with me today. I still recall the time when, while walking a foot post on one of the avenues on a quiet morning, I could see a figure ahead in the distance sitting on the stoop of a building with his head in his hands. As I got closer, I noticed a glistening stream of fluid that ran from the pants leg like a river to the curb, over the curb, and into the street. He looked like a junkie who had pissed himself, and I was about to walk by him when I saw that the stream wasn't urine but blood. The guy was conscious, and after I called for an ambulance, I tried to talk to him to see what happened. There was no visible wound to his leg, just the still blood that had run down his leg but had seemingly clotted.

After the EMTs arrived, they proceeded to cut away his pants leg. Now I almost lost it—not only was there a large grotesque sore on his leg but there were also *maggots* in the sore. After they applied some first aid and escorted him to the ambulance, I had to wonder and asked one of them if he was going to lose that leg. He explained to me that what happens with junkies is that they run out of veins that have collapsed to shoot into, so they start going to other places and don't always get the drug into the bloodstream. When it is shot in the wrong place, it can cause the capillaries to explode, which was what happened to our friend. If one doesn't seek treatment, the maggots will eventually grow out of the dead skin.

Talk about being lethargic to your wounds.

Another time, a woman and small child approached us on Lenox Avenue. The woman was complaining to us about something that disturbed her in the neighborhood. She was a drug user who seemed to be still in a drug-induced daze the next morning. A young boy was with her, wearing a suit and tie, clinging to her and being attentive when she dropped or needed something. Not that she was aware of it, but I barely recalled much she said to me that day, because I was still somewhat shell-shocked at my surroundings and couldn't comprehend the life that this boy was going to have. He seemed as a child not unlike myself when I was his age, which wasn't all that long ago, who would hold doors open for others, address their elders politely, and want nothing more than to be considered normal.

*****

My early brush with fame and celebrity occurred shortly after my graduation from the Police Academy during these first six months on the job, when the hotel workers went on strike in 1985. The employees from certain hotels went on strike, and the NYPD had officers stationed outside those hotels to keep the peace between the picketers and the hotel itself. I had been assigned to the Hotel Carlyle a few times and had met both Jackie Gleason and Art Carney, who to this day I still love in repeats of *The Honeymooners*, but met yet another celebrity a few blocks away from the hotel. On that particular day that I was assigned there, working an overtime tour (as it was on one of my regular days off that I was working), I had not come with an overtime slip to be signed by one of the supervisors for me to submit and get paid my overtime. So on my lunch break (since the hotels were taking care of us with food from the kitchen), I took a walk from the Carlyle, which was located on East 76th Street at the corner of Madison Avenue, to the 19th Precinct, which was a short distance away at East 67th Street between Lexington and 3rd Avenues, to get an overtime request slip. As I walked down Park Avenue from the Carlyle, I came upon two women who were standing at the southwest corner of East 70th Street and Park Avenue. As I got closer, I realized that the statuesque beauty standing there was Brooke Shields, who was waiting for a car with her mother.

As Brooke and I were about the same age, I couldn't help but let my boldness come out of my head in my fairly new blue uniform and stopped to engage both her and her mother in conversation. Although I was sure that there was no way that she could miss an opportunity to converse with a handsome, ginger-haired hunk in uniform, it turned out that her mother was more engaging and personable than Brooke was to me, much to my chagrin. Thinking I could sway her with telling them that no one knows New York City like a cop, I asked her on a date, sort of awkwardly through her mother, since Brooke wasn't paying me much mind. Her mom was very sweet to me, and when the limo pulled up, I held the door for them, knowing pretty well that Brooke Shields wasn't going to be calling the 25th Precinct, asking the telephone/switchboard operator in the 124 room to speak to Officer Randazzo. But I can at least say that I, somewhat, tried.

I did once meet Luis Guzman up in a club called Slopes in Hunter Mountain during the late 1980s. I don't know how, but a friend of a cop that worked in my unit, Richie, saw him and gave him a big hug before he introduced him to us. I had recognized Guzman from the movie *Scarface* at that time, but he continued after that as he largely played character roles as a sidekick in movies such as *Carlito's Way*, *Out of Sight*, *The Limey*, *Traffic*, *Boogie Nights*, and most recently, *Top 5* as himself!

My last interaction with celebrity occurred on summer when I took an overnight motorcycle trip to a friend's house in Amagansett, which is a town near Montauk. The driveway of the house was rock-strewn and a bit hilly, so I needed to park my bike behind some cars, one of which happened to belong to Fox Business News' Cheryl Cassone, who was renting part of the house. Later on in the evening, she walked from the house and approached me in a breezy summer dress and heels as I lay on the deck near the pool to ask, sweetly and politely, if I would kindly move my bike so that she could get her car out of the driveway. It was a lustful (at least on my behalf) yet innocent interaction that, years later, a mutual acquaintance by the name of Anthony Scaramucci confirmed her remembrance of the brief interlude. I had met "The Mooch" while conducting an FBI investigation during the time that he was a regular on the Fox network, and I could not resist to ask him if he would inquire with her if she remembered the incident. And, no, he was not the target of the investigation.

But getting back to Slopes—now that was an interesting place!

It has closed down since then, as well as the Heartbreak Hotel (well, that place actually burned to the ground). My friends and I would go up to Hunter Mountain for the weekends, since it was the closest mountain in New York State to the city. Although none of us knew how to ski, we'd go there and party Friday night, sleep all day Saturday, and repeat the process until we returned back home Sunday night, unless we decided that a 6:00 p.m.–2:00 a.m. tour on Monday meant a stay-over Sunday night. Skiing wasn't learned by me until I joined the FBI, and while working in California, I learned to Rollerblade in Venice Beach. When I returned to wintry New York, I just applied the same principles of turning and stopping on blades to skis, and what do you know, a kamikaze skier was born!

They also held the Police Winter Olympics in Hunter Mountain, and the guys who went to Hunter Mountain regularly from the Manhattan North Task Force would get together a team and play in the only competition that our talentless selves could enter, Broom Ball. The game is played on ice just like hockey, except with brooms for sticks and a rubber ball for a puck. It was a fun game, but we were always out in the first round, trying to maneuver around the rink in our sneakers while more serious teams, the State Troopers being one of them, would get special shoes with suction cups on the bottoms and run circles around us, scoring goals almost at will. One year, I had my employment interview with the FBI on the same day as our first-round games (in which we were eliminated as usual), so I not only missed the game but also missed one of our guys slip-sliding on the ice, smashing his face and losing a tooth! But that was okay; we were there more in spirit to party than to compete, and party we did at Slopes after the games were over!

At least we didn't have to get up early the next day to play. Since the Olympics were played during the week, there weren't a lot of people on the mountain except cops and those that wanted to be around cops. And I had been in my share of cop bars, but I never saw a place so out of control as Slopes during the week of the Police Olympics. The bouncers just stayed at the doors and made sure nothing spilled out into the street with the public; otherwise, it was mayhem on the inside. The place would be rockin', the band would be playin', people would grab the devices that the bartenders used to mix drinks and have water fights across the bar, others would dive off the lofted floor where the pool table was located into the crowd below, and shots would be poured straight from the bottle into mouths. I've never seen anything like it before or since, a crazed, chaotic free-for-all that had to have calmed down since then, but what fun it was at that time!

Speaking of MNTF, there was a cop who had worked there but resigned from the job long before he was eligible for retirement to pursue a passion that he had, unbeknownst to most of us who worked there. David Zayas had also played small parts in *Law & Order* and *NYPD Blue* before he later had a regular role as Enrique Morales in the HBO prison series *Oz* and Angel Batista in the series *Dexter*, which lasted eight seasons, as well as the movies *Stepmom*, *Rounders*, and *The Expendables*. He also appeared in the series *Person of Interest* and *NY Undercover* before he took on the role of Sal Maroni in the Batman prequel *Gotham*. I once saw him before he left New York for Los Angeles in an off-Broadway play called *Jesus Hopped the A-Train*. He had resigned from the NYPD, but I was able to talk to him after the play and wish him luck before he left for LA. It's nice to see someone who pursued their dream as he did and it worked out well. Unfortunately in LA, it rarely happens, and there's a lot of waiters, waitresses, and bartenders who know it all too well.

 I met Curtis Sliwa on an occasion when the other guys that I had season subscription tickets to the New York Rangers in 2015 (yes, we were there for Game 7 of the 1994 Stanley Cup Championship!). We would meet for cheap beers at a pizzeria that was at the bottom of the escalator that descended from the driveway that divided Madison Square Garden and Penn Station. He stopped for a slice of pizza after most of the fans had left, and we, as we usually did, took our time finishing our beers to get to our seats in time for the puck to drop. He was an amiable person, but I had found Adam Graves, a former player with the Rangers whose father was a cop in Canada, and Kiefer Sutherland, whom I met in a bar on Stone Street once and was as friendly as could be, to be genuine people. But probably the most oddly funny encounter I had with one of my "brother" officers during my probationary period occurred on one tour of duty just after midnight, when a vehicle flew past us as we were parked at the curb in the Eighties on the Upper East Side and continued to barrel down 2nd Avenue, just missing every traffic light that turned red before the car got to the intersection as it sped to try to catch up to the green lights. The traffic lights are usually synchronized to turn green so you could virtually "ride the wave" of green lights as you drive down an avenue if there are few cars on the road.

After finally getting the car to pull over, I had approached the vehicle on the driver side when a grizzled guy in his fifties, obviously very annoyed, yelled at me, "What the fuck did you stop me for?" Now I was a bit taken aback and stunned that this guy yelled at me, and as I tried to muster my composure and sarcastically respond, "Excuse me?" he immediately continued to berate me as though I was keeping him from something. "I was trying to stay up with the lights!" As I stood there still in astonishment, trying to put it all together, he then said, "I'm in the 1-9!" before turning forward and screeching away from where we had stopped him before I could say much else.

It wasn't until then that I realized that the driver was a veteran officer who was from the 19th Precinct, which had been temporarily relocated to East 95th Street between 1st and 2nd Avenues, and who wasn't used to being pulled over since all the cops in his command, and probably all the other ones who were assigned to commands along his route home, knew him and his car. At this point, all I could do was watch him catch the next wave of lights like a surfer as they continued to cascade down 2nd Avenue, laughing to myself yet again.

*****

While I was assigned to NSU 6, the "police culture" slowly began to take ahold of me—not necessarily in a bad way, just different. A former cop opened a bar on the corner of the 25th Precinct, where we had our lockers, attended roll call, and went out on patrol or "turned out," that became a hangout of sorts for the cops at that command. It wasn't so much after the 8 A.M. to 4 P.M. shifts or tours (8 by 4s), which gave you a semblance of normal life, where the sun still shone and life would still bustle as you left the command; it was rather the alternate weeks in which we worked the 4 P.M. to midnight tours (4 by 12s), which was when, and this happened often, you went out with the boys after your official tour of duty. These outings were referred to as 4 to 4s, because the last 4 hours of your "tour" were done in the corner watering hole. Not that we were on the books, but the last four hours were an unofficial extension of your regular eight.

It was at this time that the culture started to give you the feeling of omnipotence, the true Achilles' heel of most police officers who are fired and/or incarcerated. Although you're still on probation, in which time the slightest slip-up could cause you to be terminated from the job, after you've become adjusted to walking around with a shield and gun (cops do not refer to it as a badge but rather a shield), you soon develop the feeling that you can do no wrong, and even if you do, there's a way to make it right. Not to say that a lot of cops walk around as though they also hold the title of judge and jury, but the empowerment that goes along with the title, to actually be given the power to restrict, or even take away, people's freedom can put one's ego in a very different light. Toward the end of my time with NSU 6, since we all were to be reassigned to permanent commands, we went out after a particular "4 to 4" to Roosevelt Island. One of the guys had been a cop on the island and suggested we take a ride there to go by the Lighthouse.

The Lighthouse sits on the northern tip of the Island, which is sandwiched between Manhattan and Queens. We picked up more beer on the way from the bar and drove over the bridge from Queens and toward the Lighthouse.

After more drinking before we arrived there, someone got the bright idea to let off a few rounds out over the water upriver. A few more guys followed suit and also let some rounds go. I also had my gun on me, but my beer-soaked brain wasn't so far gone as to think that this was not the smartest thing to be doing. Behind us not too far away were apartment buildings. People lived on Roosevelt Island. To the left was the FDR Drive, and although it was now about 6:00 a.m., there were still cars driving by and people watching an impromptu fireworks show. Good thing this was both pre-9/11 and cell phones. And there was only one way on and off the Island, besides the tramway, but abandoning our cars there was not an option.

After getting back over the bridge before any "sector cars" showed up, we drove back into Manhattan, found a 24 hour store, and got more beer. As we hung out on the corner of East 14th Street and 1st Avenue, drinking beer pulled from a cardboard box that was now an improvised cooler, people walked past us, hurrying to their workday. We then saw what appeared to be an official-looking department car parked on the corner. Was IAD, what was then known as Internal Affairs Division, now watching us? Did a phone call come in while we were on the island, and were we trailed back to Manhattan? Paranoia set in as we watched the car, whose occupant appeared to be watching us. After discussing what to do yet too terrified to get close to the car, we finally called it a night and left in separate directions, not knowing who might visit or be there at the next roll call.

Although nothing came of it, it should have been a wake-up call for all of us, only I'm sure we all didn't awaken.

As we went along and listened to the guys who had been on the job for a while, we began to learn the parlance from which cops conversed with one another. You wore a *shield*; security guards wore a badge. If a bar or club you went to charged a cover to enter, you'd "tin your way in," showing your shield to the bouncer and asking if there was a law enforcement discount, knowing that you would most likely enter free. And the one term that was probably around for the longest and was the mostly widely used and appreciated was "on the arm." "On the arm" was a polite way of saying *free*. People would say a particular restaurant was good because the cops ate there. That wasn't necessarily true; they probably ate there because the food was "on the arm," or at least heavily discounted.

And then there was "collars for dollars"; because not everyone was paying a mortgage and looking to make as much overtime as possible, particular cops would be "looking" to arrest someone to parlay their tour into additional hours of overtime. Not that they would invent arrests, but rather, they would be more aggressive during situations where other cops might look toward mediation. And if you worked in a drug-prone area such as Harlem and Washington Heights, there was always easy collars floating around the streets; it was just a matter of how many civil rights you needed to violate to arrest them.

If you're working in one of these neighborhoods, besides the usual "Shots fired" and "Man with a gun" radio calls, you have a very good shot of finding an individual who may be in possession of a firearm on the street. A stop-and-frisk is only to be conducted when a police officer has reasonable suspicion that someone possesses a weapon. However, a police officer's perception about what may have been a weapon if articulated well enough becomes a valid search rather than an illegal one. And the fruits of that search having been validated now become admissible as evidence. I'm not saying that some police officers lie regarding the circumstances in which they find a firearm on an individual, or in a car lying in "plain view" on the passenger seat, but it doesn't take too much creativity to come up with a scenario of how the gun is found to make the search good, or legal.

And in regards to racial profiling, in these neighborhoods, which are predominantly black and Hispanic respectively, our profiling was of a different kind. Many cars with "white faces" from the suburbs of Long Island, New Jersey, and Westchester could be found trolling the streets looking to "cop" some drugs. As easy as it was to find a white kid possessing a controlled substance, to wit cocaine, heroin, or angel dust, simply stopping him and searching him was like shooting fish in a barrel. Because, back in the day, there was no other reason for him to be in that neighborhood, *especially at night.* Most of them were too scared, doped up, or just plain stupid to know. You "toss" them by searching their pockets or cars, usually without any other cause except that they were white, and more likely than not, drugs would be found.

None of these arrests would go anywhere—forget about trial.

They would get collared, you'd make your overtime, and they would plead out to a misdemeanor. Most everyone caught for possessing a small amount of drugs, it was found in his hand. The criminal complaints read like an absurdity: "Defendant was seen standing on a street corner, holding a vial of crack cocaine." There seemed to be a lot of people standing around with their drugs in their hands, because you can search someone for weapons but you can't search them for drugs, barring exceptional circumstances. So the next best exception to a search is "plain sight."

And if for some bizarre reason an arrest did go far enough that a police officer did have to provide testimony, he could testify creatively, that is "testi-lie." Everything is perception. I'm not saying that there are thousands of rogue cops out there searching people indiscriminately, putting them in jail unjustly, which is far from the case. Rather, there's a lot of hardworking officers trying to do the right thing but struggling to balance constitutional rights and keeping people safe in their own neighborhoods.

After having spent most of my time walking foot posts in the 28th Precinct under what was known as Operation Pressure Point II (OPP I having been established in the Lower East Side, or Alphabet City, as it was more commonly known), I applied to and was picked up by the unit known as the Manhattan North Task Force (MNTF). Obviously not the most elite unit, taking not only me but also two other cops I worked with who also had all six months' street experience, the MNTF was also mired in OPP II; only difference between what I was doing then to now with the MNTF was that I'd be riding in a marked car that had heat and air-conditioning rather than walking the street looking for a place to survive the elements. Not an easy task in Harlem in 1985.

The MNTF was a small unit that turned out of the Central Park Precinct, a rickety old building that was kind of quaint but not well cared for at that time. It was staffed by uniformed cops that drove around in different precincts, although at that time everyone was assigned to Operation Pressure Point II in the 2-8. Accordingly, we were not a "slave to the radio" which meant that "Central," or rather the 911 operator, didn't have us on her computer screen, and since neither she nor any of the precinct cops knew we were out there, we weren't assigned radio jobs.

Therefore, if an ambulance was needed at a residence or a burglar alarm went off at a business, a precinct sector car would be assigned, and if we wanted to, we could go too, which we rarely did. The theory behind the MNTF was that if something would happen that needed a rush of cops quickly, whether it was a spontaneous protest or a large crowd gathered at a shooting incident or there was a hostage crisis somewhere the crowd needed to be controlled. We had to be available and ready at a moment's notice, never letting the gas tank get below half-full, because you never knew how long you might have to go somewhere for a duration of time between fill-ups.

So in turn, you couldn't be stuck somewhere, waiting for an ambulance to show for an "aided case" or to safeguard a business while waiting for someone to come and fix the broken window of a shop that was broken into if an incident took place that warranted the MNTF response.

But we were able to answer jobs that a disposition would be quick, which, for the cowboy in us, were commonly "Man with a gun," "Shots fired," or "10-13," which is a cop in trouble. These were the jobs where the adrenaline rushed as you weaved through the streets, looking to be the first ones there to find a gun on someone, which is what most adventure-happy cops are looking for. Gun collars—this is the glory stat of the department. It's impressive, and if you're looking to get into a plainclothes unit like the Street Crime Unit, this is what they're looking for, guys who get gun collars. This is the "fun" part of the job.

Most of the calls are 10-90X, radio terminology for unfounded, which means either someone placed a call to 911 hoping to see all the pretty lights and cops respond at their whim or the parties involved have moved on before we get there. Usually, again, it would just be some sickos looking to make the cops run around for no reason except their own gratification. But on occasion, particularly when a description is given and it's pretty specific, you'd find your man. Some cops would patrol with an eye out, looking for gun collars.

It takes a knack, as well as patience, to stop someone in the street and find a gun on them. Or some cops would frisk any character that appeared likely to carry a gun. That would lead to a lot of unconstitutional searches, no rhyme or reason, no reasonable suspicion or fear of life, just a mope hanging out or acting a bit suspicious or just being in the wrong place at the wrong time. Not that it was right for all the people that were searched and no gun was found, but once in a while, one was.

Then there are the cops that make it an art to find someone with a gun—that's tricky. It will just start with the suspicious-looking guy, but it doesn't necessarily stop there with a frisk. Is there actually a bulge under the jacket in a spot where someone may carry a gun? If he's not wearing a jacket, is there something odd around his waistband? An object like a large uncoiled paper clip can have one end put through the barrel of a gun and the other looped over the waistband so none of the gun is seen. Does he occasionally put his hand on his person like he's checking to see if it's still there? Does his walk appear to be altered, as though he has something somewhat heavy concealed on one side of his body? Although it can be worn on the front, on the small of the back, or on either side, most mutts will conceal their guns around their waists. Finding them is half the fun.

Most of the cops I worked with were good-natured people; most of them, like me, wouldn't know what to do with themselves if they hadn't passed the entrance exam for the Police Department. The amount of drinking among us all was about the same, except a few of them, thanks to not being on the 911 operator radar, would drink *during* the tour. Now you would think that even if we're not answering any calls, the two times per tour the sergeant came around to give you your "scratches"—meaning, he would sign the next open line on your memo book, noting that he visibly saw you and that you were out on patrol—would have put a damper on that. But if you sit on the passenger side of the car and your partner, who hopefully isn't as hammered as you, can drive up, hand him the books through the window, and take off without the smell of alcohol coming near the sergeant, then you can get away with it, and in one particular cop's case, this was often.

This was a guy who was on his way to big trouble or death from a drunkin'-driving accident on his way home from work or a bar that the drinking continued afterward. Since hardly any cops take mass transit and all drive, there were a lot of potential DWI accidents out there. How this guy made it all those years without killing himself or someone else is a miracle in itself. Although he was a funny guy, he did some crazy things. While downstairs in the Transit System, he and his partner came upon a junkie who was so zonked out on heroin, while his partner spoke to the junkie, this cop walked behind him and pissed on the junkie's leg.

There was another cop who had the craziest laugh, like he was part-hyena. During these times, all cops carried revolvers, which were the guns with the cylinders where the rounds are stored. Most every cop, particularly those that rode in RMPs, wore swivel holsters, which were holsters attached to a pivot on the belt that you could swing the holster, with the gun in it, between your legs when you were sitting in your car seat. The style was made in the event that you needed to get to your gun while seated, as if someone would walk up to the car, gun in hand. The downside of this holster was that when you ate in the car, which would happen many times by the nature of the job (because you were either too busy to sit down like a human being or you eat junk food a number of times during the course of your tour), whatever fell from your mouth or dripped off from your food fell into the holster.

Now, most cops, who must qualify to shoot only twice a year, regularly cleaned out the holster and wiped down the gun. However, this cop apparently did neither. So fortunately for him, one day before roll call weapons were being inspected, which was a rarity, and it was found that his firearm had absorbed so much crap that it was actually *rusted shut*. Another cop, who was six foot six and strong as a bull, attempted to push open the cylinder of the gun and it would *not* open. If the cylinder doesn't turn, the firing pin can't go back, and the gun won't shoot. As usual, when the cop saw this, he laughed like a hyena. I'm glad he was able to laugh about it in the command and not find out on the street.

Cops use an array of names to identify the individuals that have broken, or are suspected of breaking, the law. The term mostly used and heard on television and in movies most often is *perp*, short for *perpetrator*. But there are a few other names commonly used among law enforcement, including *mutts*, *mopes*, and *skells*. But Mike was a cop I worked with who had been assigned to the New York City Transit Police Department before the three entities, City, Housing, and Transit, were merged into one New York City Police Department.

Having worked in the Transit Police Department, Mike coined his own word to describe criminals that was much less offensive and maybe even a little confusing when said. He called them hats. When I asked how he came up with that, he said that he noticed that most of the perps that were arrested wore hats, hence the moniker.

Speaking of the Transit Police, I had the utmost respect for them, and despite most recruits in the academy wanting to be assigned to the City PD first or Housing PD second and hoping not to get picked to patrol in "the hole," I secretly wouldn't have minded having been assigned to the Transit Police Department. I liked the fact that they patrolled alone, because I liked to do what I wanted when I wanted (I guess that's the only child in me!), although at least at that time there were reportedly a lot of "dead zones" in the radio communication system where, if you needed help, you really were alone! And it seemed like a good place to meet women, since nearly everyone took the train at some point, so you'd have a chance of meeting almost anyone down there. Getting paid to socialize, with life-saving moments (maybe my own) in between them.

*****

Most guys would get their assorted amount of collars and, obviously, their overtime. A number of arrests, although completely valid, were about overtime. But that was the way the system was set up, so that was the way the cops used, or sometimes abused, it. It happens in any field of employment. Some people will do it, no matter what the profession. But money can also lead to bad behavior.

During an incident where there was a drug arrest, I, along with a partner, was told to search an apartment in Washington Heights for any other drugs, weapons, and money. While we were there in the apartment, we found money that was concealed inside the pockets of clothes that were hung in a closet. The money amounted to about a thousand dollars, but instead of counting it at the scene in front of a supervisor, because there weren't a lot of cops there, we were told to take it into the station house and count and voucher it as evidence there.

As I drove to the precinct, my partner that night, who was holding the money, took it out of his pocket and counted it there. He then counted $200, folded it, and put it in his pocket. He counted another $200, folded it, and handed it to me. I played stupid and asked what he was doing, knowing at this point that since no one counted the money at the scene, no one, except for us and maybe the drug dealer, knew how much was in the closet. I then purposely sped up to the other car that we were following back to the station house, where the captain who was on the scene and the perp were sitting, and yelled, "Hey, put it back, they're right next to us!" hoping this would dissuade him from taking the money. He said, "Hey, let me know if they're right there," before shoving the $200 into my pants pocket.

I walked around the station house as guilty as a thief with all eyes on me. Any second the money was going to fall from my pocket and I would be found out. I had accepted free beverages and food from merchants before while working, but this was the first, and only, time that I had taken money, albeit not willingly. I acquiesced to accepting this money, not that it made me any less guilty. I didn't want it to happen, but I didn't resist because of peer pressure. I could only imagine how Serpico felt, and this was nothing compared to what he went through. It's a secret I've never told anyone.

Whether he just took it as a part of something that happens when the police were involved or he didn't notice it was missing, the perp never reported the money gone. Being he was Dominican, as was most of the population of Washington Heights, and that most of the police force was corrupt where he came from, he probably just figured it was gone. Since the precinct where we worked that night as well as a lot of other nights, the 34th Precinct, led the city in homicides and drug arrests for many years in a row, this was another small blip on a large radar. I'm glad this incident didn't lead to other similar challenges, because I would have had to stand up much sooner than later.

The saying goes "Where there's drugs, there's guns," and this precinct was certainly plentiful in both categories. There were plenty of characters and radio-runs to provide material for *NYPD Blue*. On one radio-run, we were able to make entry into an apartment that was used as a drug den. We could have arrested the occupants of the apartment for the drugs they had there, but instead of the cops bringing in the dopers and their small stash to the precinct and wasting our night with it (obviously, no one there was looking for the overtime), the apartment was trashed, the cops that responded with me using their nightsticks like Louisville Sluggers, smashing most everything that stood. Knowing full well that the occupants weren't going to go and make a complaint, since they were relieved that they weren't going to jail, the cops trashed the place with impunity. The stash going in the toilet, we walked out of there with our own version of "street justice" having been played out.

I've seen quite a few shooting victims and a few grisly scenes in my time, but two incidents stand out the most. On one occasion, a sector car responded to a call at an apartment. Upon arriving to the location and making their way in, they came upon a head that was cut off from the body. The one thing that made this head a little more interesting was that whoever had cut it off thought that the deceased must have needed a break, because they propped the head up on a dresser and put a cigarette in the mouth, still smoking by the time we arrived there. Talk about a sick sense of humor.

The other incident occurred in an apartment wherein the perp was shot dead by a cop. After arriving at the crime scene—and everyone knows by now from watching *CSI* on TV that people entering the crime scene are supposed to be kept to a minimum to preserve the evidence—cops were swarming all over the place to get an eye on the dead guy. He was lying on the floor against the wall, his mouth open, with what seemed like a quiet scream, a frozen look of fear etched on his face. It almost seemed like he knew that death was inevitable.

The only other guy that I saw who "lost his head" was under a train at the West 181st Street and Broadway station. Don't know if he was pushed, jumped, or fell, but there was his head, cut neatly at the neck, sitting there next to the rail under the train that had no time to stop for him. If there's any consolation, at least it's quick.

When cops speak to one another, they say they're "on the job," which can be taken as a narcissistic term by some. It means that they're a part of a thirty-thousand-strong gang, the biggest gang in world. When it's spoken, it's done so as a source of pride, because the NYPD is the best police department in the world. Nowhere else can someone experience and learn more about the human race than as a member of the NYPD.

*****

"Hey, call the Fire Department! I'll wait down here." That's what I should've said. We were on patrol in the three-four that early evening, the sun still above the horizon. Mark W and I were driving up Saint Nicholas Avenue near East 179th Street when someone flagged us down and matter-of-factly told us that there was a fire around the block. "Okay, thanks, we'll check it out," was the reply as we casually turned the corner to handle the, judging by the demeanor of the citizen, small fire in the garbage can or out on the curb.

It wasn't until we turned again onto Amsterdam Avenue that, much to our dismay, we found a fire raging out of the second-floor window of the corner building. As the flames danced outside the window, Mark radioed the dispatcher to send the Fire Department while we ran into the front vestibule.

As people ran by me, Mark and I started banging on the doors that lined the corridor of the first floor, seeking to alert everyone there that the time to leave was now. I ran up the steps to the second floor, where we had seen the apartment that was engulfed in flames. As I peered into the apartment to see that the fire was still burning out of control, one of the neighbors told me that everyone was out of that apartment and off the floor. I told him to leave and I would go up to make sure the building was clear.

Being that the interconnecting floors to the building were not that big, I figured to be up and down way before the fire would build enough that it would enter the hallway. However, I didn't take into account that the smoke would kill me before the fire did. And it wasn't until I stopped between floors to see the smoke rising like the tide, filling the hallway and immersing me quickly, making the brightly lit hallway suddenly go dark, that I realized this.

A window was just ahead of me, and I dashed up the few steps that separated us to shove my head out of the window and get a breath of some badly needed air. But as bad gets to worse, the window was opened but the opening was covered by child safety bars. Already weakened and panicking from the smoke, I first pulled on the bars, but I had to find the building with the diligent custodian that put these things on tight. I then squeezed my mouth as far through the small opening between the bars to gasp for some air, of which little I got, with the smoke enveloping me from behind.

It made me remember those times when I was a small child and got in the deep end of the pool, in "over my head," as they say. It was that same feeling, not only of helplessness, but also of having that need for air, that panicked sensation when you're crying for that next breath but know that it's not coming without a struggle. And it may not even come at all. Your adrenaline jolts you alive and your mind races, looking for a way out—there's always got to be a way out! So far, there always has been. So far.

Fearing that the fire had engulfed the second floor hallway by this time, I set it in my mind that I would have to suck in one last breath and, before I succumbed to the smoke, make a beeline for the roof and hopefully see my way out of this. Since it was now impossible to see, I would have to feel the entire way up the stairs and hope, or rather pray, that the door that led to the roof was not locked or, in some other way, obscured. Well, away we go. But just before I was about to run up, I heard my partner scream out my name. When I heard his voice coming from below, my strategy changed from going up to going down. It sounded like he might have been in the lobby, and I hadn't seen any flames yet, so I figured this might be my only shot and took off with that last breath, feeling my way along the banister and passing the apartment on fire, smoke now billowing out of it like a furnace smokestack. I kept on going down until I saw Mark's face, never so happy to see the sun shining off a lobby floor before.

Having learned my lesson about fires in Washington Heights, a few years later, I was walking a foot post with another officer, Kenny S, in Harlem when we were alerted to a fire burning in an apartment off Broadway on West 144th Street. As we approached this building, which was set back from the street by a large courtyard, the fire was again on the second floor, flames leaping out of the apartment. Whereas the other building had apartments that spindled around the staircase and were much closer to one another, this building had long hallways and the apartment on fire was at the end of the floor.

This being late at night, as Kenny and I climbed the stairs to alert the tenants, many of them ran by us in all sorts of bed-wear. As we banged on apartment doors and ran higher up the stairs, we came upon a family of a mother, two daughters, and a ninety-three-year-old woman on the fourth floor at the top of the stairs. The elderly woman, who was both blind and deaf, was confined to a wheelchair, and they could not get her down the elevator because other people were jamming into it and they couldn't get the wheelchair in. I told them to follow me down the stairs as I carried her out.

As I quickly assessed the situation, thinking the fire shouldn't have reached the middle of the building where the staircase was yet, I decided against traumatizing the woman any further by slinging her over my shoulder in a fireman's carry and instead picked her up with my arms and made my way downstairs, with Kenny leading me and the rest of the family following behind.

As we made our way down the first flight of stairs, I was wearing just a little bit carrying her that way but felt that we'd be out soon and everyone would be okay. But as we walked along the floor and prepared to descend the next flight of stairs, the smoke quickly rose and I saw the reflection of fire on the stairwell wall. We hurried our steps, and as the smoke formed around us, the weight of the woman started fatiguing me more and more. We dashed by the fire, and as we went down the last flight of steps to the lobby, my legs were now wobbling and I began to lose control as the firemen raced past me to get to the fire. As I tripped over the hoses as they were rushing to get up the stairs and fell backward onto the steps momentarily. I still clutched the woman and assured the family that we were almost there. With the last bit of strength I could muster, I pushed myself up and we made it through the lobby and out into the courtyard, breathing hard but grateful to have made it out yet again.

I would later on take the test to become a firefighter, placing number 151 out of the thousands of applicants who took the test. I was proud of attaining such a high list number but never got any closer to the job than starting the background investigation, because it was at that time that I was called to my present occupation. The Fire Department was a much sought-after job, and I remained on the list until it eventually expired, never looking back. I would have appreciated the camaraderie of the job, and especially the work schedule, but you usually never know where a path you decided not to take may have led you.

*****

On September 11, 2001, I had a morning appointment to meet with an Assistant United States Attorney at their offices located in the Southern District of New York, which was directly next to 1 Police Plaza in Lower Manhattan. Usually, we would schedule our meetings for either 9:00 or 10:00 a.m., but due to an earlier appointment for him, our meeting was not until 11:00 a.m. As I began to shave my face while listening to the Howard Stern show on the radio, I heard him say that an airplane had crashed into a tower of the World Trade Center. I turned on the television and, as incredulously as most every American who did the same, I asked myself how could a large commercial airliner mistakenly find its way into one of the tallest buildings in the world on a perfectly crystal-clear day. But we all soon after knew.

On that date, 343 members of the FDNY perished under the rubble of the edifice known as the Twin Towers. Also on that date, a sole FBI agent braved the carnage and was also killed in the tragedy. I didn't know that agent personally but had heard that he was a kind and helpful individual to those whom he worked with. He also left behind a family. I later worked on the squad to which he had been assigned, and the deference paid to both him and his legacy was astounding, the monuments left on his old desk never to be moved. Fortunately for me, my fate didn't include being entombed with so many other courageous souls on that day.

*****

I don't recall exactly when I decided I wanted to apply to become an FBI agent. I remember taking the test for the New York City Police Officer exam when I was in high school; it was the thing to do, and most of my friends took the exam, although not a lot of us took it seriously at that time. I even went out drinking with my buddies the night before and was not exactly feeling 100 percent on the day of the exam.

Most of us did.

By the time they got down the list to my name, I was finally starting to realize that I didn't have the talent I had hoped that would propel me to a career in the Major Leagues and settled for number 2 on my wish list when I was a little boy and was sworn in to become one of New York's Finest at Brooklyn College on July 16, 1984.

Although I looked forward to my career in blue, timing was a bit ill-fated when my relationship with a college sweetheart took a dramatically bad turn the weekend before the swearing-in ceremony. I had the hugest crush on her in high school, but beyond my name, she did not have much more than the faintest idea who I was. She wasn't really one of the "in" girls but rather hung out with just a couple of friends, one of whom, like her, was on the track team. While practicing indoors before baseball season one year, she and a couple of her teammates were running around the track that circled above the gym. As she was going around, I tried to get her attention by gingerly throwing a tennis ball up toward her. I got her attention, all right—got her right in the eye! That sure made an impression.

After graduation from high school, I attended a local college called Saint John's University. As luck would have it, that same girl also attended there, and having the same schedule on certain days one semester, we commuted to school together with another friend. I briefly dated the friend, who was the first girlfriend I ever had (yes, this was college, but in those days, sex wasn't as much a preoccupation as it is now and all I was ever interested in doing during high school was play ball). Well, after dating this friend, even though she dumped me for a guy that I knew, whom I provoked into a ridiculous fight in front of the neighborhood bar one night and for which I still carry the scar on my knuckle (as stupid as I was), the other girl took notice and did what most dopey college girls who were too shy to do anything about it did: she told her close friend, who told my close friend (they were dating at that time), who told me. Might not be romantic, but it got my attention.

Now, by the time she took notice of me, I was kind of over her. As a matter of fact, when this friend called me to play the "Guess who likes you" game, the girl that I had dated was my first choice. After going through a litany of girls that hung out with us at the neighborhood bar, and then a few others, I finally blurted out her name. Was I shocked! But after we finished work that night at the local Key Food store, went home, showered, watched *Miami Vice* (loved that program), and met up at the local bar, for the first time when I looked at that girl, she couldn't maintain eye contact. Who would have thought?

We dated for two and a half years after that first night, and unfortunately for me in the end, we entered this relationship with a disparity in sincerity for it, me being the nineteen- to twenty-one-year-old knucklehead who was more interested in hanging out with his buddies, and she wanting more and more time than I was willing to give. Although I treated her respectfully, I was too young to be involved in a relationship for all that time, and as it goes, eventually the time was going to be filled by someone else.

A friend of mine who worked out at the same gym as she did told me about a guy there who was paying some special attention to her. When I asked her about him, she insisted that he was "just a friend." As we got closer to graduation from college, which was now another school for me during my pursuit of the right place to play baseball, I began to convince myself, probably at the threat of this new guy, that I wanted to be with the girl more now than ever. Since I was set to go into the Police Academy and I wouldn't have time off for quite a while, she had wanted to take a trip before I started. However, my mom had different ideas and had planned for me to take a trip with her to visit her sister in San Diego. Not wanting to disappoint her, I went to San Diego but promised the girl things would be different when I returned.

Thinking about her most of the time I was away and having bought gifts for her and her mom, I was anxious to see her as soon as I returned. I called her while away, and she said that she might be going away with her cousin and might not be home when I got back. I said it was okay, that I'd see her soon after.

On the Sunday she was coming home, I called the house several times, asking if she was back yet. Wanting nothing more than to see her smiling face, I drove to her home that night and waited in my car across the street to welcome her home, knowing her family was visiting a relative and no one was there. As I anxiously fiddled with the radio while my car faced her corner, a black Celica pulled up and stopped across the street on the corner. As the passenger turned to look in my direction, although it was dark in the car, by the glare of the streetlight, I could see who I thought to be my girl sitting in that car. But my sudden dilemma was, Whose car was that? My heart raced as I got out of my car and walked toward the Celica. Immediately it took off, and as I chased it down the block, it made the light and drove away. Frantically I grabbed change out of my car and called her friends, my friends, anybody who could give me an answer about what was going on. After failing to catch anybody at home, I walked back and tried to rationalize what I saw, refusing to believe that I might have lost her.

They came back about an hour later, stopping at the same corner, only now I was sitting on her stoop, waiting for the inevitable. She walked over to me and said the lines that make you cringe when said, starting with "You promised me the world…" When nothing more was to be said, I walked dejectedly away toward my car. Not wanting to pass the driver side, for fear of acting out irrationally, and not wanting to jeopardize my appointment to the academy, which was due to start a week from tomorrow, I walked past the front of the Celica. As the headlights beamed on me and I felt like the idiot on parade, I flipped the last coin I had not used, in the futile attempt of making sense of this earlier, that was in my hand onto the hood of the car.

After I walked to my car and started to pull past them, he got out and said, "Hey, I hope I don't have no beef with you!" I stopped my car and told him not to worry; neither he nor the girl would be seeing me anytime soon, if ever. He then sarcastically responded, "Wouldn't it be funny if we were in the same class together?" I looked at my *former* girlfriend and asked her if he was going into the academy next week. She said he tried but he didn't get in. I drove off, my heart broken and battered.

I did go back during the next week and spoke to her, to no avail. She was firmly entrenched in her new camp, and I was done. I revisited the times in my head, like shortly before we began dating and she and her friends were watching us play football. She and another girl actually had words over who was going to wear my varsity jacket, which I had left on the sidelines while the game was going on. Times like that once made me laugh, until now that I was sitting in class at the Police Academy, one week of 8 to 4s, the next week of 4 to 12s (we didn't start extending our tours to drink yet), sitting there at night pining away for the days when I used to tease her with the Rolling Stones song "Under My Thumb" because she was always that much more into us than I was, and now I was left wondering what she was doing.

I've always said that timing is everything, and if the girl and I had met later in life, when I could have appreciated her more, things quite possibly would have been different. People's personalities and ways of thinking change exponentially as the years roll by. But if that had happened, I probably wouldn't have had many of the experiences that I encountered and met the people I did, professionally as well as personally, which led to some wonderful times of my life.

*****

After meandering my way through Saint John's for a year and a half and then, through the advice of my sandlot league baseball coach, another year and a half at Nassau Community College, I finally finished up in a year with a BS in criminal justice at John Jay College of Criminal Justice. Now, the only way I made it through college in four years was that the New York City Police Academy gave a number of credits for attendance there. Knowing that, as well as the fact that I wasn't going to make that dream of playing Major League Baseball, I figured out what I needed and crammed in as many courses as I could so that after the fourth year of college, all I needed was to complete the academy and then I could apply for my BS. Took me three years to realize it, but I finally took my studies seriously enough that the last year, I gave up my spot on the baseball team and instead made the dean's list.

My class at the police academy had its fill of personalities. Included in this bunch were a Russian with dark spiked hair, a bushy mustache, and a thick accent who didn't seem like the guy that you would want to fool with; a loafer whose father and uncle were both detectives on the job, and you could see that he was expecting that to carry him a long way; a class clown who liked to imitate the instructors and anyone else that would make people laugh; and a Puerto Rican who came over from the Department of Corrections and knew most everything about life and the job and wanted everyone to know that he did. I also had three friends from my neighborhood, Marty, Pete, and Mary, in our "sister company," meaning our classrooms were next to one another and we had the same instructors.

Our police science instructor was an Irish guy who sometimes seemed a little scatterbrained and discombobulated as he taught the lesson but was a nice-enough person. Although I have seen him on TV on occasion as he has risen through the ranks and become a captain, I still can't help but to remember the time he almost shot off his own foot. All the police officers at that time had two revolvers, one that was worn on duty, while working in the street, and another that was worn off duty. Although both weapons were .38 caliber, the on-duty revolver had a four-inch barrel, which was too cumbersome to wear off duty, especially in a holster on your ankle. So most cops would have an off-duty revolver that had a two-inch barrel and was more easily concealable. However, the instructors at the academy would wear the off-duty revolvers while teaching class since they were smaller and not as cumbersome as the service revolvers.

The instructor came upon a lesson that had a point about a cocked weapon. Wanting to actually show the class exactly what he was talking about, he drew his weapon from his holster, released the cylinder that housed the bullets, unloaded it before closing the cylinder, and proceeded to cock it while unloaded and continued the discussion. After finishing, he opened the cylinder and replaced the bullets before closing it and putting the revolver back in his holster. As he continued to speak, I saw the jaws of my classmates on the opposite side of the classroom drop and their eyes widen as they looked to see on the instructor's right hip that he had holstered a loaded and cocked revolver, the hammer of the gun dangling in mid-air. As they meekly pointed this out to him, he gingerly pulled the revolver back out and slowly lowered the hammer down. He never said anything about it again, and neither did we.

The law instructor was a gentleman, a soft-spoken Hispanic man who knew his lessons and taught them well. I would later see him supervising security at Madison Square Garden at one of the many New York Rangers games I attend as a season subscriber. But it was the social science instructor who was the most interesting of all. He reminded me very much of Al Pacino in his appearance, but he let his facial expressions and body language do most of the talking. He was not a man of extraneous words; he said it softly, and he said it one time only. He was proficient at sign language and would sometimes only acknowledge us with it, making us try to at least learn some of the signs. And the thing I remember most of all, he would give us little "tips" every few days, those things that were not taught at the academy, per se, but that were some important things to know when you were removed from the sterile environment from which you were learning before you hit the streets.

He had been a transit cop, which meant that when he was on patrol, it was in the depths of the city, in a place known as the subway system. I had always admired transit cops, and although most recruits except those with brain damage wanted to be a city cop and stay aboveground, where most everyone wound up, I almost secretly wished that I were selected as a transit cop. They worked patrol alone and were in close quarters with the public, which probably wasn't a bad thing when trying to meet girls. But to me, there also was this mystique about them, almost like a superhero who uses whatever powers are available to him to get the job done, and hopefully get the girl as well. Guess that was why I worked alone for most of my career in the FBI, without getting the girls.

He would give these little extra tips that I'm sure most other instructors never thought of doing. He once gave us his transit keys, otherwise known as the 400 and 475 keys, and told us that it would "behoove" us (a word I would hear most often in the academy, but not before and not much since) to make copies for the entire class before returning them to him. These keys opened most every lock in the transit system, and someday while on patrol, you might need to get into a closed station or area to assist, or apprehend, someone. And as I wrote earlier, it was also he who taught us to read the "box" signs on an abandoned building, which tell you how unstable it is, before you decide whether to go in there. A spray-painted empty box means that the building is pretty stable, a box with a half X means that you can go in but proceed cautiously, and a box with an X inside means you have a good chance of falling through the floor.

He also preached once that the best way to avoid contracting diseases while working is by simply washing your hands at every opportunity. The bacteria that makes us sick is transferred through physical contact, usually when you touch something with your hand and then touch your mouth, eyes, or nose. Most people still don't seem to understand this concept today, and he was telling me this in 1984. Whether at a restaurant, hospital, back at your command, wherever, it would behoove you (there goes that word again!) to wash your hands whenever you can. One of the many lessons, some of which I do instinctively without really remembering, that I can be thankful to him for doing the little extra for his charges.

*****

When I left the Police Department and joined the FBI on April 23, 1990, it was the first time I left home. Part of the reason for joining was to leave home and, at that point in life, leave New York. I had been living with my mother until this point, and although at the age of twenty-seven I thought it was time to leave and get my own place, I couldn't justify getting another apartment and paying more rent when my mother had a two-bedroom apartment in Queens. But if I left the job and New York altogether, it might make commuting a little harder from elsewhere.

After turning in my weapons at the 102nd Precinct for "safekeeping" until I was accredited by my new job to carry a firearm, I remember the desk sergeant commenting after I told him whom I would be working for, "It ain't like it is on TV." That just told me even more that I knew I was more than ready to get out of there. I then packed up my little Honda with the things I needed while attending the academy, shared a very tearful goodbye with Mom, and off I went to Quantico, Virginia, home not only to the United States Marine Corps headquarters but also to the FBI Academy.

I had never driven that far before, from Queens to Quantico, which is about fifty miles south of Washington, DC. After the exit off I-95, the drive is another five miles through the grounds of the US Marine Corps Headquarters until you reach the academy, which is a nondescript campus of buildings interconnected by clear tunnels. I later found out that these tunnels were the only ways to stay dry during the humid summers that the area suffered, which I would have the misfortune to experience firsthand.

On the opposite side of the road from the buildings was the firing range, where I had the opportunity to discharge more than my firearm one night with a bureau photographer from Chicago who was there for training. They did not necessarily discourage sex there, just not on the grounds. However, lust and opportunity took better of my senses, as it did for a few others there, and, fortunately for me, did not get me into any trouble on this night, or the other one in my car down the road by the lake with another trainee from Oklahoma City that was a few classes behind me. Fortunately, the Marine patrol that walked up on us was pretty sympathetic.

Each of their stays at the academy came at different junctures to my course of training. Although the interludes were brief, the relationships were both emotionally and spiritually uplifting for me, as I hope it was for them during a time of great stress for all of us.

Back behind the buildings was a fenced-in laboratory (or so they said), and we never really found out what was going on there. And then there was Hogan's Alley, a mythical little town, shops, intersections, and all, aided by role players who were civilians whose backgrounds were investigated and were paid by the FBI to participate, where agent-trainees would go through their practical exercises in regards to investigations, interviews, and apprehensions of subjects.

That first night we were there, we met with all our instructors in the amphitheater-style classrooms where we would sweat out the next four months. I left a job in New York that, although I did have up to a year to return, I would be mortally disgraced having to return as a "flunky" who just couldn't cut it. And if that didn't end my embarrassment enough, a return to my old neighborhood disgraced would definitely put me over the edge. So although you needed an average of 80 percent or better on each of the tests of the three disciplines to graduate, I had great confidence I was going to be okay. And then I came upon Mr. Rogers.

Now, while all the other instructors looked what I thought FBI instructors to look like, here was this guy who said he was Mr. Rogers, who was the physical education instructor. The guy didn't look like anything special; if anything, he looked old enough to retire already. With him having a slight build and not looking particularly strong, I told myself that this was going to be easier than the Police Academy.

This man could run like nobody's business, and whereas other instructors might do more self-defense and less physical exercise, he just loved to run. He would do self-defense as just a change every now and then and would still get a run in for that session. I was never fond of running to begin with, and now here I was with the Tiger Woods of runners. Only the gazelles in the class would sort of keep up with him; the rest of us were just hanging on until the finish. It was so bad that when we would get the itinerary for our sessions for the following week, I would cringe as I read whether we had him one, two, or God help us, three times that week.

When we went on outdoor runs, he would run like a deer, and at least with Virginia being a scenic place, there was something to look at to take your mind off the pain. And at least I knew when we saw the academy buildings again that our final destination was in sight. But for the longest time, I never understood how Mr. Rogers would decide indiscriminately when we had enough abuse when doing laps in the gym. When we ran in the gym, we did it as a group and with everyone running, as they did with almost everything else we did down there, in alphabetical order. It wasn't until toward the end of the academy, when a trainee whose last name began with T and who, therefore, ran in the back of the pack told us that when Mr. Rogers saw him throw up during the run, he would announce, "Two more laps!" as though that was his barometer of when we had enough. Pretty funny, I thought.

Mr. Rogers was always preaching about fitness and staying trim. Having a very dry sense of humor (I don't even think he knew it was funny), he once told us about the time he had a layover at O'Hare Airport. After looking at a lot of the people around him, he realized that the meaning for the name Chicago must be "city of big asses." Another story was when he had gone home to Rockaway in New York. He went outside and put his foot up on a fire hydrant to tie his running shoe. An out-of-shape individual walked over to him and asked him what he was doing. "I'm going for a run," he replied. "What for?" the man said. This was his way of impressing upon us a sound and healthy lifestyle.

And when the academy was almost over, he finally explained to us the reason that he ran us to almost death so often. As an FBI agent, you will never know if you may find yourself in an encounter with someone that could go to the death. No one around to help you, just you and him, and he's not going to let you take him to jail before one of you dies first. If this struggle continues and you reach a point where you just don't think you have enough to survive, now you know you do. Just when you think you've given it your all and you have no more to give, there's always that something extra that will allow you the opportunity to survive this fight. It took a while to sink in, but I eventually understood what he was trying to instill in us, never to give up or a never-say-die attitude, so to speak. I had hated this guy for four months, wondering why he got such joy doing what he did. Now I understood why.

The rest of my stay there was pretty basic, classes in law, procedures, shooting—all the stuff you see in the movies. We'd do our practical exercises in Hogan's Alley, the small town I described earlier in which actors were hired to play various roles and we investigated crimes that were committed there and, like in most TV shows, solved the crimes by the end of the hour, or in these cases, by the end of class. If only it were that way in the real world, as one of the instructors liked to say. There would be stressful times; no one wanted to fail and have to return to their old jobs, if those jobs were still available to them.

I would have really hated to go back to the NYPD and face my former colleagues about not making it—that would've sucked. I also took a bit of teasing from one guy in my neighborhood when it didn't appear that I was getting in to the FBI Academy. I passed my written exam and was afforded an interview, which I had thought I had done well but didn't pass. I had to wait a year to take the interview again, in which I used the time by writing to get my files from the Freedom of Information Act (FOIA) section to see what I had failed to do to gain acceptance.

Although the files were mostly redacted so as not to compromise the application process (meaning, they blackened out everything that they thought might give me an *unfair* advantage should I try the interview again), I was able to see the topics that were graded and how I scored. I did the best on current events (since I was told that I would be asked questions about both foreign and national affairs, I read the front section of *The New York Times* every day and maintained a journal on world history / politics—I was so into it!) and almost as well with oral communications (I did pride myself on speaking well), interest/motivation to become a special agent (man, was I motivated!), and overall impression, but on the topics of resourcefulness, range of interests, and accomplishments, I only received mediocre scores.

So after finding out what I thought I needed to do to pass the interview process the second time (even though I wasn't that hopeful), I passed the competitive examinations for the rank of sergeant for the New York City Police Department and entrance to the New York City Fire Department (which I thought were pretty good accomplishments), related some stories from my experiences as a cop (which showed how resourceful I could be; I took a shot with the DOA / doped-up-junkie-phone-call story), and broadened my range of interests (at least that was what I told them).

And fortunately for me, I was well prepared for the second interview and passed it. After seeing that guy again and letting him know that I was accepted to the academy, to have gone back to the neighborhood without making it, no, that wasn't going to happen.

After graduation from the FBI Academy, I was directly transferred to my first office in beautiful Stockton, California.

Now, when I was in the academy, I was told that I was going to be working in the main office in Sacramento. However, after I made contact with the agent who got you settled, he told me that there was an opening in one of the satellite offices, what the FBI calls resident agencies, in a small town called Stockton. The office was now manned by three agents and a secretary but was supposed to be staffed by four. The boss in Sacramento was looking to get someone in there who should be able to handle themselves, and they were looking for either a former police officer or military officer to take the spot. He asked me how I felt about it, but it was obviously a rhetorical question.

The bastards didn't even tell me directly. They waited until my graduation, when I came home for my four days of administrative leave to get my affairs in order before moving west and left a message with my mom. They said, "Tell your son to come to Sacramento to say hello, but don't unpack your bags, 'cause you're going to Stockton." When I had found out that this was a possibility while in the academy, a classmate named Susan, whom I nicknamed Boo because she was a park ranger from the Midwest (she didn't take kindly to the name either), had a good laugh as she told me that I better get ready for the real cowboys where I was going.

Now, before you graduate, you get a chance to "pick" where you are going to go, a so-called wish list. You get five choices, submit them to the Transfer Unit, and if there's an opening in a place that you have on your list, they'll probably send you there. If you pick spots in one region and there's no opening in a particular city you've picked but there is one in the region, they'll put you there. But if there's not a spot opened or you scatter your five picks throughout the country, then they throw a dart at the map of the country and there's your new home.

I wanted out of New York, even though I was told anyone who picked New York got it. No one from outside of New York wanted to work there, from the high cost of living to the way it was portrayed on TV (yeah, believe it or not, the outside world puts a lot of credence into what the media shows about New York). So anyone who wanted it got it, but not me. I wasn't going back.

So after I submitted our picks, on which I put my "dream" picks in rank order of Tampa, Daytona Beach, Cocoa Beach, and two other beach towns I could find on the map in Florida, my counselor came to me before lunch and told me that the Transfer Unit got everyone *pretty close* to where they wanted to be—everyone but me. But rather than being put somewhere indiscriminately that had an opening at that time, I was asked to make five more picks and have it done after lunch. I appreciated having the second chance to have a hand in where I might be for the next five, ten years, or maybe forever. Talk about pressure.

He said that there were presently openings in a couple of offices, Boston, Denver, San Diego, and Sacramento. Those openings may not be there after lunch, but I might get lucky. He also said that if I put down New York, I'd get it. He also reminded me that I once said to him that I didn't want to go back there, that I needed a change, and he had hoped that I wouldn't change my mind now, and I hadn't changed it. Boston was too close to New York, I had friends who moved to Denver for a month and all they had to say was they heard a lot about child molestation out there, and I had family in San Diego but wanted to go somewhere that was away from everyone I knew. So Sacramento was the choice.

When we got our assignments, they were handed to us in front of the class and we read them aloud. We had heard stories of people whose faces dropped when they heard that they were going from New York to Mississippi or vice versa, and also that they sometimes did a "joke transfer" to someone who vehemently said to the class (and counselors) that there were places that they would not go. Our guy was TJ, who was one of my suite mates (two rooms with two beds each were connected by a bathroom shared by all four), the tallest man in the FBI at six foot ten (he played pro basketball for the Atlanta Hawks and in Europe), who said the one place he wouldn't go was Jackson, Mississippi. No, he wasn't from New York, but he had heard about the general feelings the people there had for blacks, and he wanted no part of it. When he looked at his transfer papers, the look on his face had the class and counselors rolling. However, he wound up in St. Louis.

My roommate, Todd, who was a Maryland State trooper, was sent to Daytona Beach. He had it number 1 on his list; I had it number 2. Like Agent 86 said on the iconic show, "Missed it by that much." Everyone else got what they wanted, or near it. Even Boo got her spot in DC. And here I went to cowboy town!

The ride across the country was pretty interesting—I didn't realize how many cornfields there were in the heartland of America. During the drive across, uncertainty about my ability to do the job for which I had just completed four months of training filled my head with anxiety. It wasn't like I was going to a big office where I could just fit in like another cog in the machine. I was going somewhere I would stand out if I wasn't up for the job, and it kind of panicked me, just a little.

After the greetings were made in Sacramento with the big boss, what they call the special agent in charge, I drove down and stayed the night at a motel in Stockton. I called the senior resident agent (SRA), the guy with the most time, and he asked me to meet with him, the other two agents, and the secretary for breakfast. This should be fun, I thought.

As we met at a diner, I introduced myself to Arthur, John, Mike, and Diane. As we drank coffee—I was too nervous to eat—we sat for a while and they told me some of the basics about life at the RA. Arthur was an older gentleman, someone who, over time, I nicknamed "Casper the friendly ghost" because, although he was a gentleman who treated me well, he had an innate ability to disappear during the workday (this was especially easy, considering our direct supervisor was located in Sacramento). John and Mike were agents out of Quantico just a couple of years before me. John was a former college football player, raised in Ohio, but became a police officer in Florida where he met his wife. Mike was a former military officer raised in Boston, also married, with three daughters. Diane, the secretary, was a wonderful and generous person who had married a retired agent. I had no idea about the interesting times that I would share with these people over the next year.

I followed them back to the office, which was on the second floor of a post office building. The office consisted of one big room that was shared by the four of us *and* our equipment. The boxes that I mailed from Quantico filled with books of knowledge that I would never look at again sat on my desk, which faced the window that looked out over the park, the park that was infested with drug dealers. Although the downtown area was seedy enough, after five o'clock, it became a ghost town except for the homeless and helpless. The federal building itself, where I was once greeted in the morning as I stepped off the elevator by a young woman who raced past me while she was pulling up her pants after urinating in the corner of the elevator bank, wasn't much better. I was told that the cops had once chased a felon across the rooftop. Without even enough time to unpack my boxes, a report of a bank robbery came over the radio. I grabbed pen and pad, and we raced out the door to the bank. On-the-job training was about to begin.

After we arrived at the scene, where the local police and detectives had already arrived, we went about our business interviewing witnesses, processing the crime scene for fingerprints and any other evidence that was found, retrieving the bank surveillance camera tape to get a look at our subject, and just getting as comfortable as possible to my new surroundings. The term *subject* was new for me in my occupation as a federal agent, replacing the descriptions I had once used as a cop, such as *perp*, *mutt*, and *skell*.

I had never worn a firearm in plainclothes before as a cop. I had always worn the service revolver, a Smith & Wesson .38 caliber loaded with six rounds, while in uniform, in a holster attached to a uniform belt, and when I was off duty, I wore my Colt Detective Special, a snub-nosed .38-caliber revolver, in an ankle holster. This was the first time I was wearing the gun while dressed in business attire, on a belt. Problem was, since my personal finances weren't great, I only owned a reversible belt (black on one side, brown on the other side) that the teeth of the buckle would cinch down on the end of the belt and hold it. So now, on my first official day on the job, I had to fight with the problem of the weight of the Smith & Wesson 10-millimeter semiautomatic weapon loaded with twelve rounds in the magazine and one in the chamber sitting in the holster affixed to my belt, just being a little too much weight for the buckle. And it came loose.

Fortunately, I was quick enough to catch it before it hit the floor—how embarrassing would that be! I cinched it up as tight as I could, but it wasn't holding. As I conducted the rest of my work, mostly interviewing witnesses, I had to hold the gun against my side with my right elbow to keep it from falling, all while asking questions and taking notes. Picture that. I couldn't wait to get back to the office, sit down, and figure something out.

We finished our on-scene investigation and returned to the office. No sooner had we walked in the door than another bank robbery took place. We headed back downstairs to the cars and responded to this one. We conducted the same type of investigation, and I soon realized that, when it comes to bank robberies, the investigation at the scene pretty much includes the same type of interviews and evidence processing, repetitive but important. We finished up there and headed back to the office, only to hear about another robbery over the radio as we got out of the cars in the parking lot. Three bank robberies, and it wasn't even noon. I was assured that this was atypical, and I should only hope so!

I had to laugh. Here I was with my elbow pressed up against my side, going through this unbelievable morning. It got so that I just had to tell someone, and it wasn't going to be someone from my office. So as one of the bank employees was telling me how she saw the bank robber come up to the window, I began to tell her about my day. Since she wasn't traumatized from the robbery, I thought it was a good opportunity to let it out and make her laugh, which it did. At least the story was cute enough that she went to see the movie *Ghost* with me later that evening.

During my yearlong stay in California, I experienced a part of America I knew was out there but never envisioned myself being a part of. The two things that made California special were the climate and the landscape. It never got too cold, but it could get hot, like that dry heat that makes you feel like you're in an oven. And the landscape there was green, luscious and beautiful.

I had packed everything I owned in my Honda CRX Si, a cool little two-seater that was filled to capacity with my personal belongings. The only thing that I had shipped out there was my motorcycle, and when it got there, I did some nice cruising. A lot of paved roads through rolling hills and valleys, it was a biker's paradise. No wonder the Hells Angels started out there. I even had the opportunity to ride through and around those hills to attend the Calaveras County Frog Jump Jubilee. A whole fair centered on an arena where people brought their frogs up one at a time and let them make the jump of their little lives.

On more than one occasion, I found myself driving on some dusty road in my police-looking Caprice Classic, looking for someone I needed to interview and wondering what I was doing here in the valley. Instead of street signs, I was looking for a mailbox in the middle of nowhere. When I thought of California, Los Angeles and San Francisco came to mind, and if you were looking for a small town, there was San Diego. Here I was in Stockton, "the deepest seaport," as it was proudly proclaimed on the front of an aboveground oil tanker fifty miles south of Sacramento and ninety miles east of San Francisco. A town of about a quarter of a million people, recently known for being the catalyst for the bill banning assault weapons because some idiot shot rounds near a schoolyard. Also, a lot of colleges were there, but not much else, except for crime.

Stockton was ranked second per capita in regards to crime after Los Angeles. With both I-5 going through the west side of town and Route 99 going through the east side, there were a lot of subjects going through town, with some of them deciding to stay there. It wasn't a lot for a bank robber to come through, stop to rob a bank (like one-stop shopping), and get back on the highway. All these highways, or escape routes, which ran south from Stockton to join a labyrinth of other highways, are what makes LA the bank robbery capital of the country. Gangs would easily move through town, drug dealers—we had it all. But it did make for some fun.

Work was great; it was new, and it was busy. But after work, there was really nothing to do. John and Mike both belonged to a local gym, where we played basketball during lunch a few days a week and where, for the first time in my life, I started lifting weights. And it was a good thing, because, after work, I'd go home and make dinner while watching two episodes of *Cheers*, go for a workout, and come home to two more episodes of *Cheers* before going to sleep. That was Monday to Thursday. But on the weekends, I was traveling wherever I could. Through time I met other agents in Sacramento, San Francisco, Lake Tahoe, and Long Beach, and I'd spend a lot of time visiting them.

But after six weeks that I was there, an old girlfriend called to say she was visiting LA with a friend. I drove down there on a Friday night, met up with her and her friend, and had a great time hanging out that night. But at the end of the night, when I thought I was going to get a couch to sleep on, she told me that her friend wasn't comfortable with me there because they got the room discounted since her mother worked for the company and she didn't want to cause her any trouble if I was found there by the hotel staff. So after I dropped them off, being it was only a couple of hours until daylight, I decided to spend the rest of my evening in one of the nicest neighborhoods I could find, Pacific Palisades.

Only problem is, there weren't any motels in Pacific Palisades. So when the sun came up and I roused from my torturous sleep in the pushed-back passenger seat of my car, I called my former girlfriend, to find out that they were going to visit friends in San Diego. Since that was strictly a girls' trip, I now had an unplanned weekend, so I thought I'd look up my dear uncle Anthony. By the time I got to his mansion in Los Feliz Hills (a fancy part of LA), I found him and his wife eagerly packing for a plane trip. "Hi," "Goodbye," and they were gone. Now I was really loving it here. I then spent the next two days visiting every beach town south of LA, Hermosa Beach, Manhattan Beach, Newport Beach, taking time along the way to see what, if anything, was different from one to the next but enjoying the scene all the way nonetheless.

I finished the night in Huntington Beach, where I visited the first bar that hosted The Doors. I decided to stay at the Huntington Beach Inn, not realizing at that time when I paid the clerk that the thick plastic barrier between him and me should have been a clue. When I get to the room, the bed was surrounded by mirrors on all the walls, as well as the ceiling. Welcome home!

The next day, I continued my drive south until I ended in Laguna Niguel, a very artsy place. Whereas most of the other towns were flat and on the beach, this one had some cliffs surrounding the beach and a nice park right at the base. It was a nice place to finish my journey before making the long track back up to Stockton. During the remainder of my time there in Stockton, I learned the job from two guys who were more than willing to help me out. We basically worked alone and went about our business, but if someone was going out somewhere that he felt a little uneasy, someone else would always make himself available to go for the ride. We worked together on a lot of capers and received satisfaction whenever we were able to finish a job, especially if it was a case where another agency was looking for a fugitive and there was information that they had come to Stockton.

One of these cases involved a UFAP warrant from Los Angeles. UFAP was an acronym for unlawful flight to avoid prosecution, and it was a function of the FBI to assist other law enforcement authorities in the apprehension of criminals who broke the law in one jurisdiction and fled to another, traveling over state lines. This was the area that made the FBI sometimes indispensable to other agencies.

A man was wanted for a vicious torture-homicide that was committed in Los Angeles, but he fled to Northern California. We had received information that he might have come to Stockton and was living there. The description of him included a teardrop tattoo by his eye, a sign that he was also involved in a gang. He was also known to be a drug enforcer while he was in LA, which obviously made him what we would call armed and dangerous.

We had set up surveillance in a few places where there was a chance that he might be found. Some of these cases can be painstakingly long, where several hours, if not days, go by that you just sit in a car or van, trying to keep your focus on the pedestrian and vehicular traffic, faces and cars melting together.

On one of these operations, we had been looking for him at a place we thought he might be located. John and I sat in a car nearby after we had parked a van at the location, making it appear as though it was parked and unoccupied, with Mike in the back, peering through a tinted window.

Hours went by, and just when we were about to call it for another day, Mike called out over the radio that he saw someone that looked like our guy but he was too far away to verify that he had the tattoo. As Mike called out what the individual was wearing, John left the vehicle to get a closer look at the possible suspect. Mike and I also separately walked to areas where we would have the best chance of surrounding the fugitive if he was positively identified by John, where we could avoid any type of crossfire with one another and also lessen the chance of innocent bystanders being shot by either us or him if the fugitive was armed and decided to shoot it out. As John passed the subject and realized it was our guy by the tattoo, he gave us the signal that had us pounce upon him and subdue him before he had a chance to react.

Another fugitive case we investigated had detectives from the Portland, Oregon, Police Department having information regarding a fugitive who was wanted for a murder that was committed thirteen years ago. They had learned that he also might be residing in Stockton. As we conducted records checks, we determined that an individual that might be him was living in a trailer park just outside of town. Together with the detectives, we showed the photograph of the fugitive to the manager and she confirmed that she believed the same person we were looking for lived there. We took up spots around the trailer where the individual lived and waited for him.

A guy that looked like our guy eventually came out of the trailer and got into the vehicle that we thought he might be driving. Because we didn't want to get into a situation with him in case he was armed and was in close proximity to the other trailers in the area, we let him drive off just far enough before we conducted a "felony car stop" and pulled his vehicle over after it was safely enough away from the location. After we got him out of the car, the detectives came over and said to him as they placed their handcuffs on him, "We've been waiting thirteen years to say this to you: you're under arrest." It wasn't just satisfying making the arrest, but to see detectives who waited so long to resolve a case made it all the more gratifying.

And then there was our very own Duane Wesley Walker. Walker had robbed a couple of banks in town, and through our dogged investigation, we were able to identify him but not quite catch him right away. Walker had no permanent residence, and although he had family in town, he didn't visit them often and they liked it that way. He had robbed enough banks to where we carried his photograph with us when we went to the scene of a new robbery just to confirm whether he was responsible for another one or not.

I had kept in touch with the family in case he showed his face there. After we responded to a bank robbery that had occurred in close proximity to their house, we drove by and rang the bell. The son of his sister let us in, and we chatted with him and other family members briefly in the living room. When they assured us that they still had not heard from him, against our better judgment and not wanting to offend, we decided not to ask them to look through the place and left to return to the office. No sooner had we walked in the door than the son called me from a payphone outside the house. He told me that when we knocked on the door, Walker had taken his sister as insurance that they wouldn't say anything to us and was hiding with her in the bedroom closet. I told him to wait there, and John and I bolted back to the house.

When we arrived, John went around to the back of the house as I began to approach the front door. The sister emerged through the door with her family and said that when Walker saw her son wasn't in the house, he left through the back window. I ran around to the back of the house and saw John standing near the open window from which Walker had just escaped. As I quickly walked to the street nearest the window, John got in the car and we both began to look around the neighborhood for him. I walked down the street with my firearm at my side, the dark windbreaker with the bright yellow FBI mesmerizing the few people walking in the street, wondering what was going on.

As I reached the corner and looked down the block to my right, John approached the same intersection in the car. I saw a man across the street and halfway down the block who seemed to fit the description of Walker and, from a distance, looked like him too. His eyes caught mine in the distance, and as I looked at John and back toward the individual, I slowly walked down the block, John cruising behind me. Upon my third step, he bolted down the alleyway. As I ran after him, John drove down the block and around the corner in order to try to head him off.

As I turned down the alleyway, not knowing what was ahead of me and preparing myself for what could be a long run or a quick gunfight, I looked up to see Walker in a position I did not expect. As he tried to climb up and over a fence at the end of the alleyway, the leg of his baggy pants caught on one of the points at the top of the fence. When he fell over to the other side, the pants hung him upside down on the fence! I held him at bay until John came up and placed the handcuffs on him. We pulled him up and off the fence and off to jail.

After I received my transfer back to New York, I drove west across to Santa Cruz and down from there along the Pacific Coast Highway to Seal Beach, which was a little past LA. The drive was beautiful, the Pacific Ocean on my right and mountainside cliffs to my left. It paid to have a sunroof that day.

I stayed over on this trip in Seal Beach with another agent whom I had met through an agent in his office that I had never met. I had been working a bank robbery case in which the robbers took one of those long drives themselves from Northern California to the southern parts while continuing their spree. While I was talking to the agent who had the case down there near Los Angeles, who was undoubtedly from the South, while we were coordinating our cases of these robbers, she said to me that there was another guy in her office who had the same accent as me. Having felt a sense of loss of others who did sound like me, I said to put him on the phone. I was fortunate enough to then be introduced to Rey, who was not much longer out of the academy than I was. We became friends, and since he had the apartment with a living room view of the pier and more lively bars in his neighborhood, I became a frequent visitor and lump on his couch. The fact that his girlfriend, whom he eventually married, was a flight attendant with many friends from work only added to my distant find of utopia. Rey would eventually transfer to his hometown of New York and later was elected as president of the Federal Bureau of Investigation Agents Association (FBIAA), an advocacy organization for the improvement of conditions and issues for FBI agents.

After leaving Rey's place for the final time, I visited my uncle in LA before setting off to New York. Only this time, instead of staying in motels each night while driving to somewhere I didn't really know, I was staying with my old classmates from the academy who had been scattered across the country and, on this cross-country trip, knowing full well what was ahead of me, at least somewhat. I stayed over in Las Vegas, Denver, St. Louis, even in a small town called Carbondale, Illinois, visiting with my former classmates along the way and staying in a motel only one night in Toledo, Ohio until I arrived in Philadelphia. After staying there, I drove to the Big Apple and reported to the New York office of the FBI, where I was sure more fun was to come.

Upon my transfer to New York, I was assigned to the Special Operations Group. There are sections of that group that are known as the black bag squad, agents that covertly enter a business, residence, vehicle, or other place to surreptitiously place a listening device, or bug, or camera to allow eavesdropping on conversations regarding illegal activities. These wires are obtained by the issuance of a court order by a judge and the telephone conversations are listened to by a rotating team of law enforcement officers.

People think that the FBI has the ability and wherewithal to listen in on any innocuous telephone conversation. If they only knew what it takes to set up a wire, not only legally but practically speaking, taking into account the amount of time and personnel that you need to have sit there and actually listen to the conversations. But the thing that makes this organization revered and held in high esteem by most, and hated by some, is the perception that the FBI is capable of knowing anything about anybody, and that's something we use to our advantage.

I worked on what might be commonly called a surveillance team. We were agents who followed people full-time. Other agents, known as case agents, would be the investigators who would conduct the actual investigation in terms of interviews, evidence recovery, case strategy, and prosecution in court with the United States Attorney. The surveillance team would support their investigations by conducting surveillances for the case agents to relieve them of this often-monotonous duty so they could focus their attention to a variety of other matters.

When first arriving in New York, my team was tasked to follow the son of a high-ranking member of an organized crime family, hoping to find his father, who, at that time, was in hiding. The family had divided into two factions, and a number of people, on both our side and theirs, were looking for this individual who was leading the faction that split from the rest of the family. Our typical day would start in the morning in a small tony village on Long Island, where we would set up on the house of the son. Either in the midmorning or late morning, he would emerge from his house and drive the approximately one and a half miles to a car dealership that he owned. He would spend a good part of the day there until he left the dealership to return home. This would be our routine day in and day out until his father was finally found.

One day, while heading to the location of another monotonous, early-morning surveillance, our team was retasked to watch a bank robbery team that had robbed thirty-two banks but was still at large. Although someone had dropped a dime on them to reveal their identities, there was not enough evidence to establish probable cause, the necessary elements to make an arrest. The information that was provided also stated that they were shortly looking to rob yet another bank. At this stage in the investigation, our mission was to literally catch them in the act.

JUST ANOTHER DAY

The neighborhood in Jamaica, Queens, where these individuals lived would be in the lower socioeconomic level. As I drove to the residence of one of the subjects, I saw the van that was registered to him parked in the street. The van was white and brown, with an extended roof. It also had a very large window on the side of the van that was covered from eyes outside the van by shades. As we sat there in the area, a second team descended on the location with us. For hours, we waited for the subject to come out and get into his van. One agent would keep the eye out for anyone who approached the van, while the other agents would sit nearby in their cars. We would usually pine away the time away from the immediate vicinity of the subject who was being surveilled, waiting for "the eye" to call out some activity over the radio, by reading, eating, finding a usable bathroom, having a whiffle ball game, or throwing a football around. It was like a mobile fire company, do something to keep your mind busy and sharp while you're stuck waiting someplace, and to keep your sanity until the bell sounded, or in this case, until the call came over the radio that the subject's vehicle was on the move. Then cars would be racing around to fall in behind to tail him. But not today.

While we waited there, a call came over our radios about additional information that was received by the squad that was investigating these individuals. The information stated that another car on the same block might also be involved in the bank robberies. A decision was made by the team leaders that one team would take the van and the other team would stay with the car. Of course, with my instinct telling me that the van was going to be involved in any action today, my team was assigned to the car. During the early afternoon, as I waited in my car a short distance away from the block, a voice announced over the radio that a black male was leaving the residence and getting into the van. The male fit the description of the car registrant and also of one of the bank robbers. He started the van and took off, with the other surveillance team in tow.

Since we worked the five boroughs of New York, all of us would have detailed maps of the area. Obviously this was a time before GPS was even a concept. In case the individuals we might be following left that area, we also had maps of the surrounding counties, so we could announce the streets and landmarks over the radio to aid the team with the location of the vehicle of the subject and continue the surveillance covertly. Pulling out my map of Queens, I listened to the other team on the radio narrate their shadowing of the subject as I traced their trail through the county and, as they continued to move, navigated on the map the quickest route for me to reach their location as they moved along.

The van stopped nearby, where a friend walked to the vehicle from his home, got in the van, and they were off. They then parked by Baisley Pond Park and joined some others at a basketball court. The small crowd stood around, smoking pot, drinking from tall forty-ounce bottles concealed by brown paper bags, laughing at one another and themselves while music blared from a boom box. It's amazing what people find to do with themselves when getting a steady job isn't an option.

Continuing to listen to the radio transmissions of the other team, I heard that the two males, joined by a third, walked away from the crowd back to the van, got in the van, and left. They meandered their way from the hood to a neighborhood not too far away. They drove through the streets of Flushing like a shark swims through water, looking for prey, darting and turning until it comes upon a palatable target. I followed their every move on the map while my team watched our car, still sitting in the parking spot. I reconfigured my "flight plan" to their location for when my instinct proved right and we found out that the Toyota that we were watching was not going to be involved in anything today or when something went down with the van, whichever came first. At that point, whether we were officially called off the surveillance on the Toyota or not, with lights and sirens blazing, I planned on being where the action was going to happen.

As the van continued on its path through Flushing, I heard over the radio that a woman with a baby approached the Toyota and opened the door. As I heard this information relayed to the two separate team leaders over the radio and before the official termination of our surveillance, my car was gone in a flash, my mind racing as I dodged traffic, both vehicular and pedestrian alike. I heard my team leader announce that the surveillance was terminated on the Toyota and that we would now be joining the other team already on surveillance of the van. As he finished this announcement, I was now flying down Francis Lewis Boulevard, taking all major streets but no parkways or expressways, not wanting to get caught in a traffic jam while I listened to the radio transmissions updating me on the location of the wandering van.

As I drove west down Northern Boulevard not far from the scene, I turned off my lights and sirens as a voice came over the radio to say that the van drove down a block off Northern Boulevard and had stopped in the immediate vicinity of a bank. My heart was beating faster, and I held my breath until I saw a queue of cars, which I knew to be all law enforcement vehicles, stopped along Northern Boulevard facing eastbound. I saw both detectives and agents sitting in the cars as I made a U-turn and joined the line. I was now second from the front, behind an agent that I had worked with in the past who was on the other team that had been following the other van, Dick M. I finally had a chance to catch my breath, but it would not last long.

The same voice over the radio then began to recite the movements of both the van and its occupants: While the driver remained in the van, the other two males got out of the van and walked to either side of the front door of the bank, looking furtively in all directions. They both then walked into the bank, where they remained inside for approximately three minutes. The same males walked out of the bank and got back into the van. The van then pulled away from the curb and continued down the street.

As I sat there, wondering, since I was a late joiner to this party and didn't know what the surveillance team had as a plan, When was someone going to check to see if the bank was robbed? Another voice came over the radio and stated, "Is someone going to check to see if they took the bank?" A third voice yelled out, "I'll go!" Not being able to pull out after the van and possibly blow our cover if they didn't actually rob it, we had to anxiously wait and find out if we had a crime before we could spring the trap. A few seconds later, the last voice shouted over the radio, "They hit the bank! They hit the bank!"

The cars in front and behind me made a flying caravan down the same street the van had just gone. I followed Dick's car as he moved ahead of me, allowing him enough room so as not to smash him in the rear if he needed to come to an abrupt halt on the cluttered side street. He made a right turn at the next intersection, and as I quickly decelerated to make the same turn, my shotgun fell forward from the passenger seat to the floor. As I completed the turn and drove down Sanford Avenue, the van was stopped in the next intersection. It had been struck by two of our vehicles on either side and was locked in at the bumpers, apparently unable to move forward and now spinning its wheels in reverse, attempting to dislodge itself at the expense of anyone who might be anywhere near it.

I stopped my vehicle directly behind the van so that if it did dislodge from the other vehicles, it would lurch in reverse into my car, hopefully keeping it pinned and not able to race away from the scene down more populated streets. I then reached down and grabbed my shotgun from the floor before I raced toward the van. As I closed quickly, I saw Dick M and another agent from the Joint Bank Robbery Task Force, Mary G, at the driver's door of the van, guns drawn, yelling at the driver and pulling on the door handle. The tires of the van were spinning wildly, releasing both an acrid smell and a black cloud from the rear of the van.

As I saw the dire situation at hand, obviously everything at this point that was taught to me at the FBI Academy about seeking cover and concealment was out the window. If this situation did not come to an end very soon, one or more people, FBI, police, and civilians, could be injured or killed. At this point, they appeared to be desperate robbers looking to get out of there any way they could, and if they did get loose, who knew what could happen? Or if they decided to bail out of the van, who knew what consequences could occur from a gunfight in the middle of a busy neighborhood? With the shotgun in both of my hands, I ran next to my fellow agents. Aiming the stock, or butt, of the shotgun at the large window behind the driver on the side of the van, I struck it as hard as I could to break the window, but it didn't give way. The adrenaline still racing through me and urgency becoming ever more important, I struck the window again, this time shattering it into a spiderweb until it rained down upon the mutt—I mean, subject—sitting right there next to it. Holding what was left of the broken stock in my right hand and leveling the barrel of the shotgun and drawing down on him and the other two subjects with my left hand, I shouted, "FBI, get down on the floor!" while leaning through where the window once stood. I was so fired up that the common sense that wouldn't allow me to put my head inside a place where there were three armed guys obviously short-circuited.

Fortunately, these guys were either too shocked to see me coming through a now open window in the van, or maybe they were scared shitless that a shotgun was now pointed their way. Collectively, they decided that they were not going to try to shoot their way out and make this their last stand. For whatever reason, they froze where they were as the tall dark lanky sergeant from the Joint Bank Robbery Task Force, who was also out on the surveillance with us, reached over me and grabbed these guys one at a time, pulling them through that very same window. As police cars from the local precinct responded to the call, these mutts were handcuffed and placed into our cars.

At the conclusion of the arrest, I noticed that a crowd had gathered on the four corners that circled the scene. It's not often that the public gets to see firsthand the FBI and NYPD work together so well in apprehending violent felons, but on this day, they not only got their front seat but also got their money's worth!

I've been asked in the past if I was scared when I went after bad people, knowing that I could get injured or killed. I had once read a psychological analysis that concluded after interviewing some law enforcement officers who had been involved in violent encounters that officers are sometimes victims of omnipotence. A small percentage of people, especially males, after walking around awhile with a gun and badge and gaining some law enforcement experience, begin to feel a superman type of mentality in which you refuse to believe that anything bad will ever happen to you. That can be dangerous, for fear will provide a barometer that could guide your judgment during perilous situations.

Everyone gets scared. It's human nature. But the factor that creates tension, fear, and self-doubt is time. Often every day, when police, fire, and other agencies are engaged in dangerous situations, they are usually reacting to circumstances in which adrenaline and instinct take over. There's no time to sit back and think about the possibilities until the situation has been resolved. And if nothing goes wrong, nobody thinks about it. It's only when things turn to shit that someone may dissect the event later on and, from the sanctity of a classroom, say what could or should have been done. Every situation I have been in, I've never believed that anything bad will happen to either me or anyone on my team. Whether that's omnipotence or denial, it all depends upon your perception. Maybe it's just confidence based on good training from two very good academies and excellent training in the field. Adrenaline and instinct have a lot to do with confidence, but as I believe the self-fulfilling prophecy dictates, if you go in there thinking that you or someone else may get hurt, it will happen. The worst part is sitting, waiting for your subject to show up.

Time makes you think. You don't want to think; you want to act, act quickly, act instinctively and act decisively!

*****

While I was away working in California, my lone apprehension about coming back to New York would be getting assigned to the Gambino Squad. Queens was the hotbed of organized crime activity for the Gambino family of La Cosa Nostra, and as I had grown up there, some of my friends and associates had some affiliation with them.

But no one was more involved in it than Johnny Alite.

When I played Little League baseball, there were a couple of years when I was thirteen or fourteen that I played with a team that had a pair of brothers on it and their uncle was the coach. One of the brothers had batted third in the order, and I was in the cleanup spot right behind him. His uncle, who was a very soft-spoken and likeable man, had taken a special interest in me, even enclosing a personal handwritten letter when he was returning a money deposit he was holding for me, telling me what a pleasure it was to have me on his team. I remained friends with one of his nephews for a few years, until we reached competing high school, when we only saw each other as our schools faced off against each other twice a year.

I didn't see Johnny again until after I graduated the Police Academy. Although he was about the same height as when I last saw him, he had obviously put some time in at the weight room. His hair was cut real short and slicked back, and he wasn't in jeans and sneakers like the rest of us, now dressed in slacks and a jacket. And although we had known each other from a long time ago, he now had a demeanor that said "Don't fuck with me." The rumors were real. Again, like at Hammerheads, we exchanged pleasantries, but now we no longer had stories about baseball games to share. We had gravitated to two different, and in some respects, competing, worlds.

Over the years, while we still lived in the neighborhood, or even if we moved away, our parents would still be living in the houses where we grew up. We had seen each other now and then, always stopping to say hello and asking if everything was okay with each other's families. Although we had stepped to separate sides of the line, we always respected each other. I always asked about his uncle, his father (who had coached another team in the Little League where we had played), and his sister, Maria, whom I had a crush on from the first time I laid eyes on her when she came down to watch our games with her friends during the days of the Little League.

On one occasion, I was driving a friend and his dog to the veterinarian on 101st Avenue in Ozone Park, and I pulled up behind a shiny, brand-new black Corvette double-parked in front of the shop. The rear hatch was up, and as my friend took his dog into the vet, I peered into the hatch and saw bloodstains on the carpet. Johnny emerged from the doorway of the vet, paper towels in one hand and cleanser in the other. When I came around to the back of his car to greet him, I saw that he was visibly upset as he scrubbed the bloodstains on the floor of the hatch. As he continued to clean the blood from the carpet, steam coming out of his ears, he told me that he had purchased an expensive dog not too long ago. He brought the dog to his parents' house in Woodhaven, and he let some of the younger neighborhood kids walk the dog while he visited his parents. Unfortunately, the dog broke away from them and ran into the street. The dog was struck by a car, whose driver callously sped away, leaving the dog crumpled and dying there. The kids then ran to the house to get John.

John grabbed up the dog and rushed it here, but it died before the vet could do anything for it. He had anger for the driver who mowed it down and stopped briefly before speeding away. Unfortunately for the driver, the kids were able to get a license plate number to the car. It was widely known how, years earlier, John Gotti had once reacted when a neighbor accidentally killed his youngest son while driving in their neighborhood. The neighbor, who had shown sorrow and remorse for something that happened through no fault of his own, was later dragged into a van screaming near his work before he could escape that same neighborhood after talk of his soon-to-be demise floated around. He was never seen or heard from again. I said a prayer for that driver after saying goodbye to Johnny.

I once heard that John was able to resolve a dispute for a friend who was an attorney but he didn't need to negotiate much. The friend wanted to leave a small law firm, but he wanted to take the clients he had developed there with him, which of course the partners of that firm were not willing to do, at least not willingly. A visit by John to that firm pretty much sealed the deal that the friend was able to take the clients with him when he left at no cost to himself.

After joining the FBI and being reassigned to New York, I was placed on squads other than the one I had hoped I wouldn't be assigned. And it was only a couple of years after my return before I heard from Johnny again. I had again seen him on the streets, although it was less often, because by this time he had married, bought a compound in Cherry Hill, which is in southern part of New Jersey, and moved his family and his parents there with him. Also by this time, although we never spoke about it, we both knew where our loyalties lay, the loyalties to those other than our own families. One day, Johnny called me at my office, out of the blue. Being that he had never called me before (and, again, the days before cellular phones were available), I knew this wasn't strictly social. A visit was paid to him by a couple of agents assigned to the Gambino Squad. They advised him, as they were prescribed by law in situations like this one, that they learned of a threat to his life. Without getting into too much detail, they told him that they learned (through a wiretap, but they didn't have to tell him from where they learned of the threat) that the son-in-law of John Gotti, Carmine Agnello, had placed a contract on Johnny's life. Since Johnny had no place to go, or so they thought, they wanted him to cooperate with them, tell them everything he knew not only about his own criminal acts but also those of the family, and both he and his family would be placed safely in the Witness Protection Program.

Johnny had already told me that he said no to them. He also commented that this was the life that he chose and that he would never go against it, no matter what happened. He was not calling me to verify any information or provide him with any insight into it; he was only asking me one thing: Could they lie about this threat just to make him come in and cooperate? His relationship with Carmine was not the smoothest, but I assumed he thought could things actually have come to this? After I gave him my answer, he thanked me, asked how my mom was, and I, of course, reciprocated. We then said goodbye and hung up.

Months later, I heard that Johnny had been arrested for carrying a gun in his car. He had been stopped for a traffic violation by plainclothes cops and arrested by them. Apparently, he was being followed by an Organized Crime Task Force in New Jersey who knew about the threat that was made on his life. Knowing more likely than not that with that impending threat on his life he had to be carrying a gun most of, if not all, the time. They stopped him on some traffic infraction, found the gun in the car, and arrested him. But even after this arrest, he refused to give himself, or anyone else, up. He did his time and kept his mouth shut.

After serving his time in Rahway State Prison, where I heard he had thrown some beatings at the behest of some mobsters who were also locked up there, Johnny called me again out of the blue. He wanted to meet up with me, but because of the rules of his parole, his travel was confined to certain parts of New Jersey. We agreed to meet in a parking lot of a motel near Newark Airport.

As Johnny walked over to my car, he looked a little more relaxed in a sleek-looking Sergio Tacchini sweat suit. His hair was much longer from when he used to cut it short, and it was now exhibiting some gray. Maybe the life was catching up with him a bit. After the pleasantries were routinely exchanged, Johnny told me the story about his parking valet business. Apparently, as Johnny had established the business through his ill-gotten gains, a neighborhood guy, whom I had known in my younger days, pleaded with him to give him a break that no one else would and asked him for a job. Knowing this guy for a long time but also knowing that he was a bit of a fuck-up, Johnny reluctantly hired him on at the lowest level, letting him learn the business before he was able to let him manage some of it, considering he had the business both here in New York and Florida.

At some time, the guy was doing pretty well for him, and Johnny was able to rely on him more and more, especially after his wife contracted cancer and he needed to be with her more often. Then Johnny got arrested, and the way he explained it to me was that because he was going away for a while, he needed someone who knew the business to take care of it while he was gone. He also needed someone who he knew wouldn't even think about trying something like keeping the business but would meekly give it back when he got out. Since he had to sign the business over to keep it going, it had to be someone who he not only felt he could somewhat trust but also was afraid of him and wouldn't be stupid enough to go against him, knowing he would be coming out someday. So he signed the business over to the friend.

However, the guys from Queens, the ones who worked for Carmine, had other plans for Johnny's business. One of these guys was named Ronnie "One-Arm" Trucchio, who, as a child growing up in Ozone Park, had been the victim of an automobile accident that left him with a paralyzed right arm. But the loss of the use of his arm didn't stop him from being one of the most ruthless killers in the organization. And his reputation preceded him. A friend once told me a story about walking into a neighborhood bar in South Ozone Park and seeing an old female friend who happened to be sitting at a table with Ronnie. My friend said hello to her but respectfully acknowledged him, knowing his reputation, and kept on going about his business. The next day, he was told by someone that Ronnie wanted to speak to him at the "club" on 101st Avenue, which was infamously known as the Bergin Hunt & Fish Club, also known as the Gambino crime family hangout. After my friend shit himself, he had to decide whether to go to the club or leave town. After deciding that it might not be too bad, maybe only a slap or beating for whatever perceived wrong he did, he went to the club to meet Ronnie.

Ronnie didn't say much, didn't need to. He just made it pretty clear to my friend, "If you ever see that girl with me, anywhere in my presence, you *don't* speak to her!" Not really a rhyme or reason for that, just that crazy notion in their own heads that it was a sign of disrespect to them.

So after they got ahold of the guy that was "holding" Johnny's business for him, the money stopped going to Johnny and they were now "protecting" the guy who was once his friend, and the business, as it were, was now theirs. His question to me now was how, legally, he could get the business back. That was just like them, taking something that someone else built up, even if it was with blood money, and making it their own, often bleeding it dry until there was nothing left, just like the scene with Henry Hill and Paulie with the restaurant owner in the movie Goodfellas.

After answering his question, I had to ask about his other family members, and of course, I always asked, "How's Maria?" After our second "consultation" at the airport parking lot, he had mentioned that her last boyfriend knew little about sports and he had a tough time relating to him whenever they got together. She owned a management placement business on Beaver Street in Lower Manhattan, and after Johnny told me where it was located, I had to visit her after all these years. After seeing her, I found that not only was she very bright, but she had developed into a beautiful woman as well. We met again one night for drinks by her apartment in Battery Park City, which was walking distance from her office. She was very intriguing, a great personality with a smart business sense.

However, I knew the job wouldn't tolerate this relationship, and rather than risk having my judgment questioned, the childhood love went unrequited.

And Ronnie One-Arm—he is now serving a life sentence for racketeering. Yep, he was once a tough guy on the streets.

*****

While I was stationed in the New York Office of the FBI, one of my assignments was to a squad whose primary function was investigating major thefts that crossed state lines, which usually meant loads of merchandise that were transported by tractor trailers. Since Congress allocated our authority, as well as our budget, generally speaking, the crimes that we investigated had either a dual-state or multistate element or were simply a violation of a federal law. Generally, bank robberies are investigated by the FBI, usually jointly with the local authorities, not so much because they involve often violent and dangerous perpetrators, but because the money being stolen from the bank is federally insured. That's the nexus that gives the federal authorities justification to investigate these bank robberies: the money is insured by the Federal Deposit Insurance Corporation (FDIC). And when it comes to the major thefts, which can be anything from clothing to food to electronic equipment (basically almost any commodity), the items of value are stolen in a large-enough quantity (those trailers hold a lot of stuff) and are either traveling in interstate commerce or often transported over state lines so that they may be harder to trace and be recovered in a different locality from where they are stolen.

During the times when these individuals were identified and at some point an arrest was imminent after a long-term investigation, we would plan our apprehension like a coach would plan the strategy of a game, putting the players in the best places to succeed and allowing for contingencies. Whether it was an early-morning arrest at a residence (which was usually done at 6:00 a.m.) or a felony car stop, sometimes plans had to be altered, and we had to be prepared for that. But at least at the start of the game, agents were out there, covering all exits (so there were usually no foot pursuits of barely awake, barefoot fugitives), and the agents that were gaining entry into the residence had as best a description of the interior of the house or apartment and where the occupants in the residence could be found. This information would be gathered from whatever intelligence was available, whether it was open-source material (that you could get through either public records or over the internet, as an example) or from informants.

One of these characters that we arrested who comes to mind is an individual who was involved in gun sales that were purchased out of state and brought to New York for sale on the street. I was tasked with being the leader of the arrest team that was to bring him into court for his arraignment after an indictment had been handed down by the federal grand jury and an arrest warrant was issued. This arrest was to be done on a day that was designated as the "takedown," as he was part of a large investigation that yielded a large number of subjects who were to be arrested in connection with the same case, and therefore, a lot of arrests were coordinated the same day to get as many of them as we could before they got tipped off and possibly fled the area. Cases with a lot of violent subjects like this one also generate quite a bit of favorable publicity for the agency, which aids in the public perception that the FBI is taking care of business.

As I did my investigation regarding his whereabouts and habits by conducting physical surveillances of him to determine his comings and goings, I found out that not only was he a big dude who was bouncing at a strip club but that he was also taking stick-fighting classes on East 23rd Street in Manhattan. I was actually able to watch him go through his practices through a large window on the Second floor of a building where the school was located. His extracurricular activity was something that was definitely noted as a caution statement for his arrest plan.

On the day of the arrest, which was orchestrated with a large number of arrest teams who would simultaneously enter, by whatever means, each and every residence to apprehend their subject at 6:00 a.m., when most people were at home and, hopefully, still sleeping, we made our way to the house. The house was owned by his parents and he slept in a converted apartment in the basement. After covering all the exits, we surreptitiously made our way inside the house and down to the basement. As he awoke, he frantically rose from the bed, where he had been sleeping with his girlfriend. But he stopped in his tracks when he saw the heavily armed agents padded with bullet-resistant vests and covered by the blue windbreakers emblazoned with FBI imprinted in yellow who had made their way into the room with guns drawn on him.

As he stood in front of us, the image of this bulked-up gorilla with piercings in almost every visible place on his body (and from what I'm told by the agents who later strip-searched him, places that weren't visible as well) would have scared most people shitless, as if they were watching some warrior-demon in a horror movie who looked mean enough that he was going to rip people limb from limb. But the one thing that put this guy in real-time perspective was the plaid boxer shorts that he had worn to bed, and he was not clad in anything else, but then standing before us with his hands raised. That put a whole different spin on things as we handcuffed him and led him out of the house. I guess the idea of putting prison inmates in pink jumpsuits to stem the violence that occurs in jails may have something to say for it.

Throughout my time as an FBI agent, I had found that having gone to places in Harlem and Brooklyn, places that most other agents had never been to before, gave me a familiarity with these areas due to my NYPD background. It was an experience that gave me an advantage over those agents that came out of law school or were accountants, or even those that served in the military. For them, they were coming into a foreign environment, but for me it was like an old stomping ground.

And the training I received in both academies was invaluable to me before hitting the streets as an FBI agent. And the lessons that I learned in the field served me well when I had to serve a last-minute subpoena late at night during a trial to a witness who lived in a housing project in one of the most crime-ridden areas in New York called Far Rockaway. Gang activity, drug dealing, and muggings were the norm. As I drove out there, I could envision the headlines in the next day's paper: FBI Agent Robbed of Gun and Badge while Looking for a Witness. Or worse.

I didn't want to look like a knucklehead and walk in there with my gun drawn and scare whatever decent people I'd come across, but I also didn't want to draw the attention of some gangbangers who might target me up close or take a potshot at me from the hundreds of windows that dotted the outside of the buildings that I would be passing through. But before arriving at the projects, I had remembered during my time while working in the confines of the 34th Precinct, which encompassed the areas of Washington Heights and which, at the time I was there, led the city of New York in homicides year in and year out, that the crack epidemic was rampant and, as the adage went, "where there's drugs, there's guns."

On one particular occasion, my partner and I backed up a unit from the 3-4 on a call to an apartment building. After reaching the apartment on the top floor of the building, I stood behind the veteran cops that had just knocked on the door and stood to either side of the doorway, as had been taught to us, to avoid being a target for someone on the other side of that door who might just take a shot at the door. As we stood there, I noticed that one of the cops had his hat in his hand. As I looked closer, I then saw that he had his service weapon inside the hat, the grip held by three of his fingers, with his index finger hooked over the top of the hat and the thumb hooked around the brim so that the gun was covered from sight. I later understood that he had the gun covered but readily available so as not to either alarm anyone who came to the door or inflame them that the police was there, "ready to shoot someone." But he was instantaneously ready for any threat to him, his partner, or anyone else, for that matter.

So as I walked through the buildings and entered the one where the witness lived, I was able to conceal my service weapon, a Smith & Wesson 10-millimeter semiautomatic, behind the leather binder that held the subpoena. The grip of the weapon was held by three fingers with my index finger and thumb pinching the binder against it. If I walked into a bad situation in the elevator, or it walked in on me, or I found myself suddenly with a gangbanger in a stairwell, instead of fishing for my gun from the holster, I was ready. But fortunately on this day, the subpoena was served without incident and I returned back to the office in one piece, which is what we all in law enforcement set out to do.

One of our more interesting cases began with a phone call from Chris W, a man known to us on the squad from the past who was employed by the United Parcel Service, more commonly known as UPS. Chris was employed in what's called the Loss Prevention Unit, whose job is, like it sounds, to try to assure that those packages that are entrusted to UPS, and its employees, reach their destination without being stolen from people both outside and inside the organization. We had previously worked with Chris on a case involving a $3 million robbery of a UPS tractor trailer that contained a large load of jewelry. When we were first called for that job, one of the first questions that was asked was how many UPS tractor trailers had been robbed before this one. There were none. It didn't take long to know that, this having been the only one to have been robbed in anyone's memory, either these guys were the luckiest truck hijackers on earth to get the one that contained this much jewelry or, more likely, this was an inside job.

And it wasn't long after that before we were able to determine that a bunch of wiseguy wannabes in Mill Basin, Brooklyn, conspired with an employee who had risen through the ranks of the UPS to be a well-respected manager with the company. As it turned out, his wife got into a business that not only did not do very well but also went bankrupt, and to a point, so did they. Having a serious need for cash to continue to keep themselves in the lifestyle that they had grown accustomed to living, and with the knowledge of the inner workings of the company, he was ripe for the picking by the Mill Basin crew for the information that they thought would set up the score of their lives. But when it was all over, it cost them some time from their lives.

But one of the funniest things about this case was that we *literally* stole a major portion of the load of jewelry from them that they had kept in a van parked in front of the ringleader's house in Mill Basin. After having arrested one of the gang away from his home and job and anywhere where anyone would see and know we had him, we gave him an opportunity to help himself by helping us, if he wanted to shorten his time in a federal penitentiary, by giving us whatever information he could. That was when we found out that they were moving the jewelry to a buyer shortly and that it was being kept in a van right on the street. So instead of announcing ourselves to the ringleader with a search warrant and seizing the van, thereby shorting our investigation without enough evidence to get all the subjects, we decided to "steal" the jewelry back from them. This would allow us to not reveal that we were on to them, and we could have the one guy we had wear a wire against the other subjects and also listen to their telephone calls, now that they would have a lot to talk about if our mission was successful.

Mill Basin was a very close-knit, predominantly Italian community that was in a corner of Brooklyn that had only a few streets going in or out, and there was very little pedestrian or vehicular traffic. Also, for these same reasons, there was very little, if any, crime there. Whereas throughout most of Brooklyn you'd have to be a total ass to leave anything of value in a car, here you could be 100 percent safe knowing that whatever you left in the car would be there in the morning, since no one had the balls to steal in this neighborhood or risk a near deadly beating. That is, until the FBI knew about it.

So in the early morning hours, FBI agents and detectives from the New York City Police Department descended on this little enclave to reclaim what was rightfully not the thieves' property. And engaged in the effort to take back the jackpot was a little-known private tow truck owner and operator named Harvey, who had worked with the FBI for a number of years. Harvey often availed himself to us, usually to provide a variety of machinery, when his service was called upon in the form of towing a getaway car from a bank robbery as evidence to one of our facilities or using one of his tractors and/or trailers to help us recover a large amount of stolen merchandise that had been recovered. But on this day, he was about to go beyond his call of duty, a very special job, and like always, Harvey was up for it.

Under the cover of the night and under the watchful eye of the FBI agents and NYPD detectives, after having carefully and quietly backed up his tow truck to the van, he lifted the rear wheels and drove off with it. But as he now roared down the avenue, suddenly the lights in the ringleader's house came on and he ran out of the front door in his shorts and T-shirt, only to see an empty space where the van once sat. Having heard the roar of Harvey's engine as he pulled out but not having seen him drive away, he now saw a nondescript car lurking nearby with two guys sitting inside. With two strange faces sitting in a car right at the time after a van holding his jewelry was stolen, he jumped in his car (which probably had a gun in the glove box) and drove after them. However, unbeknownst to him, these weren't two guys from another crew that stole his van loaded with jewelry, but rather, these two guys were NYPD detectives who were watching out for Harvey, making sure he was not interfered with while grabbing the van. And not wanting to let him know that it was the cops and feds that were stealing back the jewelry, but rather hoping that he would think that it *was* stolen by another crew, off they went.

Unfortunately, he was close behind.

As I also sat in a car nearby, I heard them frantically yell over the radio that he was on their tail, driving down local city streets at eighty miles per hour with the ringleader only feet from their rear bumper. I drove off after them, tailgating his car as closely as he was tailgating the undercover NYPD car. As he looked into the rearview mirror, I could see that he squinted and peered closer to see who it was that was now on his ass. As the three cars roared down Flatlands Avenue like some sort of weird drag race, he began to let up on the accelerator, slowing his car and allowing the detectives to drive away. As I also slowed down to give room between his car and mine, he stopped his car, which was now about twenty-five yards ahead of me, opened his door, got out of his car, turned, and looked at me. There he was, still in his shorts and T-shirt, standing immediately outside his car, pondering his next move. Here I was, sitting in my car, facing him, not knowing what this lunatic might decide to do at this point.

I sat there, like the detectives, also not wanting to give up my identity so that the case could continue and we had a chance to gather more evidence and round up all the individuals involved in the robbery. But I was also not looking to have this guy run up and start taking shots at me, so I quickly placed my firearm on my lap to have it ready but prepared to launch the car in reverse and get out of there quickly myself. But almost as quickly as he stopped his car to confront me behind him, he got back in the car, slowly drove down the block, and made the turn to head back to his house. And what we had hoped he would think by the chain of events that had occurred had finally seemed to dawn on him, that a crew of thieves, much like himself, had made off with the stolen stuff and at this point he wasn't getting it back. And how poetic was it that, in his mind, the only guys that could have known about the load and its location and pulled off such a stunt would have been wiseguys, or mobsters, from his own neighborhood. Boy, did we have a laugh about what must have gone through this guy's and his cohorts' heads that night into the next day, and in their recorded conversations and telephone calls. And afterward, did I have a sigh of relief that I wasn't forced into a "showdown at the corral" in the middle of Flatlands Avenue, Brooklyn.

Years later, another call came in from Chris telling us that a package driver had come to him with information relating to massive thefts by UPS employees. I said I would be right down, and together with Pete K, a squad mate whom I had not worked with much directly in the past but knew to be quite competent, we drove down to the West Side of Manhattan in the vicinity of the largest hub or depot for UPS in the world, located on West 43rd Street, right by the Hudson River. We met with Chris and the driver, who was introduced to us as Mike K, at a nearby location. Mike proceeded to tell us about the scam that several UPS drivers were conducting while on their routes, Mike thinking that after he passed on this information, that would be the end of it for him. He couldn't be more wrong.

The area of Manhattan where the rogue drivers were working was located on the Lower West Side between 14th and 23rd Streets. The area was filled with block after block of tall commercial buildings. Also saturated throughout the area were photography stores, with some jewelry stores sprinkled in as well. Mike proceeded to tell us that each block had so many customers that one UPS package car, those ubiquitous vehicles that you could see in which the guy in the brown uniform got out to deliver your package, left the hub filled with packages to be delivered and parked on the block and remained there parked for the entire day. During the first half of the day, the driver would make his deliveries and empty his truck. Throughout the second half of the day, he would pick up packages to be delivered and fill his truck back up. Then he would return to the hub with those packages at the end of the day.

However, since the driver was there on the block for the entire day, he could get pretty friendly with the building maintenance people, whom he saw most every day, five days a week. Some of these people could be as unscrupulous as the driver, if not more so. So when he got comfortable with one of these maintenance people whom he could trust, he inquired whether they had access to a secure room that no one else had access. For those that told him that they did—which he already knew they did, but this was a way to see if they thought much the same way as him—the driver asked if they would be able to hold on to a package for them.

After it started with one package and progressed to a couple at a time, they soon started to develop a partnership in which they stored rooms full of these packages and then sold the contents to other similarly unscrupulous store owners, some of whom were on their own routes. Those store owners bought the packages back at a discounted rate and then collected on whatever insurance they took out on the package, whether it was with UPS or their own insurance carrier. The thieves could get a high value of the product from the store owner, up to 75 percent of the value, because the package was getting delivered to them at a now-discounted rate after it was claimed to be missing. And the thieves knew that since the package was going to a photography or jewelry store, it was known most likely before the package was even opened that the value of it was anywhere from the hundreds to the thousands of dollars. And according to Mike, some of these guys had been doing it for years.

Members of the Loss Prevention Unit were in the office and out on the streets, looking for patterns of loss, which were most likely patterns of theft. But when drivers were carrying packages into a building they were legitimately allowed to be in, how were they going to be caught in the act? And unless the drivers were taking in a package that was clearly not supposed to be on their hand truck into a building, how would the Loss Prevention Unit staff know unless they stopped the driver to actually read the addressee on the package? And even if they did, it could have been a simple mistake, or so they would say.

After we finished speaking to Mike and he left, we had to ask Chris the obvious question: How come UPS had been allowing this to go on for so long? Wasn't it costing them thousands of dollars in losses? And the obvious answer was money, but not in the way we thought.

The way UPS makes the money, much like many of the other courier systems make their money, is to deliver the package *on time*. Therefore, packages have to get into the hub and out to their destinations in a timely fashion. And of course, there is a tracking system in place that tells you when a package comes into a particular facility and when it leaves. And that works fine in most every hub. However, when it's the biggest hub in the world and the volume is overwhelming, and all those packages still have to get there by a certain time, then that's where the problems start and the opportunity knocks to the opportunists. And when millions of dollars of packages are going through that hub *per day*, it's not most important that every package reaches its destination; the most important thing is that most of those packages reach their destination *on time*. The fraction of packages that these guys were stealing was a drop in the bucket compared to the number of packages that were being delivered.

And when the business is based on on-time delivery, in which the most that you can insure your package with UPS is $100 and any more coverage needed after that must be sought privately, then the insignificant amount lost is simply the cost of doing business. And these money-hungry, opportunistic thieves saw the whole situation as an additional benefit, like a side job.

When Mike came forward to the Loss Prevention Unit staff and then they came to us, he said that he was doing it because he was tired of watching the thievery around him. Well, that might have been one reason. He also had a route that basically was nothing but paper-based deliveries and had nothing of high value to steal. So in effect, being a bit envious, he never had a lucrative opportunity to steal undetected like the rest of them, which probably ate at him all those years that he worked there, but it was never enough that he would actually reveal their criminal activities. But there was one thing that happened recently that put him over the edge, and wouldn't you know it involved a woman.

Mike had been involved with Karen for a number of years, having talked about marriage on several occasions. She was a pretty, petite girl who had met Mike back home in a small town in New Jersey. She worked in New York City and would sometimes meet Mike at the United Parcel Service (UPS) building at the end of his shift. If he worked late on a day she was meeting him, she would hang around, waiting for him, much to the chagrin of the management, who didn't want her hanging out at the facility. Mike was told that they would very much appreciate it if Karen would wait for him somewhere else.

Mike mentioned this situation to a close friend and coworker, Earl, who was a guy with a lot of time on the job there, as well as being the union representative. But unbeknownst to management, he was also one of the biggest thieves at UPS. Earl had so much seniority there that he had the best route and was often done earlier than the rest of the delivery truck drivers. So being the sincere friend that he was, he told Mike, "Listen, just tell Karen to hang out with me until you get in." What an offer from a good guy! As human nature took its course, Karen became romantically involved with Earl, who just happened to be a married man. Now, here was Mike, who lost the girl of his dreams to a guy that not only did he have to look at every day at work but was also his union representative, and who used to be his confidant. After that betrayal, that must have been some chilly locker room. Since Earl was not only one of the most-liked and most-respected people at UPS, as well as being the physically bigger guy of the two of them, Mike sought revenge from a different angle.

Mike wanted to pass on the information about the thefts and just stay as anonymous as could be, hoping to just watch the damage around him as Earl was fired from the company. But UPS wanted more, because they knew he wasn't the only one stealing, and they needed for this problem to be brought out into the limelight for all the employees to see. So they came to us. And our interest was to catch as many thieves as we possibly could, although we knew that the level of difficulty in making cases against Earl and the others would be extremely difficult without some avenue to get in with them. Just like with the Mob, unless you have someone that they consider trustworthy and comfortable and is vouched for by someone whom they are in with, you would be hard-pressed to get a stranger—that is, undercover agent (UCA)—in with them in a reasonable amount of time. And unfortunately, with a case like this, we didn't have the luxury of time.

At that point, we had to convince Mike that, now that he had done the right thing and shed the light on the problem by reporting what was going on, he was our only way to get in with these guys. Usually, when people wear "wires" to consensually record conversations with other people who are involved in criminal activities, they are usually doing it because they were involved in some of the same activities themselves but they got *caught*. Before that happens, they're the same people that are puffing their chests, saying, "I would never rat on my friends, and I would whack anyone that did!" Yeah, until they hear the words *years of incarceration* followed by the clink of the jail cell door behind them. It's funny what the threat of a long-term jail sentence can do to change people's convictions.

On the other side are the paid informants who are wearing wires because these people are getting *paid* for their information. And the information for which they are getting paid must be good, or else, they won't be getting paid for it in the first place. And if, as in most of these cases, this person is in a position to provide information on a continuing basis, in which he would be privy to the inner workings of some criminal element or organization, then you put him in the position of wearing a wire for one of two reasons: either to verify what he is telling you because there may be some doubt or the conversations are being recorded to play in open court as evidence, which are the purposes of wearing a wire. And in the case of it being used as evidence, the recordings have to be corroborated in court by the testimony of this person. So unfortunately, now everybody, including the bad guys, know who he is. So if you can get evidence with an informant without using recordings from him, then he can stay viable as an anonymous (at least to the world outside the FBI) informant. But with Mike, this was an operation with a shelf life, so when we were finally able to convince him that the only way we would be able to go forward with the investigation was with his cooperation, and with the promise that UPS would transfer him and we would move him to the western part of the United States when the whole thing was done and he was exposed, he agreed to do it.

Besides being paid, another rare but likely more motivational reason for someone to become an informant, which would apply in this instance, is that someone is out for revenge. While I was working with this squad, there came a time when a Mob associate named Sonny sought out the FBI, looking to avenge the death of his brother, who was whacked by some of the same people, mobsters, that they had known for years. Sonny did a slow burn for a long while, angry for what had happened to his brother and swallowing the bit about it being the life they had chosen, that it was just business and it was nothing personal.

To him, that was bullshit! For him, when someone takes away your brother, your own flesh and blood, by putting a couple bullets in his head, and leaves him for dead in some trash container, no matter what he has done, it was personal to Sonny. There was no way to separate the human emotion from "the business." Some people in that business will stomach it and not say or do a thing, because they know that if they do and the hit has been sanctioned by the hierarchy of the Mob, they'll be next. And to give up a good thing, by their standards, won't be worth it for their own self-interests. But the others, who are few and far between, know the adage that "revenge is a dish best served cold." And after time goes by and people forget and let their guard down, they will get theirs, one way or another. It could be a return bullet in the head, or if you have a group of them you want to get back, there's a way to see to it that they find time away from their loved ones too. And Sonny saw they got it.

The case with his cooperation worked out pretty well, too. The FBI rented a storefront, put in some tables, chairs, and a bar, and let it be run by a guy named Steve B, an undercover FBI agent who was also a friend of Sonny's and, as the "goodfellas" like to say in Mafia parlance, "a friend of ours." So the goodfellas were told by Sonny, "Come on in! Sit down, play some cards, and have a drink. What is it you say, got a hot load of stolen merchandise you're looking to get rid of? Steve's just the man. He can take it off your hands and for a good price. You have other friends that you want to bring in? Beautiful! Just don't mind the hidden camera taking their pictures. You got a meeting you want to set up with the other goodfellas? Hey, use our place. Just make sure you speak up so the tape recorders don't miss a thing!" Yeah, he got his revenge, all right! So when we spoke to Mike, we knew that we had to prod his sense of morality, patriotism (after all, the FBI represents America), but most of all, we had to let him know how he would feel if he didn't take this opportunity to strike back at the guy who betrayed him, who used his friendship to get close to and take away someone he loved. It didn't take much prodding after that.

Not only did he wear that wire, but he also began to identify with us, the good guys, rather than them, who slowly became his enemy. And that happens with a lot of people who become informants or cooperating witnesses (informants remain anonymous to continuously provide information, whereas cooperating witnesses, otherwise known as CWs, are someone who testifies in open court), especially when it involves payments or benefits. They eventually evolve from someone who may have turned on the people that they thought of as friends to someone who has gained a sense of joining the other team (that is, the FBI), rationalizing their covert activities to themselves by "doing what's right." Unlike most informants or cooperating witnesses, Mike had no criminal record and, as best that we could determine, had never engaged in any criminal activity with the other UPS drivers. But after a while, informants begin to feel a sense that they're not working with the FBI but that they, in effect, are a part of the FBI.

But whether they want to believe it or not, a line has to be drawn between an informant or cooperating witness and the agent who is handling or receiving information from them. An inordinate amount of time is spent together between the agent, or handler, and the informant or cooperating witness when conducting business, whether preparing them for a meeting or debriefing them afterward, either secretly on the street or in some covert location. And when you're dealing with these people, even the ones who have committed violent criminal acts, when you take them out of their "work" environment, they can become some of the most affable and friendly people you've ever met, just like the good-natured thugs seen on *The Sopranos* television series. And because of the things that they've seen and done, they can tell you stories that will keep you mesmerized for hours. It's just like in the movie *Goodfellas*.

Most people who have watched it can't say that at some points during the movie, they didn't feel something for Henry Hill, Jimmy Burke, or even the heartless thug Tommy. And even these guys will start to identify with you as the FBI. And unfortunately, sometimes agents who work with these people for long periods forget what these guys did to put themselves in this position in the first place and start to identify with them as well. And as it turned out, a few people started to do that with Sonny.

After he finished working on the street, Sonny had to be put up somewhere out of harm's way. That somewhere was what was called a safe house, which happened to be pretty far from Brooklyn, in Colts Neck, New Jersey, but close enough that he was available to us. And he couldn't just be put out in the middle of nowhere among horse farms with no transportation without FBI agents who had to take turns staying overnight there with him, either taking him to the food store or pharmacy or even out to eat. This was done mostly to make sure that, even in an obscure place, he didn't run into anybody he knew, particularly from Brooklyn. And when that much downtime was spent with someone in one-on-one situations, some agents were going to do their share of talking. And did this guy have the gift of gab with them!

When it was my turn to sit with him, I would find out more about the personal lives of the people I worked with on my squad, who had been sitting with him on other nights, than I knew from them. Whose baby was due in a few weeks, which secretary was screwing around with a married agent, and who experienced massive losses in the stock market. The supervisor had to remind agents on more than one occasion, "Do not share personal information about yourself or others to him." Although personal bonds will naturally bloom in settings where you have plenty of time together and all you have is time to talk and socialize with each other, agents, who are human, sometimes forget that he's not one of us. And because you never know where this guy will be a year or ten years from now, some personally sensitive information you tell him either about yourself or someone else may come back to haunt you, or someone else, in some way. The bottom line that has to be remembered is, he's not your friend, and if he gets an opportunity, he'll hurt you as fast as anyone else.

And if you think he'll ever forget any personal, and possibly damaging, information that he has been told, think again.

After the first couple of times Mike went out and recorded a conversation with the UPS drivers about their illicit escapades, the nervousness and inhibitions slowly melted away. After identifying the first driver that we thought would take the bait, we had Mike tell the driver that he recently met an old friend while working on his route whom he hadn't seen in a while. The story was that he came across this friend, who also happened to be named Mike, in the same area where he used to work in the Laborer's Union as a union official. However, the feds came in, kicked all the mobbed-up union officials out of the hall, and installed a monitor, who watched over the activities of the union and made sure it stayed clean. Mike was out of a job, so to speak, but found another way to make money.

So the Mike who worked for the Mafia, who was really a UCA for the FBI, was now in the business of purchasing hot items and was bankrolled well enough that he could pay a good price up front. So Mike the CW told the driver that whatever stolen stuff he couldn't get rid of, let him know and he'd tell his friend Mike the UCA.

And in not wanting to miss out on any opportunity to make money, this greedy-bastard driver gave Mike the CW some items, and in turn he gave them to us, and we gave Mike the CW the money to give to the driver the next day. Then that driver spoke to another driver, and he spoke to another driver, and before you knew it, five drivers were giving Mike the CW plenty of stolen items that they were getting the money back for promptly, just like next-day service. And of course, all these transactions were being recorded by Mike the CW.

Eventually, there came a time when we wanted to cut Mike the CW out of the scene and insert Mike the UCA to sell our product firsthand. It was great to get these guys on tape making their deals, but it would be better if we could get them on video instead. And the task of videotaping was too difficult to conduct on the street with clarity while doing it covertly.

So on a couple of occasions, we had Mike the UCA go out and meet Mike the CW in the street while doing his route, but when he was in the company of one of the rogue drivers. Well, after a short time, with a little show-and-tell between Mike the CW with Mike the UCA we had someone who looked and acted the part of a Mob guy. He had a little gift of gab and took the drivers to some nice restaurants in the neighborhood where their routes were of course, all on the FBI. Mike the UCA began to ingratiate himself with the UPS drivers, especially with the free meals. The word spread to the other drivers like wildfire! And then the coup de grâce.

Mike the UCA told the drivers that he had a warehouse in College Point, Queens. When these guys had enough merchandise stored, if they could get some type of large vehicle to do a one-stop drop-off, then they could really make some money. And when these guys loaded their stolen stuff into vans and box trucks and drove from the west side of Manhattan out to Queens off the 20th Avenue exit of the Van Wyck Expressway, they came to see smilin' Mike the UCA. And as they came, one by one, and usually with the building maintenance man they worked with, and pulled their vehicles into the warehouse after Mike the UCA opened and then closed behind them the electric roll-up garage door, Pete and I were hiding out in that same warehouse in a small room perched at the top over the restroom next to the office that was loaded with recording equipment that caught every word on videotape.

They would come to the warehouse in Cadillacs. They would come in Broncos. And they were loaded with stolen merchandise, so much so, as one driver described it, that you "couldn't fit a screwdriver" inside the passenger compartment. After driving into the warehouse, they would unload the stuff packed in large garbage bags.

Photography equipment, stereo equipment, jewelry, on and on. Sometimes it would look like a clown car because the bags just wouldn't stop coming out. And when they were finished unloading, they would sit down in the interior office with Mike the UCA and complete the transaction, all under the watchful eye of our hidden cameras that Pete and I, ensconced in a room inside the warehouse stacked with recording equipment, would be recording their every sound and movement.

And did these guys love to shoot the shit with Mike! Since they thought that they were dealing with someone from the "criminal underworld," they wouldn't miss the opportunity to brag about the things that went on at work. We put a small refrigerator in the office and stocked it with beer. Then Mike would tell them that pizza was on the way; this way, now plied with food and drink, they were encouraged to stay and relax and talk. And talk they did.

One driver spoke about how he was able to buy a boat with the money he made stealing packages from two different stores. He actually named the boat by combining the names of those stores. Another driver paid for a $40,000 kitchen renovation with his proceeds. Another driver was able to purchase his-and-hers Cadillacs, the same one that he was driving the newly stolen merchandise in to our warehouse. Still, another said that at times he wound up stacking his regular paychecks in his dresser drawer for weeks at a time because he would just live off his "other earnings." Although the drivers all worked alone and didn't conspire with other drivers, Mike the UCA would tell them to spread the word when they talked among themselves. Because he paid them a higher percentage than he normally did fencing stolen property to compete with the store owners, he could make up the difference, he told them, if they got him more merchandise. One driver stated that he had been doing this for eighteen years, and the reason he survived this long was that he didn't talk about his activities. *Yeah, that's what you think!*

Mike the UCA pretty much fit the mold of a wiseguy in his looks, of average height and build, but he had a dark, bushy mustache and a hairpiece of the same color that you could see a mile away. But he didn't have quite the demeanor that you would expect of a wiseguy, especially later on, after you saw them on the HBO series *The Sopranos*. As he recorded his telephone calls with the drivers to discuss deals and make arrangements to meet with them, he would give us the tapes the next day with a synopsis of the calls. As we listened to them before they were transcribed, we heard one of the drivers who had recently begun to discuss doing business with him. When the driver, who was known as Mike the Greek, heard the phone being picked up and answered "Hello" by Mike the UCA, he said to him, "Is this Mike the Hair?"

Now, we listened with anticipation as any self-respecting wiseguy who' had likely knocked a few people to the ground or through a window when he felt as though he had been disrespected would have likely said, "What the fuck did you call me?" or at least "Who the fuck do you think you're talking to?" And if the tone on the other end of the phone didn't change quickly, and only because the wiseguy thought he was going to make money off the stooge, would there be a second chance not to have a limb broken! But instead, after the long pause caused by obvious disbelief and embarrassment, Mike the UCA/Wiseguy sheepishly said, "Yeah." But mocking a "mob guy" without repercussions, verbally or otherwise, unabashedly did not make Mike the Greek flinch or think twice. In our case, greed was good and got another driver to bite.

That wasn't the only laugh we had at Mike the UCA's expense. At the first meeting at the warehouse where Mike the CW was bringing another driver with stolen goods to meet Mike the UCA, Mike the CW had a problem with his car and needed a ride back to New Jersey after the deal was made. Knowing that he had enough on his mind with this operation to not have him worry that he was going to be stranded in Queens, and also knowing that both Pete and I didn't live anywhere near New Jersey, but knowing Mike the UCA did live there, we told him that the other Mike would give him a ride home, not knowing how close or how far away they lived from each other.

As Pete and I were perched in our "crow's nest" recording room, listening in to the conversation between the three of them, the stolen items were inventoried and paid for before the other UPS driver asked to use the bathroom, which was, unfortunately, right below the room where we were ensconced. As the driver went into the bathroom and the meeting room remained quiet for a minute, all of a sudden we heard Mike the CW say to Mike the UCA, "So you're going to give me a ride home after this?" With the highest edge of incredulity, Mike the UCA responded, "Who, me?" As Pete and I bit our lips as hard as possible not to burst into laughter, picturing in our minds the look on Mike the UCA's face as he said those two words, we held ourselves tight until the driver washed his hands, came out, and shook their hands before leaving the warehouse. Man, the hits just kept rolling!

After we ensnared as many corrupt drivers that we thought we could get in our operation—if not all of them, at least the ones we heard about—we had to close down Operation Cover-Ups before they really screwed up the federal deficit with the money we had to pay out. So on a cool spring morning, FBI agents waited for the UPS workers to arrive at work to place them under arrest. This was the same building where they received the packages that they were entrusted by the company, and, by proxy, the public, to deliver safely to their final destination. And it was also where the undoing began between Earl and Mike the CW's girlfriend. And UPS wanted us to do the arrest there so that "the show" would give pause to any other UPS workers who might have had theft on their minds to get discouraged when they saw their coworkers getting paraded out of the hub in handcuffs. Other agents fanned out to the area to pick up the building maintenance workers who were also indicted in the thefts. And for effect and to encourage them to cooperate with us, that is, talk to us about other criminal activities that they might know about, because "the jig was up," we had Mike the UCA walk by them as they were waiting to get fingerprinted and photographed, with his FBI badge dangling from his neck. One or two of these guys actually shit in his pants when they saw him.

Unfortunately, we didn't get Earl to sell us any of his criminally obtained wares. He was skeptical of Mike the CW's friend, and especially after what transpired between the two of them, never would Earl get close to someone that was close to him. However, we were able to compile enough information that, through the "preponderance of evidence," UPS was able to terminate him. Even the union couldn't save him. So he did escape from being criminally prosecuted, but after twenty-plus years of service, he not only lost a good-paying job but was now also leaving without a pension, and he would have to start all over again while in his late forties. Ouuuuch, that hurts!

Except for one, everyone in this case pleaded guilty before going to trial. It's funny how defense lawyers are always standing up around the media to say how vigorously they will oppose these false and malicious charges that have been filed against their client by an overzealous government. Or what great character their client has and that the charges are made by overzealous law enforcement agents. That's what you read below the headlines after the arraignment of the clients—that is, the reading of the charges in court after their arrest. So as the government (represented in this case by the FBI and United States Attorney's Office) is getting their coverage to show what they are doing about rooting out various types of crime, the defense lawyers are yelling about how their clients are the victims. And then when times fade and the media moves on to the next scandal *du jour*, the "victims" all quietly pleaded guilty to all charges for which they have been indicted. In this case, all except for James A. He was a former employee of UPS who was friends with one of the corrupt drivers. When the driver brought his stolen wares to the undercover warehouse, James, who was also from Brooklyn, like the driver, was there with him to unload it from the car. Every time. And when the driver was sitting in the office after the delivery, drinking beer and eating pizza, courtesy of the government, regaling Mike the UCA about how much stuff he had stolen from people through UPS, James was there, sitting right next to him. Every time. And all on tape.

James even chimed in with a few of his own stories from when he used to work there. But somehow, they were going to convince a jury that James was an "unwitting" accomplice, that somehow he did not know that this merchandise was stolen from people, stolen from UPS. Maybe they could convince the jury that the driver was involved in the flea market business and brought the stuff from there. I don't think that his attorney necessarily talked him into going to trial instead of accepting a plea agreement, which would have saved him from the severest of penalties. But James had recently received a job as a custodian at a local school, and we surmised that pleading guilty to a felony would have surely ended his career there. So roll the dice he did.

First, there was testimony about the case, how it started, how it was conducted, and how it was concluded. The tapes of warehouse meetings were shown, the driver and James driving into the warehouse and unloading the garbage bags, one after the other, from the car. They sat in the office together while Mike the UCA paid the driver thousands of dollars in hundreds, counted out one at a time right in front of James. Then the driver bragged about how he once mistakenly stole Grandma's Cookies from a customer, thinking that they were somehow a more valuable package, and then, as arrogant as could be, said that he sometimes stole packages "just to be stupid," as though he had checked his conscience at the door.

After the undercover agent testified about the deals that transpired in James's presence, his attorney went after Mike the UCA about some minor indiscretions that occurred years earlier in his FBI career. It's called attacking the credibility of the witness to challenge the veracity of his earlier testimony. Unfortunately for them, his testimony only corroborated what the tapes had visually shown. As the entire proceedings went on, James sat there, this guy in his early twenties, clean-shaven and looking his Sunday best, not having to testify himself and explain what he thought was going on during those taped sessions at the warehouse. He just sat there and tried to look angelic.

In every trial I've participated in, the defendant never looks or acts as he will normally do on the street while he is in the courtroom.

The difference in appearance of someone who is on the street as a gang member, robber, murderer, or thief and the defendant who sits at the table in court is like night and day. On the one hand is someone who is looking to intimidate you with his facial hair, manner, tattoos, dress. On the other hand is someone that, just based on his looks, you would leave your children with for the weekend.

And the only time that they will testify in court, when you might get a chance to glean something out of him, is if the prosecution's case is so strong that the only way they may get "a reasonable doubt" from the jury is to "humanize" him. But he couldn't even take a chance here.

Although they appeal to their emotions, thank God most juries see through them, as they did in this case. A couple of the jurors answered through tears as they individually confirmed that they voted "guilty." That's the difference. People who have a conscience, although they are doing the right and just act, still feel sympathy toward someone whose act is being condemned, even though that person has brought it on himself. But other people just don't care about who's hurt by their actions.

It was not until years later, during the Shamrock Bar trials, that I was thinking back to when Ron Rubinstein defended James A. The irony was later on, when I found out that Rubinstein was a partner of the firm Rubinstein & Corozzo, Corozzo being Joseph R. Corozzo Jr., son of Joseph "JoJo" Corozzo, the reputed consigliere of the Gambino crime family, whose brother Nicholas "Little Nick" Corozzo was the one-time boss of the Gambino crime family. He interned for Bruce Cutler, the noted attorney who defended John Gotti Sr. through a number of trials when Gotti became known as the Teflon Don for winning acquittals in those trials, only to be later found out that he was being acquitted not because his attorney was winning them but because members of the Gambinos were getting to a juror each time. Their website says that Corozzo is "highly recognized for his aggressive representation of alleged members and associates of organized crime." I hope, for their sake, that he and his partner do a better job than they did for poor James A.

It wasn't until years later, while I was an FBI agent, that I happened to be sitting with the same detective from the Cold Case Squad who worked on the Shamrock homicides. One day, we were sitting in my car when he asked me, since I grew up in that neighborhood, if I knew about a homicide that involved Joseph Cervino, the same Joey I played baseball with as a kid. I told him I knew Joey pretty well while we were growing up but I never knew for sure who was involved in his murder. There had been rumors, of course, through the neighborhood and I had my suspicions. But no one except for the mutts that were there that day knew for sure. The detective said that he had the case and was looking to eventually arrest four individuals for the crime. He then showed me a sheet of paper on which he wrote the four names of the suspects.

One name that I was familiar with and had heard back then that he was involved was Sammy. Sammy was another of the many neighborhood drug dealers whom I tolerated back then because I knew him as a preteen and he was still a friend of my friends. We had known each other for a long time, and I would shake hands with him upon seeing him in the street or at someone's house. Although I'd loathe him under my breath, we'd exchange pleasantries and then be on our respective ways. He was a decent guy, but because he made money from drug dealing, especially to my own friends, I really had no use for him or desire to hang around that element.

Although I was tolerable with him with the drug dealing, it later on bothered me, more so after Joey's death, to shake this guy's hand, because I wasn't sure if he was involved in it. Even though he had known Joey as long as anyone of us, there was just an arrogance to him that I thought he could've been a part of it. I would mostly see him when he came by one of my friends' place, like when we were together watching football. But he wasn't there to watch football, he was there to sell pot to my friends. Especially after I became a cop, I'd always wanted to ask him, "Were you involved in Joey's death?" But for the sake of peace with our mutual friends, I never did. But I knew one day it would come to a head.

And I liked Joey, I really did. While we were growing up, he was in with the crowd of the older brothers of my friends who hung out in the high school yard. They never really paid much attention to my friends or me, except one of them who liked to terrorize me as he walked from his house, which was right outside the schoolyard where I hung out with my friends, through the schoolyard to the other side, on his way to meet his friends. Of course, as he was a few years older than me and much taller, I didn't have much to say if he decided on a particular day to slap me around a bit. Probably because I was the only kid with red hair, I guess, was reason enough to do it. It was the price I had to pay to be out there playing ball with my friends, and I paid the price, until the day came that I didn't have to pay anymore.

But Joey was never a bully. As a matter of fact, he was one of the best baseball players in the neighborhood. He was a stocky, powerful guy that had the nickname Bam-Bam. He loved the game of baseball and played it with the best of them, until his days of smoking angel dust deteriorated his motor skills to the point where he wasn't as good anymore. But even then, he still loved the game.

And by that time, a lot of those "friends" wrote Joey off due to his diminished mental capacity from the years of drug use. But despite the gap in age of a few years between us, we had a common bond in the game of baseball. And I appreciated his childlike love of the game and sincerity of our friendship that developed from that bond as opposed to his contemporaries.

I had been playing with a pretty hapless team at one point, just because I couldn't give up on not playing myself. Joey was looking for a team to play with; not many would have him, but my team was so bad we were just looking for people to play. I brought Joey down to pitch. He couldn't focus well enough to put the bat on the ball to hit anymore, but he could still muster a bit of speed on the fastball. If he could get the ball around the plate, all the better.

He would meet me at my car every Sunday morning during the season, sitting on it impatiently, waiting, because he wanted to get to the field. I appreciated his enthusiasm, and even though he couldn't play the game as well as he once did, he still loved playing the game. Then came the time when he wasn't around the neighborhood anymore, instead having been stabbed to death, rolled up in a carpet, and left on the side of the Belt Parkway. All for the bankroll that he kept in his pocket.

I had stopped playing baseball when I became a cop, and soon after the academy, while I was in NSU, I once had been assigned a foot post near the subway station at East 125th Street and Lexington Avenue. It was an area of Spanish Harlem where, at that time, if you didn't live in the neighborhood, then you really didn't belong there. Maybe you'd get the accidental tourist that took the 6 train uptown, not realizing that not every stop on the Lexington Avenue line was glitzy. But on this one day, who did I see emerge from the subway entrance out onto the street but Joey.

After greetings and bringing each other up on what was new with each other, I asked him what brought him to this area of Manhattan, knowing that it was not possible but hoping that he somehow lost his way. With great disappointment, he said that he was up there "buying sneakers." Yeah, I'm sure they were a one-of-a-kind pair of sneakers. Even though he was still spiraling down, this wasn't the way it should have ended for him.

In recent years I was faced with a dilemma: Should I ask someone who had turned his life around so incredibly and genuinely about something that happened in their "past life," if you want to call it that? It was obvious that he was not the same person that he was when we were younger, and what good would it do to bring this up now? I decided that there was none and tried not to think about it again, until now. As I read on after Sammy's name, I didn't recognize the next two names that were on the list. But the last name slapped me in the head; the name was someone that I had known through most of my life as a person who couldn't be that cold.

When I read Mark's name, I was shocked. This was someone I knew closely, as well as his family. He had hung out with the older tough guys in the neighborhood, the difference in our ages being about three years, but in our teens, that was a *big* difference. He had developed quite a résumé of arrests, although, thankfully, not achieving to the level of some of his friends, and was one to hit quickly and effectively, as he had done to someone once when he broke his jaw with one punch. But as far as killing one of his own friends, someone whom he grew up with and whom he had done a lot together with, I just couldn't believe it! The detective told me, when Joey died from his stab wounds, he had defensive wounds on his hands, which showed that he tried to fight off his attackers. I couldn't believe it, rushing back to me after all these years—his own lifelong friends jumped him for the bankroll he kept in his pocket.

Like Sammy, Mark had been somewhat crazy in his teens and early twenties, but he had since changed his life around, not only with his work, but also as a husband and father. He owned his own home, and I still saw him on occasion. After telling the detective that I knew two names but had only heard about one being involved with the homicide and that was only conjecture from what I had heard in the neighborhood when it happened, he told me that he was working on the case and anticipated arrests of these individuals at some time in the future.

After he left my car and walked back into the building that housed not only his Cold Case Squad but the Queens Homicide Squad as well, I thought to myself, *What now? Do I tell these guys that they might have to prepare themselves, and their families, for getting arrested for Joey's murder?* Whether the arrests happened or not, I decided that nothing good could come from that, in case it didn't happen, and if it did, letting them know that this might be coming at them down the road was not going to be helpful to them. What could they do now but worry about that knock on the door? What was the sense?

At least these were two guys who were able to pick themselves up from our childhood, unlike my two oldest friends in this life. And fortunately for Sammy and Mark in this life, the knocks on the door never came.

*****

After the FBI indicted him on charges including committing homicides in aid of racketeering, John Alite fled to Brazil. He was eventually extradited, but not before he was remanded to a jail there, from which he fought that extradition. Facing charges of life in a federal prison isn't good, but I can't imagine anyone, especially an American who doesn't speak Spanish or Portuguese, having a good time there in a Brazilian prison. He stayed there for almost two years before he was brought back to Tampa, where the charges were initially filed, and then to New York, where he was valued as a witness against the former head of the Gambino family. He had been the longtime right hand of John Gotti Jr., who was facing his fourth trial in September 2009.

While incarcerated at the Metropolitan Correctional Center in Manhattan, John would meet with an agent whom I had known for quite a while in the Queens FBI Office who was on the Gambino Squad, officially known as C-16, named Ted. Ted told me that, before he had been arrested by the Brazilian authorities, John was involved in mixed martial arts while in Brazil, where some of the best fighters in the world had trained and from where the sport originated. He was becoming quite a fighter in his own right, until his fight career came to a screeching halt. John also would regale Ted about his days as a baseball player, both here in New York, when we played together in Little League and against each other in rival high schools, and in Tampa, where he had been recruited to play in college but a career-ending injury pushed him in another direction.

John's first affair with testifying for the government came when he was called to testify at the trial of Charles Carneglia on February 24–26, 2009. I wanted to attend the trial when John testified, because I knew that the only friendly faces that he was seeing were the FBI agents, for whom he was providing the information to what he was now testifying against; the Assistant United States Attorney that, through his cooperation agreement with the government, would question him on the stand about that information; and the US Marshals that would transport him to and from court each day. His immediate family had relocated to the Midwest, and because he was a high-value witness and inmate, he was not receiving any visitors in jail. But these friendly faces had a vested interest in John: his testimony against Gambino family members. I had no vested interest in the trial or his testimony; I just remembered the kid I used to play ball with in Little League.

When I went to the courtroom located on the Brooklyn side of the Brooklyn Bridge across the street from a small park, I wanted to show John that there was someone there who had no ulterior motive or malice of the heart for him, who was there as a ray of support. I sat in the last row, just behind the podium, where the defense attorney peppered him with questions, from where I was in line that he could clearly see me while he testified. Unbeknownst to me, sitting in the first row directly behind the defense attorney was Victoria Gotti, mother to John's former best friend, John Gotti Jr., who, from what I was later told, tried her best to intimidate John while he testified on the stand.

I had missed the direct examination by the prosecution, who would first have him lay out his criminal history to the jury in order to avert having the defense attorney reveal it in a more dramatic way. This is typically conducted to "cushion the blow" of the criminal conduct of cooperating witnesses (CW), who are, more often than not, individuals who are testifying to get a reduced sentence in exchange for their testimony, a type of quid pro quo. The CW may not have much choice, unless he will consider spending a large portion of his life in a federal penitentiary. This is done preemptively in a matter-of-fact way, even though the defense attorney will have the opportunity to expound on each crime as much as possible. CWs almost always have sordid pasts because, truth be told, will most law-abiding citizens have intimate knowledge of criminal activity? So since they are in a position to have knowledge of and/or witnessed these acts conducted in the criminal underworld, who better to tell about them? Then it is up to the jury to believe that the CW is genuine in his testimony or laying the blame of the crimes that he may have committed on someone else or just plain lying to save himself.

Although I missed the direct testimony related to Carneglia, the entire cross-examination seemed entirely based on John's relationship with John Jr., almost a prelude of what was to come later that year. He testified about robberies of drug dealers, some of which he shot to make a point, the "hits" that he carried out on the orders of John Jr., and the drug trafficking that he did with John Jr., in which he controlled almost all the drug spots in Queens, which made over one million dollars per month. But this was the stuff I was expecting to hear. As the testimony continued, the afternoon became more and more surreal.

When asked by the defense attorney how many people he had shot during this time, John answered matter-of-factly, "About thirty." Although I couldn't show it in the courtroom, the answer jolted me a bit. He was then asked about the time period that he was extorting Tony from the neighborhood bar called Good for the Spirits Pub, commonly known by my friends and me simply as Spirits. It was known to me as it was my steady hangout spot Friday nights during my college years. After working my night shift with friends at the Key Food store on Lefferts Boulevard near Jamaica Avenue, which was four blocks from home, I would go home, shower, and watch that night's episode of *Miami Vice*. Then I would meet the guys I worked with, as well as others, at Spirits, which was located on Metropolitan Avenue near Lefferts Boulevard in Kew Gardens. Thoughts then began swirling in my head of the past, drinking with my friends, having a grand time, listening to the DJ spin "Smuggler's Blues," all the while John and his cronies were tuning up Tony, a paunchy but likeable guy with dark curly hair and a mustache, for extortion money in the back alley.

Then he continued testimony about shooting a drug dealer outside of the Flight 116 bar. This was the same dopey little place that I had my incident years earlier that was located at the corner of 116th Street and 101st Avenue, blocks from where John Gotti Sr.'s club, the Bergin Hunt and Fish Club, was formerly located. It was not only located either down the block or around the corner from where many of my friends had lived at that time; it was also the bar that sponsored my first softball team. However, I would only go there during the day after games, if at all, knowing the reputation the place had, especially at night. We had called ourselves the Crew, for no other reason than that we were a motley bunch that had nothing to do with the illegal substances that were being sold from there. And sure enough, John had left his footprints there as well, leaving a trail of blood spilled on the sidewalks of Queens. And toward the end, when he was asked about the illegal activities that he was involved in with the Gambino family, John actually used the words "It wasn't personal, it was business!" And although he did testify about one situation in which he was sent to kill someone for what he deemed some small infraction but instead let him live and merely sent him to the hospital, John emphatically stated that, when it came to the orders issued by John Gotti Jr., "it wasn't a democracy."

John was always a charismatic person who had a short stature but a muscular frame. He conveyed a sense of confidence as he left the stand and exited the courtroom. I could see the jurors looking at him, wearing impish smiles, as though being told tales over a beer at the corner bar, appreciating his sincerity, which was later validated by a conviction. Another guy whom we had played Little League ball with had heard that I was in touch, so to speak, with John and had some pictures of when John, his girlfriend, and their children had attended a BBQ at his home several years earlier. He asked if I could get the pictures to John, which I did through Ted. I also enclosed a note that extolled about the "better times ahead" mantra and how, God willing, after it was all over, John would be able to hold his kids again. When I gave Ted the envelope, he told me that John was very grateful for my appearance in court.

Among the columns in the *New York Daily News* about his testimony, there was an article regarding denials by Victoria Gotti, the daughter of John Gotti Sr., that she had slept with John Alite around the time of her marriage, as he had claimed on the stand. This must have been brought out during the direct examination that I missed. I then began to think about the time years ago when John called me about the "contract" that he was told had been put on him by Carmine Agnello, her then-husband, who was also involved in the Gambino family. Could this contract have been a result of this alleged affair that was found out?

Toward the end of the year 2009, John would now face his nemesis, who was once the best man at his wedding as John was married on the same day of his birthday, John Gotti Jr. During his testimony, he described the murder of George Grosso, who, along with another guy I knew from Little League named Johnny Gebert, tried to kill John as he walked down Forest Parkway in Woodhaven from his parents' house. After time had passed and a sit-down had occurred between the three of them and other higher-ranking members of the Gambino family, John described how he planned to "rock him to sleep" on a night out with friends at the White Horse Tavern in Woodhaven, Queens, which was the next block over on Jamaica Avenue from the Shamrock Bar. While they were there, he was buying shots for everyone, but he told the bartender to give him water instead in his shot glass. As he continued in his testimony, during the lead-up to this night, he actually stated the line from the movie *The Godfather* that he was doing this to "keep your friends close but your enemies closer." Although it could have been construed as a cliché, it actually applied to not only this scene but the life he was living as well. After getting him comfortable before they left the bar to go elsewhere, John sat in the back seat of a vehicle in which George was sitting in front (not smart on his part!), and John then shot him in the head and had his body dumped on the side of the road near Flushing-Corona Meadow Park.

A number of times he admitted that he baseball-batted someone to protect the drug trade that he had with John Jr. He described how he had to "hurt him bad" when talking about the vicious beatings he had given, often at the order of John Jr. As he continued his testimony about John Jr., he said that because of his greed when it came to splitting scores, Junior wasn't well liked by the other members of his crew. And right on cue, taking from a line of another movie, he said that John Jr. was feared more than he was liked.

As in the first trial, he regaled the jury and audience with stories of both giving beatings and getting beatings. His testimony at trial was, as I overheard the defense attorney say in the elevator during a lunch break, straight out of the movie *Goodfellas*.

Months earlier, before the trial, when the case agent asked me if I ever documented any of my informal "meetings" with John, I should have suspected that the question didn't come out of the blue and that there was a reason he asked me. A requirement before trial is a process called discovery, which entails that all information that is relevant to the trial is provided by the prosecution team to the defense counsel. It later became obvious to me that the defense counsel had asked if there was any such material that had been produced by me as a result of these meetings. During the years that he was involved with the crew, at some point, John had likely told either one of his associates, or even John Jr. himself, that we knew each other. And when John cooperated against John Jr. at trial, our "association" was divulged to his defense counsel, who now sought whatever records in regards to that association to determine whether there was anything in them to discredit him.

The FBI had already been mired in two other recent alleged scandalous relationships between an FBI handler and a confidential source, one that involved a New York agent named Lindley Delvecchio, who was later tried for what the Brooklyn District Attorney's Office deemed to be a collusive relationship with a Mafia hit man named Gregory Scarpa Sr. He was accused of helping the capo, who was his prize informant, kill rivals during the Colombo family civil war. Specifically, he was charged with helping Scarpa carry out four Mob hits from 1984 to 1992, at the height of the Colombo war, which pitted a group who splintered and followed Vittorio (Vic) Orena against the faction of the family loyal to official boss Carmine Persico. The allegations were that he gave the names and addresses of those who were providing information to law enforcement to Scarpa, who was aligned with the Persico faction. However, with the aid of perjured testimony by the girlfriend of Scarpa, Delvecchio was acquitted and retired from the job.

Years later, Gregory Scarpa Jr., who followed in his old man's footsteps, sought a reduction of his racketeering sentence as a reward for helping the government find explosives hidden in the home of Oklahoma City bomber Terry Nichols. But it wasn't publicly revealed until 2016 that in a transcript of the 2012 court case for the Mob informant, Brooklyn federal judge Edward Korman suggested that the government, who opposed the motion for sentence reduction, did so because the FBI might still harbor a grudge against Scarpa Sr.

The grudge was supposedly not only for his willingness to testify against Delvecchio at his trial but also due to the discovery of the explosives from the information that was provided against Nichols. Korman surmised that the FBI was embarrassed because agents failed to find the explosives when they originally searched Nichol's home in the aftermath of the 1995 bombing of the Alfred P. Murrah Federal Building, which killed 168 people.

The government is represented by the United States Attorney's Office, not only to prosecute criminal violations of federal law, but also in civil cases as well. Similar to the local District Attorney's Office, the United States Attorney's Office is staffed with Assistant United States Attorneys, commonly known as AUSAs, who prosecute the cases that come within the purview of the office. The United States Attorney's Office in the Eastern District of New York covers Brooklyn, Queens, Staten Island, Nassau, and Suffolk counties. The office in the Southern District of New York covers New York, Bronx, Putnam, Orange, Westchester, Rockland, Dutchess, and Sullivan counties.

Personally speaking, and with all due respect to the Honorable Judge Korman, from the professional experience I've had with the AUSAs who work in both of these offices, I don't see them being swayed by the FBI for these reasons and making decisions based on, for lack of a better word, revenge. And the executive management of the FBI, the agents in charge of each division or office, are the ultimate decision makers when it comes to policy issues, especially of regional or national significance. I severely doubt that these individuals, who were young agents just beginning their careers in divisions other than where these cases occurred in Oklahoma and Brooklyn, would base their decisions with revenge or embarrassment in mind. And of course, the main decision maker of all, Director James Comey, has been with the bureau only just the past few years.

From my perspective, and then again this might just be me, but as the famous saying goes, "It's just business, nothing personal."

Korman, who had presided over the Mob trial of Colombo gangster Orena in the 1990s, reduced Scarpa Jr.'s sentence by ten years. However, an appeals court reinstated the original sentence. He is now scheduled for release in 2035. Although his family had said that he was afflicted with cancer, Scarpa Sr. died in federal prison in 1994 from AIDS that he contracted through a blood transfusion.

The other case involved an agent in Boston who was a childhood friend of James "Whitey" Bulger, who was loosely portrayed by Johnny Depp in the movie *Black Mass*. Similar to the allegations in the Delvecchio case, not only did Bulger and Frank Connally exchange gifts and have dinners together with their loved ones, but Connally also allegedly provided Bulger with information including not only on his rivals but also identifying those who were "ratting" on him. Connally was obviously not as lucky as Delvecchio and is still serving time for having been convicted of aiding Bulger in committing his crimes, forty years' worth, although appeals are still in the process.

It was believed that those agents began to identify with their sources over time and almost became part of their crew. A supposed recreation of a scene was parodied on the HBO TV series called *The Sopranos*, which was about a dysfunctional Mafia crime family, when an FBI agent was listening in on a meeting involving a captain of a crime family who had gotten the upper hand of a high-ranking member of another family. The agent suddenly jumped to his feet and shouted, "We're gonna win this thing!" Although I had been around those elements much of my life, as had my father before me, their lifestyle was something that I would never have identified with, and therefore, there was no chance that there would be another scandal in my name. During the second day of trial, which I had not attended but later read about, John Alite testified about the tough kid from 62 Park named John Cennamo, who, at the age of twenty-four years old, had the unfortunate circumstance one night to be in the same bar as John Gotti Jr. On March 12, 1983, the Silver Fox Bar in Queens was the setting where Cennamo had come with a friend named Danny Silva. For whatever lame reason, Silva was knifed to death during a fight there.

Although he testified that he wasn't there at that time, John Alite claimed that when John Gotti Jr. had bragged to him about having a role in four killings, he took credit for the stabbing of Danny Silva. And on an occasion, when Alite was hospitalized at Jamaica Hospital with injuries he sustained from a brawl and Gotti came to visit him, Gotti said that John Carneglia was sent to take care of Cennamo, who had fingered him on the Silva murder, on his father's orders, with mobsters Angelo Ruggiero and "Willie Boy" Johnson also on the team of killers.

A retired cop also testified that he was pressured to write up the death of Cennamo as an "apparent suicide," over his objections. It was contended by prosecutors that members of the Gambino crime family murdered Cennamo and then staged the scene to look like a suicide. Another retired law enforcement officer testified that the Silva investigation was complicated from the start by meddling supervisors and detectives, including one who allegedly pocketed $25,000 to steer the investigation away from Gotti. Although another detective said he heard Cennamo at the bar scream out, "We all know who did it! We all know who did it! Johnny Boy Gotti!" his investigation was marked by "heavy supervision from supervisors and a lot of input from other detectives," including the detective who took the $25,000 from Ruggerio days after Cennamo's slaying. Gotti was never questioned during the investigation.

During the trial, on one of the days of cross-examination by the defense attorney, while I was sitting in the back row with other FBI agents and NYPD detectives, John was asked if he knew me, Special Agent Jason Randazzo of the FBI. The blood likely drained from my face, as I had not been prepared for hearing my name echo throughout the courtroom. Although it would make no difference in the end to the outcome of the trial, my name had now been interjected nonetheless. I sat there totally not expecting the line of questioning that was soon to follow, especially since no one knew that I would be sitting in the courtroom that day, including the defense attorney. When he was asked about the last time he saw me, John answered, "Today, in the courtroom." I'm sure that caught the defense attorney by surprise, that I was there in support of someone I knew from long ago. Or maybe he just thought that I was there in the capacity of a federal agent.

The attorney continued to ask questions regarding the substance of our relationship, looking for some type of impropriety that he could expose. John testified that I dated his sister (for which, when he was asked by the attorney how long that relationship lasted, he stated that he didn't follow his sister's love life) and that, many years ago, when I still was a cop, we ran across each other on Jamaica Avenue near Forest Parkway a few blocks from his parents' house. I recalled to myself that I was with a date, going to a friend's house in the neighborhood for dinner (which was a true occurrence that I hadn't remembered since that time, probably twenty-five years ago). He also said that John Jr. was in his company at that time (which I strangely can't remember but is still possible). Then the attorney turned his attention to a telephone call John had made to me years earlier.

He asked about that call years earlier when John had called me to validate the threat against him by Carmine Agnello. He was visited by two agents from the Gambino Squad in my office, who told him that they had information that Agnello had put a contract on him. Obviously, after giving him this information, they then told him that a way out of this situation would be to cooperate with the government and they would be able to protect both him and his family. He answered them the only way he knew how at that time, that this was the life that he chose and he would have to deal with the situation in his own way. And after we spoke, I informed one of the two agents who visited him about the telephone conversation.

When he called me, his question to me was, Would they lie to him about this threat to push him to cooperate with the government? And my answer, of course, was that the agents would not put themselves in a position of liability by telling him a false scenario that might cause detrimental results, which might include the death of Agnello by Alite. So whatever they told him should be taken at face value. He thanked me for my candor and told me the answer he gave the agents, albeit politely, with the same rationalization, that it was the life he chose. We asked about each other's families before we hung up the phone, like we had just finished a casual conversation.

This was a conversation that I had only shared with the case agent who had visited him. It really had no substantive value, but I wanted the agent to know that John contacted me after his visit, still reiterating to me that cooperation was not an option and for that agent not to hold his breath for a call. So the only way that this conversation could have come to the defense attorney's attention was through one of John's close "friends" who was aligned with him in the life at that time and with whom he felt he had confidence. The friend relayed this conversation to John Jr. many years later, since John Alite was now a cooperating witness with the government. And it was then told to his attorney.

When he asked John how he had contacted me, he said at home, though I consciously never gave him my home telephone number, knowing it could lead to the appearance that I was traveling down a "bad road" with a close, personal association with him. I vividly remembered sitting at a desk in the old FBI office on Queens Boulevard in Rego Park, astonished to the subject of the conversation with him. When the attorney continued asking him the basic context of our haphazard meetings in the streets of Queens, John said I was often chastising him for living "the life" and tried to get him to leave it, offering for him to stay at my house while he slipped away from those that he knew in the life. I knew for a very long time that he was entrenched in the life, not only because of the wealth that he had attained but also because they would never let him just slip away, and it was only wishful thinking that he could leave it behind and something I would never say to him. Perhaps he was trying to put a spin to it, as though I was a good soul.

When the attorney asked him if he had trusted me, he gave an answer that I was a bit surprised and caught off guard to hear but then understood from his perspective. He said, like anyone else, he didn't trust me and even suspected that I might have been "working" him, just like other law enforcement personnel had tried before. Wow, to probably this day, he hadn't recognized the sincerity in my concerns, wishing that he had traveled a path more like mine rather than those of the knuckleheads of the old neighborhood. And the epitome of our divergent lives was never more apparent, that I was able to trust certain people with my life but he had no one at all.

Although I had known him through the different stages of our lives, he looked at me sideways just as he did everyone else.

When the court recessed for lunch, a man approached me where I had been sitting in the rear of the courtroom and asked me if

I was Jason Randazzo. I was now standing in the courtroom, feeling a bit vulnerable after hearing the testimony and still in a slight state of shock that I hadn't had a chance to shake off yet. I didn't want to acknowledge him, but not wanting to lie, I nodded. He then introduced himself as a *New York Post* reporter whose name I recognized from the daily articles he was writing about the trial. He asked me if I would answer a few questions.

Mercifully, one of the detectives who had been sitting in the back row with me saw the situation and called me to the vestibule immediately outside the courtroom. After excusing myself to the reporter, I joined the detective in the vestibule. The reporter, passing us on his way out of the courtroom, gave me his business card and asked me to give him a call.

I can only assume that the defense attorney was on a fishing expedition that day for a third scandal in the FBI, much like the other two. Fortunately, the moral compass that had been provided to me by my parents, especially my mother, ensured that if there was a scandal of this nature in the FBI, it wouldn't be at my expense.

When I returned to the office later that day and read through my e-mail, I received a forwarded message from the office media spokesman. The same reporter had asked him through the e-mail some confirming questions, including the correct spelling of my name. After I called the spokesman, he stated that he did not answer the reporter's request and did not intend on answering it. No article had been written mentioning my name or association to John. I called that reporter a few weeks later, late at night, to ensure he wasn't there. I just wanted to leave him a voice mail message and apologized if I was rude to him in the courtroom on that day.

He called back and left a return message that said the apology was not necessary but that if I should like to meet with him for coffee, he would be available. That message was left unrequited.

In the spring of 2010, I was descending in the elevator that not only housed the newer office of the FBI located on Kew Gardens Road but was also the same building where the Queens District Attorney's Office was located as well. I had gotten on an empty elevator on the twelfth floor, the top floor of the building, and on its way down, it stopped on one of the other floors where the DA had offices. Three rather young-looking adults, two women and a male, who were probably law school interns working for the office, also got on the elevator, carrying case file boxes, about six boxes in all, that appeared to be material from the DA for an upcoming trial.

Each of the boxes had the name John Burke written on it. *Here it is,* I thought, *the next round from the hood for John Alite.*

*****

One of the quickest adrenaline rushes on this job comes from chasing fugitives, especially when you know with reasonable certainty or positively that your guy is in the dwelling. Fugitive investigations used to take a lot of time and patience, but through the advent of social media and cellular phones, it has become more of a real-time effort. Before the changing times, you would look at a person's personal information and copy it down on reports and "wanted" flyers so often that you would know it as well as your own. If your guy was bad enough, and many of them were, you could have him profiled on the TV show *America's Most Wanted*, and many tips, mostly anonymous, would lead to many false leads but it was hoped that someone truly knew where he was and would call in to the show. Going to places, discreetly if possible, and talking to people, whether they were former wives, associates, people who might have an interest in reward money looking for someone who could place your guy (and infrequently, girl) somewhere, even if it was a location that was visited from time to time, and you would have to sit and watch and wait for hours, maybe even days, at a time. And it would all be worth it when you had your man in cuffs and another fugitive case was put in the books.

Through the evolvement of technology also came the advent of a tool that expedited a number of quick-moving investigations, called Triggerfish. This truly amazing invention revolutionized the process for hunting fugitives or searching for kidnap victims through the cellular phone and often catching the mutts by virtue of their own hand. It also prevented many lost hours when some idiots would get a novel idea of calling their family members themselves or have other people call for them and say they were kidnapped and ask for a ransom payment, thinking they would get some quick money for their desperate needs. The idiots would sit, in a hotel room somewhere with their boyfriend or girlfriend, and wait to make another call for the "drop," only to have the anvil drop on them. The technically trained agents and their use of this tool was invaluable to aid in the solution of these type of cases.

The tool itself reminded me of a Polaroid camera, for those who remember the instamatic photographs before digital photography. After the telephone company was able to provide the general area of the location of the phone through the "ping" that the phone gave off, which came from the cell phone tower that was local to that particular telephone, the tech agents would drive into the area, usually in a blacked-out SUV, and circle around as the location of the power source became stronger. Eventually, it would lead to a specific location, then to a specific floor, then to a specific room. My initial experience with Triggerfish occurred after a bank robbery in Queens, when we were given information regarding a fugitive from Baltimore for a robbery/homicide whose cellular phone was "pinging" in Brooklyn.

As we completed our crime scene investigation at the bank, I was told that the tech agents were already out there in Brooklyn tracing the phone. As I drove over and contacted them on my cell phone, the tech agents said that they had the phone of the fugitive at a location and were awaiting my arrival. As I continued my way there, they gave me a description of their car, a blacked-out SUV, of course, and where they were now parked. I parked my own car around the corner from them, put on my bulletproof vest, grabbed a couple of extra magazines of ammunition for my firearm and made my way to their car.

As I jumped in the back seat, the passenger had the camera-looking device pointed toward a house on the corner that we were facing. The driver said that the phone was on the second floor of the house. As I brought up the "wanted" flyer of the fugitive that was e-mailed to me on my cell phone and thought about what our plan of action might be, a couple appeared through the door of the house and walked down the steps of the front stoop. As they walked down the block along the sidewalk across from us, I anxiously looked at the photo of the fugitive and then the individual walking along with the girl. As my eyes darted back and forth, I could not get a good-enough look at him to determine if this was our guy and whether I'd be blowing this whole operation up by jumping out and grabbing the wrong man. But when I looked at the tech agent in the passenger seat, he seemed to be following the couple as they walked with the device, not saying anything at this point. Finally, he said out loud, "The phone is moving down the block!"

With his confirmation that the phone was moving and a positive identification from the flyer that it was our guy, knowing that the rest of my squad had not yet arrived, we watched the couple as they turned the corner. Knowing that under normal circumstances, their part of the job was done when they identified the location of the phone and it was then the part of the investigative squad to take action, I asked them if they had my back as I exited the car. Jogging ahead with my gun down to my side (not up next to my face like the Hollywood actors, for many a good reason), I quietly and cautiously came up behind the couple, wanting to close the gap as quickly as possible and avoid a foot chase into the unknown. As I came up on him, from around the corner of a parked car in front of the couple came one of the tech agents, gun drawn down on the male, announcing our presence.

"STOP! FBI!" I was able to reach out and grab him as he began to put his hands up and push him over the hood of that parked car, the other tech agent tending to the female and making sure she didn't become a threat to us. After searching him for weapons and handcuffing him, I asked the male if he was the man we were looking for and if he was from Baltimore, just to confirm we had him. After he had lied to us about who he was and as we walked him back to our cars, the other members of my squad pulled up to the scene. Ryan bounced out of his car, brought the "wanted" flyer of the fugitive over to us, and said, "Gotcha, motherfucker!" He grabbed the guy, threw him in his back seat, and off they went to his journey back to Baltimore.

After that time, we were able to locate kidnapping victims through either their cell phone (the kidnappers thought they were crafty by using a victim's cell phone so it wouldn't be traced back to them through telephone records but didn't think that we might be able to find the location of the actual phone while it was in use) or the telephone of the kidnappers if we could identify them and track their phone. Or the rapist who had fled from California during his trial, only to be found talking on his cell phone while he was drinking coffee at a table in the Starbucks that was on the first floor of the Empire State Building. But no apprehension of a fugitive was as gratifying as the murderer named Jorge Aldea from Philadelphia, who had killed a female witness while she worked at a convenience store; she was to testify against him at a trial. For a twenty-year-old kid, he had a lot of killing under his belt already.

After we were alerted that a Violent Crime Task Force in Philadelphia was looking for this guy and they got a "ping" in the Bronx, I called our tech guys with the information they needed to head out to the general location and start sniffing around. As they circled the area searching for the phone, I maintained contact with both them while coordinating with my squad mates who were making their way up from the Manhattan office. Of course, they then keyed on a particular building and called me just when I finally got a chance between calls to them and calls to my squad mates to get out of the car and fetch my vest out of the trunk and quickly throw it on before losing touch with anyone. Much to my chagrin during that two-minute interval, I missed a call from, of all people, one of the tech agents.

"I tried calling you, and then I called someone else from your squad. Nobody's picking up the fuckin' phone!" he yelled out when I called back. Just to placate him, because we needed these guys more than they needed us and they always had another operation they could move to if they didn't get the response they were looking for, I apologized for my insolence before he got around to tell me that they have focused on a location. As I raced over to the location from just blocks away and phoned one of my squad mates to give him the information, I pulled up just in time to see one of the tech agents out front of the building, moving with the device like a Geiger counter looking for uranium. Although I would like to have waited for others to get there before going up inside the six-story building and after this guy, there was no waiting; I was the sole hunter following the golden retriever who was sniffing for our prey.

We combed the flights of stairs until we reached the fifth floor, where he said the cell phone was in an apartment. He pointed to the apartment closest to the stairs, motioning that the cell phone of the fugitive was there, before looking at me dismissively and asking through gesture where the rest of my squad was. When I motioned back that they were on the way, he derisively whispered to himself loud enough for me to hear "Reactive squad," a sarcastic response with the moniker given to the few squads in the office that reacted to crimes as they occurred—i.e., bank robberies, kidnappings, and fugitives. The reactive squads were opposed to most other squads that investigated crimes proactively, which is to say they looked for crimes that were either in the process of happening or hadn't yet been discovered. However, either way, it was not quick enough responding for him.

Although I had only met him a few times before, I grew respect for both his craft and the value in the expertise for which he honed that craft, and, despite the derisive comment, I actually liked him more as we moved on to other fugitive cases. He also reminded me a lot of the actor Greg Kinnear, both in looks and, in some movies, mannerisms.

A young boy suddenly came out of that apartment with a cart full of laundry. He didn't look older than fifteen. I stopped and questioned him about the people in the apartment; however, after he went back and took us in there to see that the only other person in there was his much younger brother, the tech agent insisted that the cell phone could then only be in this other apartment directly above us. We continued up the stairs and stopped on the landing between the fifth and sixth floors.

As we stopped and I listened through the door for any noise on the other side, he placed the device against the wall and said it was in there. My squad mates and detectives of the New York City Police Department Bronx Warrants Squad also got there and formed up behind me on one side of the door and across on the other side. After personnel went through the apartment below to get a "visual" of the only other escape route from the apartment through the fire escape, the lieutenant from the PD whispered to me that someone should cover the roof in case he decided to attempt an escape to the roof. I said I would cover it but before I proceeded up the one flight of stairs, he warned me about the door likely having an alarm. Whether he said to me that the alarm would be activated by my opening the door (which I had thought I heard, and therefore, I was going to position myself directly inside of it, prepared to move as soon as they gained entry into the apartment) or by my approaching the door by stepping within range of the motion sensor of the alarm system (which would have meant staying on the steps before the first landing and then running up after they made entry through the door, therefore setting off the alarm after they entered the apartment and not possibly causing the fugitive to be "raised up" before gaining access to the roof) is known to only him and God, because all I heard was that the door was alarmed and not to go through it before they hit the door.

The lieutenant turned his attention toward the door of the apartment as I crept up the stairs, and as I approached the landing that led to the steps directly to the door that led to the roof, an ear-splitting sound rang out from an alarm! Duh, I just set off a motion detector alarm on the landing that leads to the door of the roof. Now as I sheepishly stood there, gun in hand, the alarm went off blaring loud enough that it could be heard not only in the entire building but probably down the block as well. I was embarrassed to no end, and the lieutenant mouthed to me from the door that the alarm should go off on its own after about a minute or so. So as everyone waited in place and I stood there getting more red from the embarrassment of what felt like a "rookie mistake," the alarm kept going…and going…and going for minute after minute. Although a few people exited other apartments on the floor, no one came out of this one. I came down from the landing to discuss with the lieutenant about having someone get the superintendent to silence the alarm. Finally, the alarm stopped. Still, no movement was heard within the apartment.

At this point, feeling directly responsible for having stirred up the building and, very possibly, the occupants of the apartment that we were standing immediately outside of, I asked a junior agent to cover the fire escape from the roof, but as he moved to take a closer position to the door of the roof, I grabbed him by the arm to ensure that he didn't make the same mistake as I did. As he moved to the steps below the landing to the roof, I moved to the opposite side of the apartment door from the lieutenant, now positioning myself to be the first to encounter whatever was on the other side.

We banged loudly on the door, yelling out both "Police, open the door!" and "Policia, abra la puerta!" After about a minute, which felt much longer, a young-looking girl, maybe out of high school, maybe not, answered the door, with an older couple standing behind her.

After she said that it was her aunt's apartment and they were just there visiting, we showed them the "wanted" flyer with the photograph of the fugitive, whom they all stated they had never seen or know of. While the lieutenant continued to talk to them, I quickly looked around the apartment from where we were standing, gauging where the fugitive might be, if he was truly there. As I glanced at the tech agent, he was still motioning the device like he was looking for the holy grail, walking just behind me as we now entered the living room of the darkened apartment. She yelled out behind us, "Do you have a warrant to come in here?" I looked ahead to see two rooms that were padlocked from the outside in an alcove in the rear of the apartment. Keeping my gun drawn as we crept closer, knowing that if he was in there he'd be pretty alert now, moving left foot forward, right foot to left, and then left foot forward again, I kept the sights of my firearm trained on the opening, glancing intermittently to my left to eventually see the tech agent reach the wall with the device, steady himself, and mouth to me, "It's there!"

I took a position on the opposite side of the opening to the alcove, peeked in quickly (not to leave my head hanging out there like a target at the carnival), and saw a door to a room directly on the other side of the wall from where the tech agent stood. As I cautiously moved to the side of the door where the knob was, the lieutenant slid in near me so as not to be in front of the door but ready to spring. The door was locked as I tried the knob, and the lieutenant pulled out a small knife and worked on pulling the latch back, bravely exposing himself to fire from the other side of the door while I trained my weapon on that doorway. As he was able to pull the latch back and pull the doorknob, the door flew open and a darkened figure sat on the closed toilet just inside the doorway. We reached in and grabbed any body part we could to pull him out, my left hand quickly moving from whatever part of clothing on his torso that I grabbed to pull him out to scoop the back of his neck as I trained my .40 caliber to his head. He meekly lay there as the others quickly searched him for weapons, handcuffed him, and moved him away to the more open area of the living room, where he could be more thoroughly searched. Despite intelligence that he claimed he would be going out with a bang; instead, he went out with a whimper.

At first, he denied that he was the person we were looking for, but the star tattoo under his left eye pretty much gave him away. We later discovered that the older couple that were there did not admit to knowing him because he had threatened them if they did say anything, but the younger female was his nineteen-year-old girlfriend, who not only knew why we were looking for him but was also later discovered to have participated in the killings with him, stashing the guns, acting as a lookout and driver. After he had been brought in the living room, the lieutenant and I searched the bathroom in which he was hiding. Inside the vanity, there sat a loaded 9-mm handgun, immediately adjacent to where we pulled him out, four rounds in the magazine and one in the chamber.

Fortunately for us, he turned cowardly when his adversary was also armed, unlike his victims. However, I could not understand how his callous girlfriend could let us go back there, knowing that we easily could have engaged her psychotic boyfriend who was armed with a semiautomatic handgun, in a gun battle that would surely have left him dead and some of us with a husbandless wife or a fatherless child. Amazing how some people just don't care.

But sometimes technology can only go so far and good old gumshoe work has to take precedence.

An agent on my squad had a lead on a guy who was wanted for a homicide twenty years ago in Baltimore, named Jose Sean Pellet. Some recent checks had possibly placed him at one of two residences in Brooklyn, living with a woman there. The agent and I sat out at those residences for hours, looking for him, but came up empty. That agent, not to be deterred, did some cross-checking between the name of that woman and other databases and service lists and came up with a new address for her in a different part of Brooklyn. A couple of checks later found a six-year-old child that was listed for that woman at a school nearby to her residence. And the topper was a callout to modern-day technology when the fugitive had conveniently listed a Facebook page under one of his aliases, which provided us with recent photographs of him and his children.

On an early Tuesday morning, members of our squad fanned out around the residence in our tinted-out cars, armed not only with our sidearms but with the photographs taken straight off the Facebook page as well. Most of us had placed ourselves in the streets between the residence and the school, where we had hoped to see the fugitive walk with his son. The case agent and another squad mate sat in an obscure van in front of the residence, calling out possible targets bundled up on the cold March morning as they scurried through the front door of the five-story apartment building and out into the brittle air. The first few were either checked out by the roving units as they walked and crossed off or sat in cars parked nearby while warming their engines, unaware that they were being watched and evaluated. None of them were him.

After a few hours, a man about the same height as our subject walked through the door with a small child in tow. Two cars with two agents inside, me included, drove and watched the individual continue south down the block after the agents in the van called them out. As one car kept the eye on them, we circled around to get a better look at them from a parked front view. When I looked at the man and then down at the photographs in front of me, I called on the radio, "This is our guy!" Our only plan up until that point was to wait until he had walked the child to school and then grab him a short distance away so that the child would be away from harm should his dad choose not to go quietly, but also to save his father some shame when the handcuffs were placed on his wrists. However, as usual, contingencies happened.

As they zigzagged across streets and made their way in the right direction, they mysteriously turned down a subway station entrance and descended below. The agents in the two cars darted from their respective vehicles and closed the gap as quickly as possible, anticipating any type of situation that might arise. As we made our way down the stairs and approached them from behind with our guns to our sides, aided by the small steps of the child, which afforded us the time to catch up to them, we grabbed him before he got to the turnstile and pushed him to the tiled wall. As he was handcuffed and searched, confirming to me when asked for his true name but denying he was ever in Baltimore, his child cried in shock at what was happening to his father, not understanding who we were and what we were doing. It saddened me to see that and to allow the manacled dad one last kiss with his son before he went on his way back to his mother, and the other another way, to prison for a long time. But I'd rather do that than give a stroke to an eighty-one-year-old woman who thought the shop was getting robbed by me.

We were looking for another fugitive out of Virginia for murder, named Udeil Yates, when his cell phone began pinging one night in the tony town of Roslyn, found in the suburbs of Nassau County, nestled in what's known as the Gold Coast. Why this heavily tattooed guy from Virginia was found in this neck of the woods would be an interesting story, once we found him! My squad and other agents from the Long Island Resident Agency (LIRA) met the SO agents in a parking lot near a pizzeria and watched as the phone that had been discovered in the area was pinned down to a residence. But the phone was located now in Citi Field, home of the New York Mets, who were playing the Washington Nationals that night. We listened to the game to gauge when he would be leaving there (of course, it was a close game that night, so he might not be leaving early!). Then toward the end of the game, the phone left the field and proceeded down Northern Boulevard to the intersection of 108th Street, where it suddenly went dead.

Could he be on a train in a tunnel coming back? With no idea and hoping he was returning to the residence, we fanned out and lay in wait, three agents from my squad in each of two minivans on a completely darkened street at opposite ends of the block as the LIRA agents covered the outer perimeter. We kept the engines running to keep ourselves fairly cool as we waited in our bulletproof vests and equipment for a car to enter the block and turn down the driveway to the residence, where we suspected our guy would come back. Cars came and parked in their own respective driveways, people stepping out, into their houses, I'm sure wondering why a minivan with tinted windows was parked on their block with the lights off. It was so dark here that we had to improvise covers for the lighted dashboard so as not to illuminate us, a problem never dealt with in the five boroughs of New York City, where the streetlights always splashed plenty of light on the cars and people below them. We waited most of the night and early morning to see if someone came back to the residence, but no one ever came.

We finally broke off that morning until the cell phone came back on when, as I was leaving my house to go to the gym, an e-mail came over the Blackberry that the signal reappeared that morning in the same area where it disappeared the night prior. The SO agent had gotten out there early on his own and located the signal in a salon there. As I went back inside my house to "gear up," frantic e-mails were coming from other agents that they were coming but were on their way from New Jersey. Many of the New York-based agents lived there because the main office was in Downtown Manhattan and the adjoining state was pretty accessible to it. As I was the only agent on the squad who lived on Long Island, my commute to the location was much quicker than anyone else on the squad.

I drove around the corner from the location, spotted the SO agent and parked my car on the side street. He told me that he was parked on the block where the salon was located, a U-Haul truck sitting directly in front of the salon. And there was Greg Kinnear sitting in the tinted-out SUV about fifteen yards from the truck without an obstruction or concealment between them. He was sitting alone at that time as I circled the salon without wearing any identifying clothing, including my vest. I got into the front seat next to him and he told me that the fugitive, who he said was wearing a black shirt with red wings on it, was seen moving boxes from the U-Haul truck into the salon but he hadn't been seen for about ten minutes now. There was no activity around the truck, but a Hispanic woman with bleach-blond hair was standing next to it with a baby stroller, looking up and down the block, glancing at us every so often. I knew we were parked too close to the salon, two white guys in a predominantly Spanish neighborhood looking for a black guy who was going out the back door of the salon any second now, if he was not out the door already. She walked into the salon with the stroller but then came right back out with a cell phone to her ear and casually strolled toward our SUV, peering at the tinted windows and the laptop that was on a stand between the two front seats, I'm sure wondering why these guys were sitting there. After about two minutes, she walked back into the salon.

As we sat there and I processed the situation, another car with an agent came into the area and parked behind us. Unable to see what was going on in the salon from our vantage point, I sat and thought there must be a way to see in there without getting made when a tall heavily tattooed black male walked out of the salon and down the sidewalk in our direction. This guy looked like our guy, but he was wearing a white shirt. The SO agent said to me that he believed that it was our guy. I was hesitant because of the wardrobe change and not wanting our fugitive to get away through the back if he was still in the store. As the male walked near our car, with no time to give the other agent in the car behind us a warning over the radio that we were about to engage this guy, I pushed the car door open, my Blackberry with his picture bouncing from my lap onto the sidewalk as I raised my SIG Sauer 22 up to place him squarely in my sights and shouted with authority, "FBI! GET DOWN ON THE GROUND!

Now!" He stopped in his tracks, earbuds still in place, my voice and presence obviously commanding his attention, and dropped down to the ground. As the SO agent came from around the other side of the SUV to bring his hands behind him, and knowing that the agent in the car behind us would be right there, I ran toward the salon, making sure anyone else in that store stayed there in case this wasn't our guy. As another guy came out of the front door to see what was going on, I gave the same commands to him, dropping him immediately to the pavement as well.

As I looked behind him into the salon, I saw the same woman who had been outside earlier run toward the door and begin to push it close. I ran toward the door, and seeing her pushing it through the glass, I kicked the wooden frame around it, thrusting it open and throwing the woman back. I ran inside to find the woman with her sister and eighty-one-year-old mom cowering as I yelled for them all to get down on the floor. I continued to the back of the store, making sure that there was no one else in there, before asking the women for the name of the guy in the doorway. When the blond woman said he was a friend from the neighborhood, I asked her who was the guy down the block in the white shirt. She responded that she didn't know him. I asked the guy in the doorway the same question. He responded it was his cousin. Since the place was secure and I was feeling more sure that we had our guy down the block, I walked down where the SO agent still had him on the ground.

When I first asked him his name, he responded it was Jimmy Mays. After a smack in the back of the head by the SO agent and a second question from me if that was an alias for Yates, his head dropped down to the pavement, him resigned to the fact that he had been found. Going back to talk to the women, I found out that they had no knowledge of the guy being a fugitive and were wondering, being that they were a part of the neighborhood for forty-three years, who are the guys who are sitting in the SUV. They thought that they were being robbed when I came to the door with a gun in my hand. Lucky for me, they didn't keep a gun under the register.

Lastly, when you think you've seen it all, we went to the Bronx early one morning, looking for a guy who had been running with a crew, doing home-invasion robberies. The rest of the crew could be found in jail, and this was the one guy that was still on the street living in an apartment with his girlfriend and their kid. We stood around the case agent as he gave out the description of our guy and warnings about him during the briefing outside the Kingsbridge Armory before the raid. We were attired in our green bullet-resistant vests emblazoned with FBI on both the front and back, adorned with equipment such as radios, handcuffs, flashlights, and sidearms.

He gave me and a new agent that was along for the ride the all-important task of watching the windows to the street on the front of the building in case the guy decided to jump out one of them when they entered the apartment. There were no other ways to get out of the residence besides the front door, he said, so with that, we lined up in our vehicles and drove in a caravan to the location on Davidson Avenue.

As the agent and I took a position behind an SUV immediately outside those windows leading out onto the street, the rest of the party entered the building through a gate and made their way through the lobby to the apartment door, which was just inside. We heard the typical shouts of "Police, open the door!" repeated twice before the loud thunder of the tools used to gain access to a dwelling when the occupants didn't readily come to the door.

Boom! Boom! Boom!

Funny, I thought to myself, *I hear dogs barking, so someone must live there. No one is sleeping through that, but no lights are coming on in the apartment.* And then as I saw flashlights shining through the windows and around the rooms, I heard indiscriminate yelling of "Police, hands up and get down on the floor!" Okay, they were in the apartment and no shots were fired; the apartment must be secure by now, and hopefully he didn't sleep somewhere else last night or was still out partying and the first part of our day was done with an arrest. However, the call went out over the radio that he was not there.

While we were standing outside, contemplating our next move to see if we could still find this guy somewhere this morning, one of the agents inside noticed that a window was open, which was a little unusual even for a warm apartment, being it was a cold morning in mid-March. As they questioned the girlfriend and asked her about the window, which led out into, for lack of a better word, an alcove that was not accessible from the street, she said that he was here but he jumped out that window when we came to the door. As the call immediately went out over the radio that "he went out the window," the agent and I looked at each other before looking at the three windows that were our entire assignment and then again at each other, as if to say, "Did we fuck up somehow? How did he get out the window without us seeing him?" The radio transmission continued that the window was on the side of the building.

I took off to the side of the building to find an open gate that accessed the back of the adjoining building. Running to the back of the building with my gun in hand, I slowly peered around the corner there, past the high chain-link fence topped with razor ribbon that separated me from the backyard of the apartment building we had just entered. Well trained in the art of clearing an area without exposing myself to an armed adversary, I "cut the pie" (the technique for clearing an area as safely as possible) until I came into full view of the perp running away down the few open yards behind the buildings in a light T-shirt and shorts. As I shouted this out over the radio with the description of his attire, I ran back to the front of the building to see if he ran back out onto the street and if we were covering as many routes for him to escape as possible.

Agents ran down the block and around the corner to Jerome Avenue, where they continued up the block to an open parking lot that was located on the back side of the apartment buildings. As they checked there, I took a position on the corner of West 184th Street and Davidson Avenue, where I could see both the street that ran up the front of the apartment building, in case he ran out that direction, and along West 184th Street, the direction that I had seen him fleeing, in case he came out that way. They checked the lot to no avail, and as it appeared that he must have made it off the block before we could secure a perimeter, we regrouped back in front of his building. We then checked the alcove, which we were able to access from a door in the lobby of the building, and the two adjacent yards with what we called negative results.

We again stood there in the front of the building, contemplating our next move as a helicopter from the NYPD Aviation Unit hovered overhead. We decided that we shouldn't readily surrender to the belief that he made it off the block without thoroughly checking the backs of each building, although most were secured with locked gates and the ubiquitous fences with razor ribbon. We got the superintendents to allow us access to the alleyways and yards and checked each of them. The two buildings next to our perp's building, in the direction he ran, were open to each other, and there was a wall back there which was topped with razor ribbon. The yards were separated from the parking lot which led out onto Jerome Avenue, but there was a tree right next to the wall that had some ribbon wrapped around it, but not enough to where I could see he could make it up and over the wall. However, if he hadn't yet made it off the block and into either a livery cab or a friend's apartment nearby, he couldn't last long the way he was dressed in this weather.

After having checked most of the alleyways and backyards, a few of us walked down one alleyway that had been opened by a superintendent of the building and looked again. As we walked back toward the street, one of us noticed that something that he had seen before on a fire escape this time just didn't look right. Balled up, perched on a fire escape that was so short that it led to only one apartment, our guy had curled up and gotten small when agents twice walked up and down the alleyway, one of them later admitting that he had looked up but just saw what he thought at that time was something stored on the fire escape. Upon hearing the dog of the NYPD Canine Unit, which had been called to come to the scene and attempt to follow his tracks from the open window, we were able to "encourage" him to comply with our demand to come down, and promising that the dog wouldn't be unleashed on him, he grabbed the lowest rung of the fire escape, hung down, and dropped to the floor, clad in the same T-shirt and shorts that I had seen him wearing. Now we found out that all he had on his feet were his socks. As the handcuffs were slapped on him, it was still pretty cold out, and at least an hour had passed since he first jumped out that window. He was shivering pretty hard as he was brought out to the street to sit in the rear of a nice, warm FBI vehicle.

Another lesson to be learned by us: don't always look at street level; sometimes ya gotta look up!

A few years later, I met up again with that same lieutenant from the Bronx Warrants Squad, as our organizations joined once again to hunt down Tommy Smalls, who was part of a four-man crew that carjacked two livery cabs in the Bronx and callously shot to death the drivers, dumping their bodies in the streets. They then used the cars as they committed armed robberies of convenience stores before leaving the cars behind. Since carjacking was a federal crime, the case was worked jointly by the FBI and the NYPD and prosecuted in federal court by the US Attorney's Office of the Southern District of New York.

After the other three mutts were meekly arrested, this one had to run. And while he was on the run, he had help from a female acquaintance in hiding him. But we had informants helping on our side as well, and they pointed us to a building located in the projects at Columbus Avenue and West 102nd Street. We gained entry through the front door of the building and made our way up to the Ninth Floor, where members of the Warrant Squad and FBI lined up in the narrow hallway as two detectives up front took turns putting their ears to our side of the door to the apartment as they intently listened for any signs of movement. After confirming that there were people in the apartment, they signaled back to the lieutenant, who then advised the personnel that were outside the building, watching the window, that we were about to gain entry, before signaling back to knock and announce.

As they banged on the door, seconds ticked by until after yelling that the door would be coming down unless someone came to it, a petite girl opened it as the line pressed into the apartment, pushing her aside to the living room on the right as each of the three bedrooms were searched for Smalls. Two other people, a couple who said that they had just gotten there to visit the girl about ten minutes ago, were also herded into the living room. The detectives who were ahead of us swept through the rooms while they checked all the traditional hiding spots until they came upon one bedroom that had a master lock on the door (obviously, this was a place without a lot of trust!). As both the other detectives, agents, and I shouted at the three of them, asking where Smalls was and what was in the locked bedroom, they all repeatedly said that they didn't know where he was and that her brother was sleeping in the room. When no one came to the door, they breached the lock, and again the room was flooded with agents and detectives, restraining the brother and verifying his identity as others searched the room, to no avail.

As the brother appeared dumbfounded, saying that he went to sleep hours earlier and didn't hear the banging going on outside the door, everyone fanned out again to the other rooms to again check and make sure nothing was missed. As one detective went deeper into a closet and saw what appeared to be a filled laundry bag in the corner, he pulled on it to make sure it was clothes that was in that bag. As the pull revealed the bag to be a little heavy, sure enough, the contents were found to be five-foot-six, 130-pound Tommy Smalls in the flesh.

It was fortunate that he wasn't armed with a gun that he could have trained on us as we left that bedroom and went to the locked one, but unfortunate that none of the weapons were found on any of the mutts during each of their arrests. I guess although they shot and killed unarmed men, they didn't want to be caught in a situation where the fight was more even.

Most of the time in the movies or on TV like the series *Law & Order*, when the good guys are on surveillance for a subject or perp and you see them sitting there in the unmarked police-looking car directly across the street from the target location in plain view (and the subject/perp never sees them as they walk out the door), it seems like they just got there a few minutes ago, with enough time for one of them to go get cups of coffee for each of them and just get back in the car, when the person they're looking for shows up. Despite what's seen in the media, it never happens that way, and you can sit on a surveillance from a few hours to all night, except for one occasion.

The squad I worked on through the final years of my FBI career was the FBI/NYPD Joint Bank Robbery Task Force. The task force was a squad that comprised of both special agents of the FBI and detectives from the NYPD that worked side by side, an agent partnered with each detective. We investigated the bank robberies in which the robbers actually displayed a firearm or another weapon to rob a bank. The unarmed bank robberies, which had the term *note jobs* since, normally, the robber gave the teller a note that read that he was committing a robbery and threatened violence but an instrument of violence was not displayed, were capably investigated by the NYPD Major Case Squad. Although our title only referred to bank robberies, we also investigated kidnappings, fugitives, and extortions. But when the Major Case Squad developed a case that involved a serial bank robber, even though he might not have displayed a weapon while he was committing those robberies, we would combine forces to identify and arrest that individual.

And in February 2015, we had such an event when Alfred Brown was wanted for a string of ten bank robberies.

The Major Case Squad had identified the bank robber and that he was possibly "laying his head" at night at two locations very close in proximity to each other in Harlem. One of the locations was on Bradhurst Avenue, and the other location was on Frederick Douglas Boulevard, which was a continuation of 8th Avenue north of Central Park. We met on an extremely cold morning, during the coldest February in New York in eighty-one years, at the Rucker Playground, which sat across Frederick Douglas Boulevard from the Polo Grounds Towers. The Towers were now run by the NYC Housing Authority but was once the site of the heralded field where the New York Giants played baseball for seventy-five years before leaving for sunny California, and the other New York Giants played football there before leaving for Yankee Stadium, after which the stadium was left to be demolished in 1964. But athletics were still known in the area as the Rucker Playground, later became known as the spot where some of the best basketball players in New York City came to play and hone their skills, many of which went on to the NBA. We met there with the case agent from my squad, who was working with the lead detective from Major Case.

With his mother living at the location on Bradhurst Avenue and several agents and detectives setting up to watch for him from their vehicles over there, I was assigned the residence located at 2855 Frederick Douglas Boulevard, just a few blocks south from where we met. Being that it was almost 8:00 a.m. and most of the people working this operation didn't stop for food or coffee on the way there, I already picked up my favorite newspaper, the *New York Daily News*, and had made myself a large cup of fruit and a turkey sandwich with whole wheat bread.

I pulled up and double-parked down the block from the residence, where I could clearly see the front door of the apartment building, tinted windows all around the car concealing my presence except through the front windshield. After I set myself up there and got settled for the day, I took out my fruit and relaxed a bit as I started reading about Alex Rodriguez and his return to the New York Yankees in spring training after a yearlong suspension for PED use, glancing at the front door between paragraphs. I was sitting there, just watching, reading, and relaxing for maybe ten minutes when *Thwack!* I look up to see that my collapsible driver-side-view mirror was knocked forward but at least not gone!

As I looked at the empty space where the mirror had been before while also incredulously looking at the idiot livery driver who just came so close to my car that he banged the mirror out of place to drop off his passengers in front of the same residence that was being watched, I also looked at the passengers getting out of the car. As the driver got out of his car and walked over to the other side to look at his mirror and then briefly looked at me to see what I was doing, I was looking at the guy who got out of the back seat of the car with his girlfriend, both of them with a big "Ohhh" on their faces, like they were mimicking "No, you didn't just hit that police-looking car."

As I looked up and down at the male passenger and the "wanted" flyer with his photograph sitting on my console, I suddenly realized that he was our guy.

He was the first one out of the car and, maybe by nature, close to the door of the residence, his girlfriend still a bit in shock to the livery driver's stupidity. I must now weigh the fact that when I got out of the car to approach them all with my white face, wearing khaki-colored range pants in a predominantly black neighborhood, which, aside from the large dents on the left side of my car and a missing hubcap from a previous accident, screamed "Cop!" or "Five-Oh" as the police had become affectionately known based on the TV series of the police in Hawaii, he might take off like a jackrabbit and disappear into the building, thinking that we were on to him. But I thought of a scenario that might work, not alarm him that he was being sought by us, and deflect from the obvious, that I was the police. I thought I would quickly call the case agent and detective, Kevin and Jim, and tell them to get over to my location. "Our target is here, but act like you're there because I had an accident with my vehicle."

While I was sitting in a banged-up Ford Focus, his eyes widened as he looked at my vehicle, curiously watching me while standing close to the female he traveled with in the livery car. As he lingered there, I pulled my car behind the livery car, got out, and started yelling at the driver about how stupid he was (which was not far from the truth!) before quickly shouting to him and his girlfriend not to go anywhere. "You guys are witnesses to what just happened! Yo, yo, yo!" I yelled directly at him, "My supervisor is coming right over to take a statement!" As he, thankfully, listened and did not walk away from the livery car, I assured them that the supervisor was only a few blocks away and it would take two minutes once he got there.

As Kevin and Jim pull up in their darkened Ford Explorer and got out, clipboards and pens in hand, our prey seemed to be a bit at ease that it didn't appear that we were looking for him. As soon as they got within arm's length to them to take their witness statements, *bam*, they dropped the props and grabbed all five foot five of him in the blink of an eye. What could've been an all-day surveillance if he had walked into that building with his girlfriend, waiting for him to pop his head out, running on us in one direction or another, maybe back inside and into the apartment if we didn't box him in somewhere and what might have turned into a dangerous situation became an innocuous arrest that was over in minutes, or at least that's what would have happened if it was an episode of Law and Order.

And maybe it would have saved us from spending the rest of the day sitting in front of the building.

After the livery struck my mirror and pulled in front of the building, Brown cautiously but quickly walked toward the front door of the building that we were watching and lingered close to that door instead, where he waited for the same female he traveled with in the livery car. I could see that he was wide-eyed with paranoia and that, since he immediately moved toward the apartment building once he exited the livery, once I tried the same tact of trying to get him to come back as an accident witness, he would be gone in a flash! Once inside the building, he could either disappear into the catacombs of apartments inside there or come out on the roof and disappear into another building down the avenue or up the street. So I, too, acted cautiously and took that path, letting him go for now but planning on catching him later in a safe manner. I felt confident that he'd slept somewhere else that night and that he'd leave the building to go somewhere instead of staying inside the entire day. And how wrong I was after he disappeared into the building as we waited… and waited…and waited as day turned to night, and we continued to wait.

Other cars on the surveillance switched around and took breaks so they could be fresh, but the lone idiot that I was stubbornly sat by myself in the same spot, relieving myself with a wide-mouthed plastic bottle and snacking on fruit and power bars, obsessed that the minute I switched out with another car, he would emerge from the building. A minivan full of detectives waited double-parked across the street from me, facing the opposite direction from down the boulevard. I saw them motion from the car window to a guy on a bike to come over to them. Seeing he was a deliveryman, I thought they were going to show him a photograph of our guy to see if he knew what apartment he might be inside the building. Next thing I knew, the deliveryman was handing them bags through the car window—they ordered takeout while we were sitting out here!

Finally, after eleven hours of our sitting in a car, he emerged from the building and turned south onto the boulevard, catching the eyes of the now well-fed detectives in the minivan positioned in that direction. One of them shouted his location into his radio as they got out and moved toward him from across the street. As he saw them coming, he bolted right back to the building doorway. As soon as I heard the radio transmission which positively identified him, I swung the car door open and my feet hit the pavement, with the intention of beating him back to the building door. But a funny (or not so funny!) thing happened to my legs after eleven hours of inactivity, as they felt like pure jelly when I stood on them, and I moved (barely) in the wobbliest foot pursuit to that door that I now had no chance of winning. As I steadied myself against a parked car on the way to the door, rubbing my temporarily (I hope!) crippled legs and hoping I didn't give myself a case of deep vein thrombosis, Brown darted through the door unmolested and disappeared. However, after securing the roof and perimeter and canvassing the building on the floors that he was last seen or heard running up the stairs from, we found him by virtue of an informed neighbor who shifted his eyes to the apartment he was hiding without saying a word.

*****

Technology has taken some away from the old-style fugitive investigations, which would involve time-consuming endeavors like showing photographs to people, talking to both associates of the subject and local cops, going to former places of employment, all being done rather discreetly so as not to alert the individual that he is actively being sought. Surreptitious surveillances on what may be a current address, perhaps provided by a tip (anonymous or not), could lead to many hours of monotony (like sitting in a car for eleven hours). But the gratification felt when the handcuffs were slapped on the subjects we sought were priceless.

Understandably, the events of 9/11 changed the landscape of the New York Office of the FBI forever, in which the executive management made a major shift of resources away from the Criminal Division, which the Fugitive program was under, toward Counterterrorism and other related programs. Traditionally, the office was split into two major divisions, one that investigated strictly criminal activities and the other that conducted foreign counterintelligence operations, with one squad, the Joint Terrorism Task Force, concentrating on domestic terrorism. Although it was a move that was needed to be done at that time due to the tragic events, condensing the criminal division had a partially shortsighted aspect in that a fair number of terrorists have some type of criminal element that could originally expose themselves through the violent crime arena in some way before they rise to the level of a terrorist operation. So it is possible that they can be thwarted earlier through various criminal investigations.

When the FBI shifted those resources, the United States Marshal Service (USMS) took the opportunity to expand their fugitive program, where we had abdicated much of our own. The objectives of the USMS are the care and custody of federal inmates, including their transportation between courts and correctional institutions (as was dramatized in the movie *Con Air*), the security of the federal courthouses and its judges, and the apprehension of fugitives. Now the men and women of the USMS do a great job when it comes to putting their heads down and pursuing, locating, and apprehending fugitives. Their shortcoming, however, occurs because they are not practiced in conducting investigations. And at times, there should be some investigation conducted in conjunction with the arrest of the fugitive. That is where the lack of experience hinders the process of information development that could take an arrest even further. And the USMS does have task forces that incorporate the resources of other federal, state, and local agencies, but for some reason, there has been a slight rivalry that has prohibited the two services, the FBI and USMS, from working together in a task force setting.

As a cinematic illustration that displays the epitome of what I am trying to convey, the situation is never more apparent than the scene out of the movie coincidentally titled *The Fugitive*, with Tommy Lee Jones playing the role of Deputy US Marshal Samuel Gerard hunting down the fugitive Dr. Richard Kimble, played by Harrison Ford. Gerard corners Kimble in a large sewage pipe that lets out over a large cliff but loses his gun in the struggle to arrest Kimble. As Kimble points the gun at Gerard before jumping through the end of the sewage pipe, he says to Gerard, "I didn't kill my wife!" Gerard responds, "I don't care!" It's a funny exchange, and as the movie follows along, Gerard and his squad, somewhat reluctantly, do conduct an investigation that is funneled to them by Kimble that determines the real killer. But as their training and mind-set fall short in interviews and interrogations to where the primary and only function is to "get their man" and return him/her to the jurisdiction that wants them and the case is considered closed, for us, in an effort to elicit admissions of guilt or incriminating statements against others, we may be able to extend investigations or potentially begin new ones. That is where opportunities may be lost.

They do know, however, how to employ one charge of the Federal Criminal Code and Rules, the federal penal lawbook, which is Title 18, United States Code 1001. This statute states that "whoever, in any matter within the jurisdiction of the executive, legislative, or judicial branch of the government of the United States, knowingly and willfully, (1) falsifies, conceals, or covers up by any trick, scheme, or device a material fact; (2) makes any materially false, fictitious, or fraudulent statement or representation; or (3) makes or uses any false writing or document knowing the same to contain any materially false, fictitious, or fraudulent statement or entry, shall be fined under this title or imprisoned not more than five years, or both." This is the statute that makes it a crime, unlike local or state law enforcement officers, to lie to a federal official.

Although most people who will remember the case in New York involving Martha Stewart will think that she was convicted of insider trading, that is incorrect. Ms. Stewart, who was accused of insider trading, whereby she had sold four thousand ImClone shares one day before the company's stock nosedived, had her securities fraud charges thrown out and was tried for lying about the stock sale. She was sentenced on July 16, 2004, after being convicted for conspiracy, obstruction of justice, and two counts of making false statements to a federal investigator to five months of incarceration, two years of probation, and five months of house arrest. Although she requested to serve her sentence at the federal prison in Danbury, Connecticut, made famous in the television series *Orange Is the New Black*, she served it at a federal prison camp in Alderson, West Virginia.

And with that in mind, if a friend, relative, associate, et al., of a fugitive knowingly and willfully lies regarding the location or whereabouts of the individual, they can be charged with the same statute. So if you're on the run from the Marshal Service or us and you think so little of someone that you want to put them in a position of following you to the federal penitentiary, go to them. After they are visited by us and don't give you up but make us risk our lives and possibly the lives of others who come into contact with you, then we will build a case against them. And if the surveillance cameras don't catch images of you there, which they will, there'll be enough pissed-off neighbors or other evidence that we'll come back for them with.

With that said, and I cannot stress this enough, as I would never besmirch the reputation of the Marshal Service, who, in working several joint investigations with the men and women of that agency, I found to be the most eager and tireless workers in the federal criminal justice system, it is simply a matter of their job description being different from ours. They are great at what they do, which is different from what we do. And in deference to them, I can honestly say that I liked working with them as much as with the agents on my own job.

*****

I met Melanie through a mutual friend. She was a pretty petite Hispanic girl who lived on Long Island, not far from me. I had given her my business card in hopes that I'd hear from her again, only not for the reason that she called me. When she called me and left a message, I could hear in her voice that there was a problem probably for which she was calling. And the problem wasn't just some overzealous ex-boyfriend; he was also a blood family member of one of the most ruthless Italian organized crime families in Brooklyn, the Persico family.

She then told me of the story where she used to work at a club on Long Island not too far from her house called Club G. She had met this guy, Teddy, over a year ago there and had begun dating him. Although he had told her that shortly before meeting her, he had spent the previous eighteen years behind bars, and that she had noticed law-enforcement-type vehicles sometimes following them or parked outside his house, the thrill of being with the king of Club G or the money that he flashed must have been too much for her to refuse. But his constant obsession had become too much for her and she wanted out, but he wasn't letting her go.

I found out that a personal friend of mine was on the Colombo Squad, the name of the crime family from which the Persicos ruled. Not only was he familiar with Teddy, but he also knew who Melanie was, although she was not involved in any illegal activities with him. He had told me that he had heard numerous conversations between them over the time that they were dating. He said that he was scheduled to be listening to "the wire" the next day, and if I came down to the wire room, he could play me some of the tapes. The wire room is located in the depths of 26 Federal Plaza in Manhattan. I met him there the following day, a room linked up with all technical equipment and computers for agents to listen to Title III telephone calls, those that are granted by a court order through a judge which are recorded and then transcribed. We sat down in front of a computer, and he picked out a recent call between them from the calls listed on the computer screen. As the call came up and began to play, there it was: their rocky history was there for us to hear, in tape-recorded conversations between them on their cell phones. As I listened to conversation after conversation played by my friend in the wire room, the obsession was worse than I even imagined.

Call after call to her cell phone, Teddy would ask her, "Why are you being that way?" and would continuously ask her to talk to him, while she pleaded for him to leave her alone. She would scream into the phone that he had to stop calling her before hanging up. After a few seconds, a number was heard being dialed again and Melanie would answer, repeatedly asking why he wouldn't stop calling her. This would go on for an hour at a time, usually ending with Teddy telling her that he would always be around and would never leave her alone. This was a very creepy and ominous statement, considering he had no value for other human beings, or life for that matter, and she was the object of his deranged affection. He had put bodies in the ground before, as a matter of business, and I had no doubt that, if he didn't think he could have her, based on his calls, he would have no problem putting one in the ground that actually meant something to him.

My friend told me that in other recorded calls that he had with family members, they asked him to forget her and move on. It was the conversations that we all have in our adolescence when we experience a bad breakup, "Plenty of fish in the sea...," "Time to move on..." But Teddy was different; he was prepared to stay with it and make sure that she wasn't with anyone else but stayed alone to come back to him someday, threatening harm to anyone that she might date.

Soon after I had heard these calls, Melanie would call, frantic, that she had heard strange noises outside the house late at night. Although the house where she lived with her parents was close to the route that Teddy would take home to Brooklyn from the club, which, according to sources, he would visit any of the nights that it was opened, possibly her paranoia was getting the best of her. This was until one morning, when she called me to tell me that two of her car's tires were flat, while it was parked in her driveway close to the house.

I called in to the office to give them a little heads-up on what was going on and where I would be that morning. I drove to her house, gun concealed in my holster under my jacket, and changed her tires, which had obviously been slashed overnight, for her. It rained that morning, but she held an umbrella over us so that I only got partially soaked. After taking a flat tire to a local store and having it replaced, we went back to her house to put that tire on and, with the aid of a spare, drove to the store again to replace that tire so she'd have a spare, just in case. We talked about what she could do, in which I could only allay her fears as best as I could with "I'm only a phone call away, and the police, via 911, are that much closer." I told her that she could tell him that we were now dating, that maybe hearing that she was with an FBI agent would keep him back. But she worried that hearing this might infuriate him even more, at not only her, but at the both of us as well, and continued to deal with the harassment.

When I talked with my friend and his partner, they said that an indictment was soon being prepared for Teddy that would put him away for a while, possibly ten to twenty years, and hopefully long enough for her to move on with her life and him to do the same. My only recourse, unless things escalated with him, was to reassure her that he was going to do some heavy time but that it was going to take a few months for them to complete their investigation and put him behind bars.

It worked out well in the end; he didn't physically approach her, and his campaign of harassment was only through the phone. Maybe it kept him busy and preoccupied enough that he didn't focus on being arrested until it happened. He was sent away again for a good stretch, and Melanie, at this point now, could go on to have a family and enjoy her life without fearing a predator known to her only too well.

It was a kinder fate for her than it was for many friends from my old neighborhood. One of the funniest people I ever knew was a friend named Lee, who was my oldest and closest friend since kindergarten. We were best friends through the years of hanging out in the schoolyard. Unfortunately, he also had an addictive personality that came with all the humor. He got caught up in the web of illicit drug addiction with the escalation in drug activity moving from the use of mescaline, mushrooms, LSD, and Quaaludes to heroin and crack cocaine. The mixing of the drugs in a single day was not an aberration. The drug usage not only unquestionably damaged our relationship but also led to his personal demise.

He used to go with another friend that we all grew up together to "Pitkin and Pine," a notorious intersection in East New York, Brooklyn, that was well-known for the drug trade at that time. He constantly borrowed money from me, usually telling me he was short on the rent that month or other excuses, money that, after a while, I realized I wasn't getting back. The last time that I brought it to his apartment, we cried as I challenged him on the reason he needed the money, knowing that he was lying to me, Lee knowing that I knew but still insisting the lie was the truth. I guess I gave it to him still because I wanted to believe him but, in the end, I was angrier than sad when he died at only forty years old. Although we were told that he accidentally struck his head on the edge of the kitchen table and bled to death as he laid there unconscious in his basement apartment, like his excuses about the money, I wanted to believe it wasn't due to a heroin overdose. But I've never convinced myself that it was the real cause. What did matter is that the lifestyle that he once lived, in my eyes, definitely led to his untimely death.

George Maple was another poor soul who, although I wasn't nearly as close to as I was to Lee, was an eccentric but colorful character whom I enjoyed meeting haphazardly on the streets of Richmond Hill when I still lived there. After moving away, I didn't have much contact with him but heard he had fallen on hard times, living on the streets until he finally passed away there. I had played Catholic Youth Organization (CYO) baseball with one of his brothers, Frank, and knew his other brother, Kenny, and sister, Ann Marie, but never got to meet the eldest, Jackie Maple. Jackie became an NYPD legend who created CompStat, the statistic-based crime-fighting tool that changed street policing forever in 1994, during police commissioner William Bratton's first tenure there during the Rudolph Giuliani administration.

He had risen to the rank of lieutenant in the New York City Transit Police Department, which was a separate entity from the NYPD at that time. Bratton, who was the TPD commissioner, noticed his crime-fighting strategy of mapping crime. When Bratton left to become the police commissioner of the Boston PD in 1992, he took Maple with him. When he returned to the NYPD as the police commissioner in 1994, he made Maple a deputy commissioner, and CompStat received national attention while dramatically reducing violent crime. When Bratton was forced out in 1996, Maple left with him and they consulted police departments across the country.

Jackie Maple died at the age of forty-eight in 2001. He was later recognized, and his legacy lived on when the street where he was raised, 108th Street near Park Lane South, was renamed Jack

Maple Place. George was a much lesser-known figure than Jackie, and although not memorialized, he's still remembered as well.

Speaking of other kind souls who have caught, and made, bad breaks, Tony moved into my new house in the apartment that was upstairs from me with Paulie. Now, Paulie, I didn't know very well; I knew his sister dated my friend Butchie and that he was the cook at a well-known local restaurant on Jamaica Avenue in Richmond Hill for a long time. That was until his fiancée's father opened a restaurant in Ozone Park and had Paulie running the shop. Besides having the gift of gab, Paulie could really cook; he could make something out of nothing and make it well. Although he wasn't well-read, he knew the restaurant business, and the restaurant on Liberty Avenue thrived for a long time until the engagement fizzled. Then so did the restaurant eventually.

And he did make some amazing meals for us, whether it was at the house or in the restaurant. He knew his way around the kitchen. I didn't really get to know him until he lived above me, but the guy could make friends with a stranger in the street—he could talk to people that easily. He was a real character, and I was glad to get to know him.

But even he had his problems, those issues that just hang until they finally blow up on you. Well, not just any you. After having stayed away from cocaine and crack for all those years, he relapsed. And it wasn't pretty!

When I found a large amount of crack cocaine in his bedroom (yes, it got to the point where I knew he was on something and I had to know if it was in my house), I knew it was bad enough that he wasn't just using the stuff; it looked like he was selling it too. He had to go, and as politely as I could, I asked him to pack his belongings and leave. He did. It was a hard thing to do to let someone you know is going to find trouble go find it, which was inevitable, because the only people that he was going to stay and live with were the same ones with whom he was using the stuff. I had put myself in precarious situations in my life, most of the stupidest episodes when I was a kid before I became a law enforcement officer.

When I was growing up, my friends and I did nothing but play ball from day into night all summer long. Eventually, it slipped to playing ball during the day and my friends buying drugs that night. Finally, we stopped playing ball altogether. I never understood the drug use, as it all seemed so very unnatural to me. But they enjoyed the high and craved for more. I stayed there for a long time and watched the odyssey until there came a point when I knew it was time for me to leave, and no one said a word, much less noticed.

During that time, I never did anything harsher myself than smoke pot a handful of times.

Fortunately for me, it just didn't take. And when I was asked if I wanted to smoke, I said that I was feeling pains in my side after I smoked it while playing ball. Gratefully no one argued with it. When I was hanging out in a group and a joint was being passed around, the person next to me would reflexively hold it for me to take when they were done smoking. They would be blowing out the smoke, enjoying the sensation for a second or two, while the joint would hang in the air. Then they would look up to see what was going on with the person next to them that the joint was still in their own hand. I would hear "Oh!" as they stretched their arm with the joint across me to give it to the next person.

But peer pressure still took hold when I was one of the few of us who had a car. I was asked on a few occasions to take friends to drug locations so they could buy whatever they were using that night. I was lucky never to get arrested, never to get robbed for doing it, but it was some of the stupid moments. But now, Paulie was bringing that risk back, and another day could not pass with this situation literally hanging over my head.

A short time after he left, I heard he was arrested in East New York for robbery and impersonating a cop. I couldn't see how anyone would've thought he was a cop, but obviously, it didn't fool those that mattered most. I called the ADA in Brooklyn who had his case and told him who I was and where I worked but that I was not calling in an official capacity. I talked to him about Paulie, how I knew him, from where I knew him, that he was a deeply troubled individual who never harmed anyone but himself in the past and had done it to himself again. He had no history of violence until now. I implored him to have Paulie sent to a drug rehab, that he had skills to offer society. He told me that he would see what he could do.

That ADA was transferred from the case, and another ADA was assigned, and he was told not to take any of my calls. As a result of my effort to see that he got cut a break, Paulie did six and a half years in the New York State prison system. We wrote letters and kept in touch until he got released. He understood that I had too much to lose and appreciated that I didn't forget about him altogether despite his slip from grace. He got his job back at the same restaurant where he was working before he was arrested. The owner there, Vinny, ran a family business, and he knew not only that Paulie was a good worker but also that, deep down, he was a good person. I still see Paulie from time to time; he lost a lot of that prison muscle (with the bald head, he looked like Mr. Clean!), but he still has a good heart—they didn't take that from him.

I hate to admit it, but it wasn't the only time the wrong side of the law was living above me.

After Paulie, I had another friend from the neighborhood move up there. Marty, an ironworker, was down on his luck after having blown a workplace accident lawsuit of $180,000 in two years and now needed a place to live. After he had cried to me that no one who was around while he was spending that money was around anymore, I reluctantly took him in even though I knew better. And how was I repaid?

Early one morning, after having lived there for a few months, police officers of the Warrant Squad of the Nassau County Police Department knocked on my door. They had an open arrest warrant for him from Queens County that they were looking to bring him in on so that NYPD detectives could pick him up and take him back there. Although there was an outside door that they had other members of their squad ready to go through to enter the apartment, they wanted to post other members at any other door from which Marty could exit. So I let them in to walk up the staircase that led from my living space to his space.

As I walked ahead of them, I realized that my Smith & Wesson 10-millimeter semiautomatic handgun was sitting prominently on the dining room table. I wanted to get them up there and out as quickly as possible without going through the embarrassment of identifying myself as a federal law enforcement officer who had this idiot living above me. So with the sweatshirt that I happened to have in my hand when I answered the door, and walking a little quicker ahead of them, I was able to launch the shirt ahead, falling perfectly over and covering the gun for no one to see it. They went up, knocked on the door, and in a moment's flash, I was rid of another occupant that I then realized I didn't need to be around with. After I stacked a few garbage bags of his belongings in the garage and told him where to find them, it was time to move on from another small dilemma.

That wasn't the only issue, but it was the final one. Marty had lived a few blocks from me with his sister growing up, down the hall from my mother and me in the apartment building, and then above me. He did clean up after our parting, which was a final wake-up call, bought a house, and was married for a short while. But Marty died later when he was only fifty-two. I had heard that he was found sitting in his car on the block where he lived at that time. I could only speculate on what caused his death, and although I did go to his wake, I was never told and never asked.

These are people whose frailties are toxic only to themselves and those who are close to them. Some people pull themselves up, and unfortunately, for others it leads to their demise.

*****

On May 7, 2012, the trial of John Burke began in the same federal courthouse in Brooklyn where Charles Carneglia was found guilty a few years before. John had been in the New York State prison system for a marijuana bust that violated his lifetime parole for a drug conviction. He was one of the guys in the neighborhood that was feared. It was rumored that when his father got pissed off in a local bar one time, he went back there with a rifle. I didn't hear that he shot anyone that day, but knowing how his son had a passion for the criminal element where he became a known associate of the Gambino family, I wouldn't have doubted it. John had been imprisoned for a variety of crimes, including murder, but a judicial technicality lopped off thirteen years from his sentence and he was now eligible for parole in 2013. The Gambino Squad of the FBI now had an opportunity to put him away for a long time in the federal system, or else, a man who had known nothing more than dealing with people in vicious ways, which would surely continue if he was released, would be a dangerous problem for those in his way.

He was charged with gunning down Bruce Gotterup, who had fallen behind in payments for selling cocaine and marijuana in locations controlled by John Burke in Woodhaven and Forest Park, in 1991 in Rockaway Beach, and John Gebert was gunned down in 1996 outside a bar on Jamaica Avenue for selling drugs and not making any payments to him. They also added on the murder of Danny Z and wrapped it into a RICO (racketeering-influenced criminal organization) case. Of course, like Jimmy Burke, who was portrayed by Robert De Niro in the movie *Goodfellas*, he would always be an associate and couldn't be admitted as a made member in the Mob, despite his credentials, because he was Irish.

On the eve of the first day of the trial, I called his brother Tony to see if he was going to be at the courthouse. Although his brother John was violently psychotic and it was rumored that his father had a penchant for settling arguments at the end of a rifle, Tony was a relatively quiet person. Although we didn't maintain regular contact, I still called him every once in a while just to see if he was still doing well for himself. Years earlier, Tony was a slick, good-looking kid who was well-respected around the neighborhood, especially behind his brother's reputation. He dated one of the prettiest girls in the neighborhood, and I guess I was more jealous of him growing up than anything. But years later, while attending the wake of a family member of one of our mutual friends, I came across him, now sporting a paunch and balding on top. After exchanging the same pleasantries that we had over the years, I noticed that his demeanor seemed to be different, the self-importance now gone. He seemed much calmer and more at peace with himself. He sat down with me and spoke about how his life had changed from those days. He had married another woman he had dated from back then, but his partying ways were wearing thin on her and the marriage. There came a time when he decided that a life change was needed to not only save his marriage but also save him. Tony had become a legitimate born-again Christian.

He gave up drinking. He gave up smoking. He devoted himself to his wife, his marriage, and the church. However, after some time of following this lifestyle, his wife decided that she didn't like him so far removed to the other end of the spectrum and she divorced him anyway. But years later, Tony found someone who appreciated his life for what it was, and he remarried. While talking to him, I could sense the change. He had his own business and was living well, with God. After telling him how I'd been trying to get a mutual friend of ours to come to my house to do some work, Tony volunteered to do it himself. He came by the following week and got the job done. When I asked other people about him, they would say that it was all true, and a miracle how he changed.

Tony was incensed at the way John was portrayed by the government in the papers and that "double jeopardy" should have taken place in regards to the Danny Z murder, since his brother had already been acquitted of that case in state court, not realizing that with a RICO charge, he wasn't necessarily being charged with the murder itself but it was being produced as a part of the activities involved in the once-continuing criminal enterprise. He was also very unhappy that one of the daily newspapers printed an article that stated that a key witness had been threatened during that trial and the government was seeking the judge to provide extra security during the proceedings to prevent that from happening during this trial. The article had mentioned that the witness was threatened by a "family member" but didn't further identify who was that family member. To Tony, the case was a vendetta against his brother.

I went the third day of the trial, while one of the cooperating government witnesses testified. I had not seen John in over twenty years, and when he came into the courtroom, it took me some time to recognize him. He was much heavier and balding on top, but his face stood out to me. He didn't immediately recognize me, but through the afternoon session, through the corner of my eye, I saw him look at me for a period, probably saying to himself, "I know that guy, but he's sitting with the government agents, so where would I know him from?" Although his brother Tony wasn't there, his mother sat with his sisters on the opposite side of the courtroom gallery. I was not familiar with his sisters, but I had met his mother on a couple of occasions at a mutual friend's house in Richmond Hill, usually when I stopped by there on a celebratory occasion and the mother would come by as well, until she moved from the neighborhood.

She didn't seem to recognize me, even when I held a door open for her during a break in the trial. She probably assumed that she would not recognize anyone sitting on the opposite side of the gallery and hadn't seen me enough times to put it together. I was intending to come to the trial when John Alite testified, as I did in the other prosecutions, but it was decided by the prosecution team that they had enough cooperating witnesses who were looking to help the government for special considerations and didn't need him to testify this time. He was pretty happy about that, since he was released from prison a few months earlier and was now firmly looking to put this "life" behind him and find employment and lead a quiet life in South New Jersey.

When I met with John Alite soon after his release, he was relieved to be out of prison after ten years but realized, after he decided not to enter the Witness Protection Program, that life would not be easy. Before he went to jail, John had made money like there was no tomorrow, spending cash, buying properties, and even being smart enough to stash money away. However, through the larceny of his "friends" from that life whom he thought he could trust, besides what the government seized as his ill-gotten gains, John was left practically penniless except for whatever money the government was paying him for his prior cooperation. Between that and his wife's job as an office manager, there wasn't a lot to keep his family comfortable in the small apartment that they were living in. He had called out to people—I even called a friend with a moving company to see if I could get him a job there—but once the situation came out about his past life, no one wanted to take on that. And although he didn't have enough fear of retribution from the Mob to go into the program, he knew he was limited in his choice of jobs in that he couldn't be tied down to one place where he had to be routinely, in case someone did recognize who he was and made that known to those who would want to do him harm.

After the jury came back from their deliberations, they found John Burke guilty of the charges. The sentencing would only be a formality now, as he would surely spend the rest of his life in prison, and on January 25, 2013, that was what he received. As the saying goes, guys from the old neighborhood are either dead or in jail, or lucky enough to have a second chance.

And speaking of second chances, karma does have a way of bringing things full circle. In March 2013, Bobby Vernace, who beat the state murder rap in 1998 for the murders of Richie and John and had risen in the ranks to be a boss in the Gambino crime family, operating illegal rackets in Glendale, Queens, was facing his own RICO charge, which included their murders in 1981, again not being charged with the murders themselves but rather as part of the activities with which he was involved as a pattern of the continuing criminal enterprise, and again, like Burke, double jeopardy didn't apply here. One of the reluctant witnesses that would be testifying was a girl who was there with her sister, who had since passed away. They were friends whom I had lost touch with over the years, and I didn't learn of the sister's death until this trial came around. When I spoke to the FBI case agent who was working with the US Attorney's Office in the Eastern District of New York in the prosecution of this case and learned about her reluctance, I had no issue with going with him to speak to her about coming forward. It was an odd and sorrowful reunion, sharing a few laughs and tears. But with some assurances from me, her reluctance waned and she became one of the prosecution's witnesses against Bobby Vernace.

And the once-reluctant witness with the threatening surname, Linda Gotti, who had recanted her identification of all three mutts, Ronald B, Frank Riccardi, and Vernace, shortly after the killings but, after the passage of three decades, was finally ready to tell the truth, was also expected to testify at this trial. With her uncle dead and her father in jail for life, they could no longer talk her out of testifying this time. And apparently, she never got over the fact that her boyfriend was killed over something so stupid. However, with another star witness who had also come forward after the passage of time, it was decided that his testimony itself would be able to stand the test of time and fear.

The bartender, who had testified thirty years earlier at the state trial but feigned amnesia, testified again at the federal trial with a memory like it happened only yesterday. In the early morning hours, the three mutts walked back into the bar. Riccardi spotted John toward the front of the bar and pointed him out to Vernace, who then grabbed him with a gun in one hand and pushed him onto the pinball-style bowling game that ran along the wall. While he viciously pistol-whipped him, Rob B, who had been watching the other mutt's backs, held Richie and the rest of the crowd at bay with his revolver. Suddenly, a shot rang out, and John slumped over the game, struck in the face with a bullet from Bobby's gun. Richie jumped over the bar, but before he could reach his mortally wounded partner, Rob stopped him in his tracks with a round to the midsection. He fell to the floor, also gravely wounded from a bullet.

The crowd in the bar, as well as the bartender, stood there in shock as the carnage unfolded before them. The bartender knew who they were right away, having seen them not only in the bar there but also from the Patio Social Club in the neighborhood. Rob B let a shot go into the ceiling as they left the bar, a signal that it would be unwise to follow them out. Richie and John, who had also slumped to the floor, were left behind to die.

The bartender was never directly threatened, but days after the killings, he received a message from Ronnie "One-Arm" to see him at the club. This was the same individual who asked Scott to come to the same social club to castigate him merely for saying "Hello" to a girl that was with him. The bartender went to the club as he was told but found no one there, but the message was clear and indistinguishable without Ronnie resorting to actual witness tampering: "Shut the fuck up about what you know and what you saw!" And when large no-neck men sat in the front row at the state trial of Bobby Vernace in 1998, that sealed the deal that the bartender needed to watch out for himself.

Another testimony at the federal trial told that the mutts escaped to another neighborhood social club in their blood-splattered clothes, where they were chastised, not for killing Richie and John instead of giving them a beating, but for coming there to the club immediately afterward, as was reported by an informant who was there at the club, possibly putting the "heat" on the place.

In April 2013, largely through the testimony of the bartender and without the testimony of Linda Gotti (although she did want to testify now, the prosecutors didn't want the trial to become a circus with Victoria Gotti having to defend herself, which she most fervently would do, regarding her telling her niece Linda that she didn't have to testify all those years ago), Bobby Vernace was convicted of racketeering, which included the two murders at the Shamrock bar. His days on the street were now behind him.

And as for the patron Frank Riccardi, he had beaten the state murder trial but died in his midfifties. But from what I was told by the same FBI case agent about his physical appearance, his guilt about what had happened that faithful night had taken a toll on his health. Whereas Bobby and Rob went about their criminal business from that night, Riccardi devolved from being disrespected to reeling pangs of guilt. Although he wanted to act like one, he wasn't a hardcore guy like the others, and unfortunately for him, his actions that night dramatically changed the course of not only his life but the lives of many others as well.

An appeal for Vernace went all the way to reach the United States Court of Appeals in 2016. His argument was that he was wrongly convicted of the murder "in aid of racketeering" and that the slayings of Richard Godkin and John D'Agnese in the Shamrock Bar stemmed from a personal dispute, the spilled drink, and were not related to the Gambino family. But the three-judge panel found that the violence burnished the mobster's reputation in the street and his later rise to power. "A reasonable jury could have concluded Vernace went so far as to commit murder in a crowded bar because such a public display related to preserving (and even enhancing) the reputation of the Gambino crime family and its members." Appeal denied!

Justice does prevail, more often than not. On May 27, 2014, Bartolomeo "Bobby" Vernace was sentenced to a term of life imprisonment plus ten years. He was a mere Mob associate when he killed Richie and John, but the brutal killings proved his mettle with the Mob and, over the next three decades, helped vault him to a seat on the Gambino family's ruling panel.

Although both he and Riccardi had each beaten the murder raps in separate state trials in the 1990s, the guilt caught up to Riccardi, and a finding of guilt did the same to Vernace. The judge sentenced him after rejecting defense motions to set aside the verdict for insufficient evidence and because it was disclosed after the trial that a key government witness, Francesco Fiordilino, was committing crimes while in the Witness Protection Program.

Fiordilino, who was a Bonanno crime family mobster, pleaded guilty to illegal gambling and collecting debts for people he owed money while he had been testifying for the government at the murder trial. He finally admitted to committing these crimes after he testified about Vernace's involvement with lucrative baccarat games run by the Gambino and Bonanno families in social clubs and coffee bars because he feared he was going to get whacked over the money he owed. His testimony about how he experienced a "metamorphosis" from lowly coffee boy to a respected thug after committing a murder supported the government's theory that Vernace's status was enhanced after the bar killings. Although Fiordilino's crimes committed while in the federal Witness Protection Program could have tossed the conviction into jeopardy, the conviction and sentence stood after appeal.

*****

It was around this time that the Central Park Five, as they came to be known, settled with the City of New York for $41 million for having been wrongfully convicted of the rape of the Central Park jogger in 1989. According to newspaper reports, doctors who had treated the victim said that the different injuries sustained on her head were from more than one instrument and that bruises found on her body, including her legs, also showed that there was more than one perpetrator involved in the rape. However, they were discounted strictly on the basis that the only DNA found on her was from one person, who conveniently took the entire blame for the incident even though he was already serving a life sentence in prison and the statute of limitations had long passed for him relating to this crime; therefore, he had nothing to lose.

It was later revealed that lawyers representing the City of New York had gathered information regarding the incident over a number of years and felt well-prepared to defend the city against a lawsuit. They also had compared other cases of false imprisonment to this case and had decided that fair compensation, if it was reached before going to trial, would be $15 million.

But they were "encouraged" by the mayoral administration to settle the case and give much more than they had felt was a fair settlement. The news reports called it a political settlement.

The assumed reasoning behind the settlement was that a civil trial would have muddied the waters of the complete "innocence" of the Central Park Five, as they had become to be known. The sole individual who had confessed and was then tied to the crime by his DNA was implicated in ten other rapes, none of which had the same modus operandi but were all drastically different from the case of the Jogger. Yes, of course, he was there, but did he really act alone?

Although the top city attorney, known as the corporation counsel, approved the settlement, other city lawyers had argued in a memorandum that the city had a strong case if it chose to take the civil rights case to trial, which was probably why the mayor's predecessor, Michael Bloomberg, wouldn't settle the case and the current mayor at that time of the settlement, Bill De Blasio, made it a priority during his campaign for mayor as part of his "progressive agenda." A question immediately raised with the settlement was, If there was no evidence of police or prosecutorial wrongdoing, why was the settlement such a drastically high amount? The other question was, with twenty white cops, some of whom had no contact whatsoever with any of the defendants, having been named in the lawsuit for racial bias, why were the two black arresting officers, who actually put handcuffs on some of the defendants, not named in the lawsuit? One of those officers, a retired detective, asked that question, especially in light of the fact that he admitted to first using the term *wilding* and to call them a wolf pack. At least, this is what I learned through reading various periodicals that reported on the incident and its aftermath.

*****

During January of the following year, both John Alite and John Gotti Jr. wrote their own autobiographical books. I read a few excerpts from Junior's book, in which he complained that everyone was out to get both him and his father. He seemed to be under a particular delusion that I was John Alite's FBI contact as a confidential source until I handed him off to another agent on the Gambino Squad, Squad C-16. Thereafter, I then conspired with that agent through my contacts with the Federal Bureau of Prisons at the Metropolitan Correctional Center to wield my influence and have Junior subjected to inhumane treatment by the staff during the time of his federal incarceration. But since Gotti Jr. had never met me, it was quite presumptuous of him to believe that his physical and mental condition was so important to me that I would jeopardize not only my employment but, quite possibly, also my liberty for him. His self-aggrandizement severely misjudged my character and overstated his importance.

As a rule of discovery, when he went to trial, his defense team was provided any and all documents relating to any contacts that John Alite had with anyone and everyone in the FBI. They never received a document with my name on it because I never had a professional relationship with John Alite. If John Alite called me about anything other than a personal matter involving either of our families or friends, I informed the case agent at that time of the contact. Since nothing factual was ever told to me by him, I simply relayed the nature of his contact to me.

By then, I had assumed all along that John Alite had told Junior about knowing me, just in case it came up somewhere. It would be a preemptive act to let your team know that you have a history with a player from the other team but that you are securely aware of where your loyalties lie, like I did when I told agents of the Gambino Squad of my history with him. But maybe on his team, which I never realized before, our true relationship might have been seen as a vulnerability. Knowing how much John Alite knew about Junior's criminal activities and the jeopardy it created should I be able to convince him to turn toward the government, no matter how good a soldier he might have been, might not have been worth the risk of that happening one day.

And in keeping with the family tradition, on March 2, 2017, Mob boss John Gotti's namesake grandson received an eight-year prison sentence after pleading guilty on charges of running a $1.6-million-a-year oxycodone ring in his own Queens neighborhood of Howard Beach. The son of Peter Gotti was caught in Operation Beach Party when cops raided his residence and seized five hundred oxycodone tablets and forty thousand dollars in cash. He also agreed to forfeit $259,996 in drug profits. All accomplished at the age of twenty-three.

But it didn't just end there, of course. Barely two weeks after the sentencing hearing, he was charged with other crimes committed with a Bonanno family capo who recently became a semicelebrity after being acquitted at trial just sixteen months earlier for his part in the infamous 1978 robbery at the Lufthansa terminal at John F. Kennedy Airport, which was portrayed in the movie *Goodfellas*. Vincent Asaro was the only individual ever charged in that robbery, mostly because the others involved in it were all dead. He and Gotti were implicated in the torching of a car on April 4, 2012, after a road rage incident and a bank robbery of the Maspeth Savings and Loan Association that occurred two weeks later.

Asaro, who had been inducted into the Bonanno family more than thirty years ago, had been driving in Howard Beach when he was cut off by another driver as they were coming to a red light. The incident so enraged him that, after he was able to track down the residence of the other driver, he assigned a Bonanno associate to torch the car. The associate recruited Gotti, who provided the getaway car, his own Jaguar sedan. Although spotted by an unmarked police car, Gotti was able to elude the pursuit when it was terminated for safety reasons due to his reckless driving. He was then able to dodge the arrest for five years.

Two weeks later after the torching, he held up the bank with two Bonanno associates, one of them the same person who ignited the gasoline that was splashed on the vehicle in the arson case. The robbery netted them a total of $5,491, but the best part was that Gotti's girlfriend worked as a teller at the bank, had access to security protocols, and knew the amount of cash on hand. Although you would have thought the score, loot, would have been a bit bigger. So one chapter ended for Asaro, who was now eighty-two years old, and another continued for Gotti, when on December 28, 2017, at a sentencing hearing in the United States District Court in Brooklyn, Asaro was sentenced to a term of incarceration of eight years for his crimes and on March 13, 2018. Gotti was sentenced to a term of incarceration of five years for his crimes in that very same court. The end of one era and the beginning of another one.

*****

Justice never did prevail for Joey, as no arrests were ever made in his killing, which had long been forgotten by most. But it might have all been for the best for all parties here on earth, for Joey's family would have relived the tragedy and learned that his "friends" killed him for money. And for most of those who were involved who, as senseless as the murder was, had later on turned their lives around and were not only responsible human beings to themselves but, most importantly, had also become so for others who were now dependent upon them, financially and otherwise. I guess no good would have come from it now.

Even some of my legitimate, law-abiding friends amazed me! Having responded to a bank robbery during the course of my workday, I was late meeting a friend whom I had attended New York

Ranger games with over a number of years. And we were season ticket holders with two other friends whom we normally met at the games. We would drive along the Long Island Expressway, heading to the Queens-Midtown Tunnel, which would leave us driving westbound on East 37th Street toward Madison Square Garden. In response to the reason for my lateness, my friend said to me, "My cousin was a bank robber!" Since he was already many Bud Lights into the ride, I didn't even bother inquiring further into the absurdity of what he was talking about and wasn't going to ask again when he returned to sobriety.

Some months later, as I was channel-surfing, I stopped on an episode of *American Greed* when I heard an all-too-familiar raspy voice that was unique to my friend and his brothers, which numbered to be seven of them, so I had a lot of experience with this discernible way of sounding. As I stopped to look at the person from which the voice emanated, I also noticed that this person had the same facial features and mannerisms as one of my friend's brothers. When the program showed the name of this individual, Stephen Trantel, I came to realize that this was the cousin that my friend was talking about.

I gazed in amazement as Trantel told the story of how he transformed himself in 2003 as a commodities broker on Wall Street who lost his job to becoming a prolific bank robber on Long Island, committing ten robberies in five months throughout Nassau County! After losing his seat on the exchange, he needed $20,000 to get back there. As he sat on a bench outside a library in Freeport, he decided that robbing a bank might be a quick and easy way to get the money. He researched it online and saw that it was advantageous to use gloves (no fingerprints) and to leave the getaway car away from the crime scene (so no witnesses will see you getting into it close to the bank). He was successful in ten bank robberies and stole $65,000; however, paying the mounting bills prevented him from actually getting his seat back, that and the vacations he decided to take with his wife. He left a fingerprint on the last note, obviously getting a little careless and probably putting it on the piece of paper before he decided to use that paper as a demand note. Although he had no violent criminal history, he was arrested twenty years earlier for driving under the influence, which produced an old fingerprint card and there was the match. However, at first the investigating detective was incredulous, as he tried to figure out how a man who had a nice family in a good neighborhood and who was a successful commodities broker could be robbing banks!

After his arrest and sentencing in 2004 to nine years of incarceration, Trantel summed up the loss of freedom, future payment of restitution, divorce, and loss of his family by saying he tried to save it all but instead lost it all. And that just about said it all.

*****

There were a couple of guys from the neighborhood, both of whom would be mentioned in amusing interactions, whom I would label as hang-arounds, as they were called in the FX channel series *Sons of Anarchy*. They would hang around the same people, clubs, and hangouts where the gangsters also frequented, in a small way to feel as though they were a part of "the life" without really being in it. They gave you the feeling that they wanted to be in it, but I got the sense that the commitment, although feigned to seem appealing, wasn't really worth the pitfalls of incarceration or, possibly, death. I think they knew that once you were committed, there was no going back to legitimacy.

Although one of them, Jake, acted in a small way that he was a part of the family, he couldn't really be considered for membership because he was a redheaded Irishman. The Ravenite Social Club had been the official headquarters for the members of the Gambino crime family since the 1970s. It was located in Little Italy at 247 Mulberry Street. But in Queens, Jake hung around the gangsters when he could, either outside the Bergin Hunt and Fish Club, which was the clubhouse of John Gotti during his reign as the head of the Gambino crime family, or another associated social club located two blocks away on the corner of 99th Street on the opposite side of 101st Avenue. When I say he hung out outside the club, that's because I don't think he was a part of it enough that they would let him inside the club.

The Gambino crime family was the namesake of Carlo Gambino, who ruled the organization from 1957 to 1976. Before his death, he had anointed his brother-in-law, Paul Castellano, as the next boss. Castellano was portrayed more as a greedy businessman than a wiseguy, which infuriated many of the members, to include upstart capo John Gotti. Gotti then orchestrated the assassination of Castellano and his driver in front of Sparks Steak House in 1985 before ascending to the top of the enterprise.

Outside the Bergin Hunt and Fish Club, Gotti and his crew would have an annual fireworks display every Fourth of July. One year, I decided to take a look for myself, so I hopped on my 1984 Honda Nighthawk and rode down to 101st Avenue. I later graduated to a cruiser bike to make long overnight trips out of state but never veered toward Harley-Davidson bikes. In his autobiography, called *Hell's Angel*, Sonny Barger, national leader of the Hells Angels, wrote that he himself rode Harley-Davidson because "that's the image" but they should have switched over to Japanese models when they began building bigger bikes, because they are so much cheaper and better built. Harley-Davidson, however, had "the personality," and that was why, regrettably, they stayed with it.

So as I rode over to the corner of 99th Street and 101st Avenue, lo and behold, there was Jake standing on the corner next to the associated social club. I pulled up close to the curb alongside him as his eyes moved from the burst of the fireworks high above to my helmeted head. As he stood there alone, I'm sure his concern was the thought of his "friends," who might or might not know who I was and what I did professionally, wondering why I would stop there next to him. As he panicked a bit and looked around every which way for any of the "goodfellas" to be standing within earshot of the two of us, he said only as loud as I could hear him, "I don't know you and you sure as hell don't know me," before turning and walking away as calmly as he could muster.

Today, a shoe store now stands in the place where the Ravenite Social Club once stood and the Bergin Hunt and Fish Club has since been separated into two storefronts. And while on the topic of Italian social clubs, restaurants, and catering parties, Aldo's Pizzeria, the scene of the interminable luncheon, was in the news again years later in 2016. A waiter who was also a grandson of the owner committed arson when he torched a luxury car that belonged to the owner of a rival pizzeria. The act, which he admitted in federal court after surveillance video captured the arson in which he accidentally set himself on fire, was in retaliation for taking a $1,300 catering order away from Aldo's. The only other irony was that his sister had been arrested a month earlier with her boyfriend, John Gotti, the grandson of the late Gambino crime boss, after engaging in the illegal oxycodone peddling ring.

The other interaction began one day when I was walking to a printer that was by the desk of that very same agent with whom I had "conspired" against Gotti Jr., and I saw on the top of a stack of surveillance photos in a box a photograph of the brother of a friend, Aaron. It was a headshot, but you could see that he was dressed in typical wiseguy fashion, a black turtleneck underneath a black blazer. Incredulous at the sight of a photo of someone I could not fathom any reason for its' presence there, I asked him why there was a picture of Aaron here. He responded, "Oh, that's Peter Gotti's driver. It was taken at John Gotti's wake."

Now, I knew that Aaron (the other hang-around) did hang out a bit with Peter Gotti (as they were friends who happened to live in the same neighborhood) and he was on a few episodes of the series starring Victoria Gotti called *Growing Up Gotti*, but knowing both his family and him personally, I was sure that he wasn't doing anything sinister with the crime family. He was a guy with a city job who lived commensurate to his means, which he assured me himself when I spoke to him later on after this skeptical moment. But for the moment, my fears that he was involved in something stupid were allayed.

Sometime later, while attending a party at a mutual friend's house in my old neighborhood, I saw Aaron, still flying right and, to the best of my knowledge, not under any clouds of doubt regarding his participation in any illegal schemes. As I smiled and shook his hand, I said to him, "Hey, Aaron, what are you up to?" He responded without a pause, "Makin' sure that guys like you aren't lookin' for guys like me." I shook my head as I laughed, knowing that if any guys like me were looking for him, it wouldn't be me.

It was a sometimes-delicate balance between lifelong friendships and allegiance to the job, which, in the end, would always win out. I wouldn't have looked too good in an orange jumpsuit, anyway.

Throughout my career with the FBI, besides working the bank robberies, fugitives, extortions, and kidnappings, I also worked quite extensively on violations of the law that occurred on US government property within the five boroughs of New York City, most prominently the federal prisons located in downtown Manhattan and in Brooklyn, the VA hospitals located in Brooklyn, the Bronx, and Queens, and the US Army forts, one of which was Fort Totten, which was located in Whitestone, Queens, but was later decommissioned, and Fort Hamilton in Brooklyn. During that time, I was responsible for investigations that involved a number of cases involving people who were responsible for killings, rapes, serious assaults, and even a case involving a serial child sex predator. The arrest and subsequent successful prosecutions of those individuals who sought to abuse the innocents and bring them to justice for those that couldn't defend themselves were the most gratifying moments of my life.

And through the times the stories unfolded, both personal and professionally in the FBI.

There was the UPS driver who had a crooked cousin who convinced him to give him information on a high-end truck that delivered valuable merchandise. He set up the fellow truck driver that was robbed, and when we caught him, we gave him an opportunity to help himself before he was sentenced by "wiring up" against his cousin. And at first, he did a good job recording some incriminating conversations, but at some point, he felt a greater obligation to his crooked cousin than he did to himself and told him about the recordings. We still had enough evidence to convict the both of them, but his cooperation agreement was torn up and he served more time in prison than his cousin, the individual who actually did the robbery. Obviously, self-preservation was not on his mind.

There was the murder-for-hire case in which we were able to place a UCA in contact with the target of the investigation. The UCA was picking up the target for a first-time meeting by her residence in Brooklyn to lay out the terms of the deal in a vehicle that was wired for "sight and sound." I went to the meeting location in a tinted-out van and parked at a hydrant across the street from the residence so that the bureau photographer that was concealed behind a partition directly behind me could document the meeting with photographs as well. Not only would we have both the audio and video recording of the meeting itself, but also photographs of the target leaving her residence to get in the car and leaving the car to go back to her residence to document that it was, in fact, her.

As the UCA drove past her residence, he missed the house numbers and didn't stop until he drove a bit farther up the block. We pulled in behind in the middle of the block, and as she walked down the steps, looking for a waiting car, the photographer rapidly snapped away as she looked up and down the block but didn't see a double-parked car on the tightly packed street. She then looked up at the van sitting on the hydrant across the street, squinted, and then proceeded to walk toward the van. As I was asking the photographer if he was getting good shots of her, I suddenly realized that the UCA must not have described his vehicle to her. And, since she saw a car idling directly across from her house, she was now coming over to the undercover van!

I held on to my panic when she reached for the door to open it and hop in, to which she would probably wonder what a tinted-out black van with a multitude of equipment in the front compartment that made it look like a cockpit of a 747 was doing there with a guy with a holstered gun. Just before she grabbed the handle of the door, I slammed my hand down on the door lock button on the door console. When she found the door locked, she put her face to the window, trying to look past the tint. But before she was able to focus her eyes through the tint, I yelled out at her from inside the van as loud as the Who's Roger Daltrey would, "WHO THE FUCK ARE YOU?" She jumped back, startled, looked up and down the block again, and then saw a double-parked car down the block. She raised a quick hand and mouthed *sorry* to the voice inside the van before quickly walking off to get into the other car. As I started to calm myself, a voice from behind the partition said, "I got some good close-ups!"

On a personal note, after I attended the funeral of a relative on Long Island, my cousin was heading back to Brooklyn, and since she came by train, I offered to drive her back since I was going that way. As we talked and she asked me about my job, I thought it would be interesting to her to tell her about a recent bank robbery that occurred near where she lived on New Utrecht Avenue. There were multiple robbers involved in the robbery, all of whom were caught at that time through the investigation, except for one subject, and I happened to have the "wanted" flyer with his name and information, as well as his photograph, in the car under the passenger-side visor.

As she peered at the flyer, I noticed a chilled look on her face and her mouth dropped. I asked her if she was okay. She responded, "I'm Facebook friends with this guy's sister. We all went to high school together!" She said that she hadn't seen him in years and that he aged quite a bit but she did have contact with the sister on occasion. I could see how shaken and nervous she was about it. I knew that he was "on the lam" without much resources or money and that, since he knew we were looking for him, because we had talked to all his relatives, it was only a matter of time before we either found him or he surrendered himself. I couldn't put my cousin in a position of trying to elicit information about his location from the friend, even if the sister knew where he was hiding out. I kiddingly said to her, "Well, there's a reward for his capture," before we changed the subject. He was arrested without incident not long afterward. Small world, but the stories could go on and on!

I didn't see John Alite much again after taking him to a New York Rangers game at MSG shortly after he was released from jail. The funny part of it is that I had him meet me at the house of a friend whose brother had openly said, in a somewhat-allegiance to the Gotti family, what he would do if he ever met John since he was released from prison. I felt pretty comfortable that nothing would happen and had John meet me there, as was my common ritual. John might have even enjoyed meeting with an unarmed detractor, kind of a "Here I am, what do you have to say?"

Prior to that, we had met for lunch in New Jersey, and he had been looking for work; the money he was paid by the government for his time testifying wasn't going to last long with a number of children in his care. At that time, he couldn't work at a place where he would be stationary every day, as there were people looking for him, and if they found him somewhere, that would be it for him. So finding a job in which you were constantly moving, unless you were a door-to-door salesman, was not easy to come by. I had asked a friend who was an executive of a moving company in New Jersey, but for obvious reasons, even his friendship with me was not enough to take a chance like that.

He had dropped from contact with me (maybe to protect me, maybe to protect himself), but I heard years later that he has opened a business in Queens, is now pretty much out in the open, and from what I have heard, is doing well. Even though we don't speak anymore, I'm glad for him.

I had great satisfaction in my years of law enforcement, six with the NYPD and twenty-eight with the FBI. It was not only adventurous but was also just plain fun. It was a lot of work, but if that's not what you set out to do, what's the point of being there? Although there were some agents that I met along the way that made me wonder why they got on this job if they didn't want to work cases.

Which leads me to remember one particular axiom that was said in the old-time FBI that, although it was only repeated sarcastically, reflected the confluence of administrative burdens, meddling supervisors and executive staff, the few non-interested bureau support personnel, and a few Assistant US Attorneys who are supposed to aid your cause instead of hindering it: "Big cases, big problems. Little cases, little problems. No cases…"

About the Author

The author was born in Brooklyn and raised in Queens, New York. Through his adolescent years, he tried to compete athletically in baseball and football, hoping to one day play one of the sports professionally. During his time in college, where he bounced through three institutions of learning over four years, trying to find his footing in sports but never quite securing it, he finally got serious about his second choice in life and was able to earn a bachelor of science degree in criminal justice from John Jay College of Criminal Justice. The degree enabled him the opportunity to follow the foundation of learning street-level local law enforcement with the New York City Police Department which developed into a career conducting investigations involving bank robberies, fugitives, kidnappings, extortions, and other assorted personal crimes with the Federal Bureau of Investigation. Since his retirement from law enforcement and government service, besides maintaining his fitness with both the gym and sports to keep his physique in top shape, the author enjoys driving both fast cars and motorcycles in the New York area while also keeping a residence there on Long Island.

CPSIA information can be obtained
at www.ICGtesting.com
Printed in the USA
LVHW040852300720
661936LV00002B/271